# CRIME BUSTER

Best wishes

Bob Taylor

23. 5. 02.

# CRIME BUSTER

Inside the Minds of Britain's Most Evil Criminals

## BOB TAYLOR

PIATKUS

Copyright © 2002 Bob Taylor

First published in 2002 by
Judy Piatkus (Publishers) Limited
5 Windmill Street
London W1T 2JA
e-mail: info@piatkus.co.uk

**The moral right of the author has been asserted**

*A catalogue record for this book is available from the British Library*

ISBN 0 7499 2279 6

Text design by Paul Saunders

This book has been printed on paper manufactured with respect for the environment using wood from managed sustainable resources

Typeset by
Action Publishing Technology Ltd, Gloucester
Printed and bound in Great Britain by
Mackays of Chatham Ltd

*I dedicate this book to my wife Sheron and my children*
*James, Frances, Robert, Joseph and Finlay*

# CONTENTS

# ACKNOWLEDGEMENTS

The inspiration, guidance and support of my wife Sheron in the writing of this book was the most important factor in its conception and completion.

My many years as a police officer and especially as a senior investigator brought me into contact with some exceptionally professional and dedicated police officers. I also had the privilege to work with pathologists, psychiatrists, psychologists, forensic scientists solicitors and barristers who all contributed to the successful investigation and prosecution of the cases I was involved in. I would wish to pay tribute to their excellent work and that of their colleagues.

The victims of crime and their relatives are drawn into the tragic investigations enduring endless hours of questioning at times when they really want to be alone in their grief. Their co-operation and assistance is vital to crime investigations. I would like to thank all of them but most of all Julie Dart's mother and grandparents, Lynn Dart and Harvey and Margaret Atkin and Wendy Speakes's daughters Tracey Millington-Jones and Leah Speakes.

The victims of the sexual crimes cannot be individually named for legal reasons but their fortitude, resilience and bravery must be acknowledged; in some cases it saved their life, in others it helped them endure their ordeal and return to a normal life. Sadly for some the scars of their trauma will never heal.

A personal note of thanks goes to Robert Smith, my literary agent, Alice Wood and Gill Bailey at Piatkus Books, Phil Callaghan and Alan Spain for the book cover photographs and design. Also, my family and friends, my mother and father Marion and Eric Taylor, sister Judith Mitchell, auntie Doreen Smith and my friends Andrew Sheldon, True North Productions, Tim Grogan and Ron Burks.

# INTRODUCTION

I have had the best of times and the worst of times. Murderers, rapists, drug barons, terrorists and the full array of the criminal spectrum have all passed through my hands at some time in my working life.

At times, it has been distressing to see the brutality one person can inflict on another. But my faith in human nature is restored by the goodness I see in those wanting to help bring about justice for a victim.

As a senior detective, I led over fifty investigations into murder, kidnapping, rape and other serious crimes, and many suspicious deaths, and achieved a hundred per cent record in solving all these cases. In more recent times I headed the Northern Area of the élite National Crime Squad, investigating serious and organised crime, predominantly drugs. Over the course of my whole career I worked on over 150 murders, and of those only one remains unsolved.

In March 2001 I retired from the police just two days short of thirty-one years' service. Of my time, twenty-six years were spent in CID. I served at every rank as a detective and retired as a detective chief superintendent.

It all began one rainy Saturday in January 1970. I caught a No. 39 bus from Halton in Leeds to the city centre and made the short walk to Brotherton House, the headquarters of Leeds City Police. I still do not know why I decided to become a police officer. As a teenager, I began working for my father, a hard-working and honest man, who was building up his own plumbing business. He fell victim to an unscrupulous builder who, despite knowing he was going bankrupt, contracted us to do work he knew we would never get paid for. The money he owed my father was equivalent to over a year's wages for me. My dad eventually got £12 from the Official Receiver. The unfairness and sheer crookedness of it all shocked me.

I knew a police officer, a neighbour of ours, and I used to think how smart and authoritative he always looked. I liked working in the family business but was looking for an independent challenge. So I signed on the dotted line, returned home and, with some trepidation, told my parents that I was leaving the family business. As throughout my life, they gave me their full support and were delighted for me.

It was a proud day when I returned from training as PC 1008 Robert Taylor. The number before mine was allocated with a wry smile to PC 1007 Bond. Our boss said they wanted to save 57 for anyone called Heinz who joined. But John Gott was PC 4 and was, naturally, nicknamed Forgot.

For three months I accompanied a tutor constable before being unleashed alone on an unsuspecting public to patrol the mainly inhospitable streets of the Gipton estate in east Leeds. In those days we would parade over twenty officers on nights; now, sadly, the force would be lucky to parade half that number, even though crime has since soared.

A sense of humour remains a vital tool to cope with life in the force. Two new officers to the division were paired together, PC 353 Mick Bradney and PC 53 Ray Wood. The sergeant explained: 'I'm putting you together 'cos if you get lost put your numbers together and that's the station's phone number. Ring us and someone will come and get you.'

Characters in the service are few and far between. I hope I was one, but also that I did a good job. I worked in most CID offices in Leeds, the Area Robbery Squad and the Regional Crime Squad. I have worked with the good, the bad and the downright ugly.

I have felt pride in the achievement of taking a killer off the street and a heavy heart when I spent a Sunday afternoon at the mortuary, looking down on a murdered young child, with hair the same golden colour as my daughter's.

I even managed to fit in time to complete a law degree, attending polytechnic two nights a week for several years – the revision in the pub afterwards was murder.

It is one thing to aspire to being a detective, another to become one. A well-earned track record in arresting criminals used to be deemed a necessary qualification. Unfortunately that does not seem to matter now as force after force has introduced tenure, which ensures that good and bad detectives have a set time in CID before returning to uniform duties. I compare this scheme to telling a soccer player he can play seven games for England but will eventually have to leave the team, no matter how good he is.

I have seen every crackpot idea put forward over the years by senior police officers and politicians – the wheel has been reinvented that many times the tyre is bald. The role of the detective is yet again under threat from the same fickle individuals, who have still not been convinced of the need for such a being, seeing it as creating an élite class or, as they prefer to regard it, an underclass of ordinary uniformed officers in comparison.

I have heard many unenlightened senior policemen say, 'You don't need to have been a detective to detect a murder.' I often wonder whether, if they were laid on the operating table, would they prefer a surgeon or a butcher to wield the knife? Some cases detect themselves, when witnesses know the killer. Stranger murders are the ultimate test of a detective's skill. Most will not deal with one in a career. I had two.

Of all the many cases I have headed, some stand out because of the special nature of the offender or the unusual features of the crime. But all my cases have played a part in moulding my career and defining my philosophy of crime investigation. Eliminate the obvious, then contemplate the ridiculous.

I have found my time as a detective fascinating and challenging, from the hunt to the conviction, and have tried to understand what makes criminals tick. I have dealt with many killers and rapists whose true motives are often not obvious. If you look in the eyes of a newborn baby there is no way of telling whether it will grow up to be a saint or a sinner. I believe there is a little madness in us all, but most of us can control it and live normal, civilised lives. But killers and rapists have an inability to control their streak of madness and, coupled with a character defect, this manifests itself in their committing gruesome criminal acts.

Madness may come from nature but badness comes from a lack of nurture, exposing a child to evil and negative influences in their formative years. Such people grow up knowing that what they do is wrong but not caring, as they have not been taught to. Does it matter whether the crack in the teapot occurred when it was made or during the time it has been used? Either way it is still a cracked pot.

Despite all the evil I have seen and dealt with over the years, I have not become cynical, failing to see the good in the world. I was able to switch off between cases or when I returned home of an evening, but when I was involved in an investigation I would be totally focused until the job was done.

And so, as I handed in my warrant card, I had a heavy heart but a feeling of a job well done.

# chapter one

# LETTERS FROM A KILLER

## Tuesday, 9 July 1991

A prostitute was his best chance. A young one, not one of those hard-faced types who'd be difficult to control. Like the one he'd nabbed a few weeks ago. He'd learnt his lesson from that fiasco. Selecting his prey, a street-walker, and getting her in the car had been easy enough. He'd pulled the knife and ordered her to strip. She did as she was told, no problem. But then he slipped up.

Stupidly, he let her out of the car to undress and she ran off. She'd even been cheeky enough to throw a brick at his car. Have to get that dent sorted, he noted. Yes, he'd been foolish with her, but no way would he make the same mistake twice.

Cold air filled the former stables even though it was sunny outside. It mattered little to Michael Sams. He had a job to do, a plan to fulfil, and, if it worked, his life would be irrevocably changed. He'd be rock-eted to national, maybe international, infamy. He'd get the respect, the dues, he'd been unfairly robbed of. He'd show everyone what he was really like.

As the easy sounds of Radio 2 filled the brick building, Sams methodi-cally set to work. Everything must be perfect. After all, he thought with a grimace, it would not do to break down with a hostage in the back. He'd hardly be able to call out the AA. He'd had one such close call back in 1976, and it was something he did not wish to repeat.

His plan back then had been simple – to turn the windowless cellar of his large, stone detached home into a prison. His victim, a millionaire mill-owner's daughter, would be kept naked, bound and gagged, while he pursued his elaborate plot to get his £30,000 ransom. His first marriage was on the rocks. He was mixing with local criminals who always seemed to have money – and he wanted a piece of the action.

The mill-owner would have to go to London's St Pancras station, pick up a two-way radio from a left-luggage locker and take a train to Leeds. At some point on his return journey, he would be radioed and ordered to throw the money from the speeding train.

Sams knew about trains. Indeed, he classed himself a clever fellow, owner of a quick, shrewd brain. He knew exactly how long it would take a train to stop when the emergency cord was pulled. He would be long gone before anybody worked out where the money was.

But back then Sams had felt he needed an accomplice to help carry out his plan and there was no one he trusted enough to involve, and so he had aborted it. This time, he reasoned, it would be different. It would work. He had been through the plan so many times. It was foolproof. His teenage college years spent studying pure maths, applied maths and geography at A-level had not been wasted, he told himself. The ransom money would be the passport freeing him from his troubled marriage and allowing him to move to Thailand, where he could start his new life. The only person he would miss would be his mother. Sams would do whatever he needed to do to succeed.

He put the final touches to the wooden box, screwed the sides together and stood it in the corner of his dark, gloomy workshop. If she escaped from the box, the passive infrared sensor (PIR) would pick up her body heat. She couldn't go anywhere. There was no way out for her. And no way out for him now.

It had been worthwhile having that dummy run, Sams mused as he pulled on a pair of cotton gardening gloves, sat at his typewriter and gently eased in a sheet of paper. Carefully, amid the clutter of his tool workshop, he began to type. 'A young prostitute has been kidnapped from the Chapeltown area last night ...'

He did not know her name yet. Even worse, he did not care.

*

Like Michael Sams, I was preoccupied with my work that afternoon. But while he was preparing to travel down the road to criminal infamy, I was seventy miles north, settling into my new job and wading through a raft of paperwork.

For both of us, that day in July would be a turning point. Like him, I felt a sense of trepidation mixed with excitement. But mine stemmed from my arrival for my new job at Millgarth police station in Leeds city centre. Only the day before I had been promoted to detective superintendent, in charge of sixty detectives at four stations, covering some of the most crime-ridden areas of West Yorkshire.

Life was never dull at Millgarth. I had last been there four years earlier as a detective sergeant. In the intervening years I had experienced what some might say was a meteoric rise through the ranks to my new post – boss of my old stamping-ground.

By 5 pm, Sams and I were finishing for the night. While he was returning to his unsuspecting wife Teena, I strolled to the eighteenth-century Whitelocks tavern to mark the end of my second day with a pint of Yorkshire's finest.

A couple of miles away, Julie Anne Dart, a fresh-faced eighteen-year-old, was enjoying what was to be her last meal with her boyfriend Dominic Murray at his flat in Gipton. Though she was unemployed, Julie's dream was to join the army, and she was waiting to hear whether she'd passed its entrance exams.

That week passed quietly, giving me an opportunity to size up colleagues who would smile at your face and mean it and those who'd smile and then stab you in the back. The police are no different to any other organisation. There is always someone carrying a grudge because they joined the force or had their last promotion before you and now see you holding a more senior rank. By Friday teatime I'd seen many meaningful smiles and felt little cause for concern from those I earmarked to keep an eye on. The weekend off was welcome.

Within hours of the second week kicking off, the division's reputation for crime was restored. And in some style, as it was to turn out.

I was called to a meeting at Weetwood police station on the outskirts of Leeds to look at two letters – one typed, one handwritten. A young woman might have been kidnapped and the letters could be connected, I was told. The first was addressed to Dominic Murray:

Hello Dominic,

Help me please I've been kidnapped and I am been held as a personal security until next Monday night. Please go and tell my Mum straight away. Love you so much Dominic

Mum phone the police straight away and help me. Have not eaten anything but I have been offered food. Feeling a bit sick but I'm drinking two cups of tea per day.

MUM – DOMINIC HELP ME.

Dominic my mum will be in at 5.00 everynight or phone yes phone her. If not there leave a message. If not working go to her house.

Love You all
Julie

The letter was postmarked Huntingdon, 7 pm, 11 July 1991, and seemed to be in three parts – firstly to Dominic, then to Julie's mum, Lynn Dart, and finally to both of them. It had landed on Dominic's doormat the previous Friday. He followed its instructions and immediately called Lynn. She was initially sceptical that it was Julie's writing, but when they realised that neither of them had seen her since Tuesday, they went to Gipton police station and reported her missing.

Lynn had not approved of Julie's relationship with Dominic, so the teenager had told her mother she was staying with a girlfriend that week. When she left Dominic's home that Tuesday night, Julie told him she was going to work at the Leeds General Infirmary. Police checks showed she had never worked there. Julie further told Dominic she was going home that night. This small deceit was enough for neither Dominic nor Lynn to realise Julie was missing until he received the letter.

As I looked at the letter, the first thing that struck me was why would a kidnapper allow his victim to write and actually encourage her mother to go to the police? This girl was being held as personal security, but for what? No money was demanded. I read the second letter, addressed to Leeds City Police. Littered with spelling mistakes, it was also posted in Huntingdon.

A young prostitute has been kidnapped from the Chapltown area last night and will only be released unharmed if the conditions below are met, if they are not met then the hostage will never be seen again also a major city centre store (not necessary in Leeds ) will have a fire bomb explode at 5.am 17 July.

1. A payment of £140,000 is paid in cash

2. £5,000 is put in two bank accounts, 2 cash cards and P.I.N. issued these two bank accounts to allow at least £200 per day withdrawal.

Next Tuesday 16 July a WPC will drive to Birmingham New Street station with the money, and await a phone call at the Mercury phone terminal in the waiting room on platform 9, she must wear a lightish Blue skirt with the money in a sholder bag. She must be there at 6pm and await a call at 7pm, she will then be given the location of the next phone call, (after receiving the call she must drive north out of the city on the A38M Aston Expressway, to join the southbound M6, this information is given to avoid her getting lost in the city.) She must have at enough petrol for at least 200 miles driving and a pen and pad may also be carried, but no radio or transmittor,

All phone calls will be prerecorded and no communication will be possible or answered. No negotiations will be entred into. Any publicity or apparent police action will result in no further communication.

He monies to be in equal quantities of £50/20/10 used notes and the cash cards to have their P.I.N. marked on them in marker pen. The money to be wrapped on polythene of at least 120 microns the taped with parcel the bank cards to then be taped to the polythene then the package to be wrapped in brown paper and tied as in the diag at the end of this message. The whole package to be no more than 350mm X 350mm X 90mm.

Once the money has been received Leeds will receive a phone call at around midnight of the name and address of the store with the fire bomb five hours should be ample time to gain entry to the store. The hostage will only be released when all monies have been withdrawn from the accounts.

The hostage will be well fed and well looked after in a home rented for the purpose, she will be guarded 24hrs a day by P.I.R detectors connected directly to the mains. Once the monies have been withdrawn you will receive the address of the hostage, BEFORE ENTERING HOUSE THE ELECTRICITY MUST BE SWITCHED OF FROM OUTSIDE before opening the door or any movement will activate the detectors.

LEEDS CITY POLICE
HEADQUATERS
LEEDS.
(page 2)

Tuesday the WPC will at all times carry the money package with her, she will be sent to various phone boxes for phone messages at one box a small plastic box with a small green L.E.D. illuminated will be inside the box, this must be picked up and placed ontop of the instrument panel on the car dashboard and must be visible through the front windscreen, this box will also have a large red L.E.D. (antitamper) and a large amber L.E.D. (Transmitter detector) if either of these two illuminate the no further messages will be received. The money package as I said must be carried at all times and at one destination it must be clipped to a dog type clip that will be hanging from a tree, no downward pull must be made on the rope. The WPC must then return to the car which must be some 300 metres from this point within 60 secs and drive a further 800 metres before removing the plastic box with the L.E.D.s

The money will be picked up by some-one unconnected with the writer but will be the male person who parks down this "lovers lane" each Tuesday for a few hours, His female companion will be held hostage until the money is picked up from him, he will have a short range two way radio which I can direct him. Should anything go wrong these two hostages will not be harmed.

This action has been planned for some time, but obtaining a small hand gun plus ammunition took longer than anticipated. If anything goes wrong or the ploice are not able to meet the demand then the hostage will never be seen again, plus the store will be fire bombed, the action will then begin again next time an employee of say the Electric/Gas/Water Companies will be used, to kidnap them in the course of there work will make the company pay the ransom.

No publicity must be given until the money has been received then a press statement may be released but must mention that no monies were handed over.

The extra £5,000 must not be added in cash with the main money as the main package will be buried for a long while so that serial number will not be traced, serial number in cash dispencers cannot be traced.

As I laid the letter on the table, it seemed surreal. A young woman was missing. She had lied to her mother and boyfriend. She was now apparently writing home saying she had been kidnapped. Why should we believe her?

And why were the police being blackmailed? I could have done with more time to think about it all, but I had only until 6 pm the next day to decide what to do and put together a plan.

I scanned what I'd noted down. The second letter did not mention Julie by name though the chances of two unconnected letters posted in Huntingdon on the same date and at the same time about a kidnapping in Leeds were remote.

The second had been addressed to the former Leeds City Police, non-existent since 1974, when it amalgamated with the West Yorkshire force. Maybe the author knew my old force.

He addressed it to 'headquaters'. Was it penned by an ill-educated person or was it done on purpose? But use of terms like '120 microns' and the mention of the £140,000 being in equal quantities of fifties, twenties and tens did not suggest a lack of education. I had no problems with his demand for no publicity. Going public would have made it difficult to control the spread of information, even with a press embargo.

The definite threats to kill the hostage and fire-bomb a store had to be taken seriously. We knew Julie was missing and had to assume she was the victim. He even threatened to kidnap someone else if this failed. He meant business.

Julie had no history of prostitution or convictions, but enquiries revealed she had been spotted in Chapeltown, Leeds' infamous red-light area. So what took her there?

Why demand £140,000 plus £5,000? It was not exactly a rounded sum. Asking for it to be in equal quantities of notes was odd, as £140,000 does not divide by three. But Detective Constable Dermot Fairhurst calculated that 1,750 £50 notes, and the same number of £20 and £10 notes, when added up, came to £140,000.

I realised our letter-writer was no fool.

I returned to Millgarth and discussed the matter with my divisional officer, who was sceptical that the letters were genuine. 'If I was you, I'd throw them in the bin,' he advised. But I was not prepared to risk either Julie's life or my career on it being a hoax. There was no reason to think it was. But then again, what sort of person would kidnap a girl from a working-class background, demand money from the police and expect them to pay up?

I stared at Julie's letter. 'Mum phone the police straight away,' she pleaded. I had a daughter a few years younger than Julie and did not want to imagine the fear she and Lynn must be going through.

If Julie was a hostage, she'd hardly sneak out to post the letter and then freely return to her prison. It must all have been done under the kidnapper's control. It was he who actually wanted the police to be involved. How bizarre – a man committing one of the most serious criminal offences who wanted us to know and get involved.

Did this person really think the police would give him the money and let him walk away? He was taking us on and must be confident of success. He must realise he would be hunted until caught. Was it a grudge thing, a disgruntled police officer? Could Julie be part of it? It just did not make sense.

I decided I would take the case on, but I would need the help of the Regional Crime Squad (RCS) with its officers specially trained in kidnap to provide me with a courier.

An old schoolfriend of Julie's told the police he had seen her a few days earlier on Spencer Place, the main drag in the red-light area. She was standing at a street corner only yards from where Yorkshire Ripper Peter Sutcliffe picked up two of his murder victims.

The omens were grim, and I cast my mind back sixteen years to the hunt for Sutcliffe. I hoped I was not now about to get embroiled in a similar case.

Kidnapping and extortion are, thankfully, rare crimes. Those being carried out while you investigate them involve you taking an interactive role, playing out your part directly with the kidnapper. What you do or do not do can determine the outcome, and at stake, more often than not, is somebody's life. There is little margin for error.

Certainly, if we were to follow the instructions, we were left with just twenty-four hours to plan for the rendezvous at Birmingham New Street station. It could all be a con, but I knew I would not take that chance. I saw Norman Mould, the RCS co-ordinator, and one of his detective superintendents, George Newbold, at their offices that afternoon to arrange for a courier.

I knew exactly what their capabilities were, having worked with them on two previous operations when extortion demands were made on a major food store. Both resulted in arrests and successful prosecutions.

By 6 pm on Tuesday, police courier Annette Zeknys was at New Street station, in Platform 9's waiting room. Her first problem arose when station staff announced they wanted to close the waiting room. Annette persuaded them to keep it open without revealing her true purpose. I could have laughed at that – if it had been the only hurdle she was to face that night.

At 7.06 pm the phone rang. She answered: 'Hello, who is that?' There was no response. She quickly asked again, but still no response. The phone went dead. She waited another hour, hoping the caller would call back, but he didn't.

As the evening's events played out, I waited at Millgarth. When I heard what had happened, I was disappointed. We still had no idea whether this was a genuine kidnapping or not, but one thing was certain – Julie had been missing for a week now. I wondered uneasily what might happen next.

If he was not a hoaxer, how much longer would he keep Julie hostage? I had no option but to telex all UK police forces to warn of the threat to fire-bomb a store on the seventeenth. By Thursday, 18 July, no store had been bombed, thankfully, but we still had no news on Julie, so I decided to put out a missing-persons report to the local paper. We made no reference to the letters.

At 8 am on Saturday I was in my office working, being on call over the weekend. I ordered the scene-of-crime officers to go to Lynn Dart's house to fingerprint personal items on Julie's bedside table. This would give me a set of prints for her, and we could see whether any matched the ones found on her letter. I still had no news of Julie, and her family were understandably anxious.

I scanned the pile of daily telex crime reports from police forces across the country, with details of overnight robberies, rapes and other crimes. My gaze focused on one from Lincolnshire. A naked woman had been found dead. She was aged between eighteen and thirty, wrapped and tied in a sheet and left in the corner of a field near Easton, a mile from the A1. I felt a chill go down my neck. Had Julie Dart been found?

I rang the Lincolnshire incident room and told DCI Gordon Reedman about her. He said farmer Robert Skelton had gone to his field at 7.45 am the previous day and found a bundle by an oak tree next to its entrance. No attempt had been made to hide it. Mr Skelton thought it was grass cuttings, wrapped and secured with green rope. He slit the candy-striped sheet and saw the outline of an arm.

Lincolnshire Police were treating it as murder, and forensic scientists and the pathologist were at the scene. As Gordon talked me through the details, I stared at Julie Dart's missing-from-home report. The body was naked, but on the woman's right middle finger was a metal ring with several stones in it. Julie had a similar ring, but that was not enough to be conclusive.

'The head and upper body are in a bit of a state. We cannot do a normal facial identification so photographs are no good, but her lower body is well preserved,' explained Gordon.

'What colour is her hair?' I asked.

'Most is missing, but brown, I'd say. I think she was killed elsewhere and dumped in the field. We don't have any suspects and she died from a couple of blows to her head with something like a hammer,' he replied.

'Time of death?' I needed to know whether it fitted our timescale.

'Seven to ten days ago,' said Gordon. It did.

'Is there anything unusual about the body?'

'At the post-mortem I noticed she had a chipped front tooth.'

A cold shiver went down my spine. 'Just a minute,' I said, as I thumbed through the report. There it was – Julie had a chip on one of her upper front teeth. We agreed that I'd send down officers with fingerprints and dental records so a comparison could be made. In my own mind, though, I knew it was Julie.

I went to tell my team. To get Julie's dental records we had to ask Lynn who her dentist was. She naturally wanted to know why we needed them. Though Lynn sensed there was more to it than she was being told, and there was not going to be a happy ending, I was not sure enough yet to tell her any more.

The sad truth came at teatime. Fingerprints confirmed that the body was Julie's. I would have to tell Lynn – but what was I going to say? I reflected on this as Detective Inspector Paul Maxwell drove me to Lynn's. A secretary at the then Leeds Polytechnic, divorcee Lynn was raising her son Paul and Julie alone.

My heart was heavy as I knocked on her back door. There is no right, best or easy way to tell a parent their child is dead, a victim of murder. I had to do many 'death knocks' during my years in the police, and it never, ever got any easier. I still had not worked out what to say when Lynn opened the door and quietly ushered us into her small, tidy kitchen. I could see the tension in her face. I glanced into the lounge – the TV screen was framed in the doorway. The local ITV news programme, *Calendar*, was on, and a reporter was telling of a young woman's body being discovered in a Lincolnshire field.

Lynn caught sight of it and knew immediately. She looked straight at me and mumbled, 'It's our Julie, isn't it?' 'Yes,' I replied, sorrowfully. She broke down and wept, and my mind raced as I tried to find some way to ease her pain.

'Can you tell me how and where she died? Did she suffer?' pleaded Lynn. I knew she would have questions, most of which I had no answers to at that time, and I told her so. I tried to offer some comfort: 'I don't know where she was killed but she was struck on the back of the head with something heavy. She would have been unconscious before she realised what was happening,' was the best I could offer.

As if it were a consolation prize, I vowed: 'Lynn, there is one thing I don't want you to worry about. I can assure you we will catch Julie's killer.' I said it with force, with anger at the loss of life of a young woman on the brink of adulthood, and for a mother who'd lost her only daughter. And I meant it. It was my pledge to Lynn – and to Julie.

I knew I could not intrude too long on her grief, but I had to explain where Julie was and what would happen next. 'Can I see her?' Lynn asked. I did not have the heart to reveal the state her pretty brown-haired daughter had been left in. Lynn would find that out soon enough. And time would not soften those details. Lynn proudly showed me a picture of Julie. I lied and said she couldn't see her daughter yet as her death was now a murder inquiry.

I also felt that Lynn needed to remember her daughter as she really was – a promising schoolgirl athlete, spirited and lively. It was months before I told her the truth, and only when she commented about being denied the opportunity to see Julie for one last time. Paul and I left the devastated Lynn with her family to grieve together. Returning to the car, Paul remarked: 'That might be a tall order, boss, catching the killer.'

'Yes,' I said, 'it might be. We'll see.'

I began putting together my team, which would grow to fifty officers at its peak, and we moved into the infamous incident room at Millgarth. This room has had more media exposure that any other in the country, as it was from here that the hunt for the Yorkshire Ripper was conducted. I had worked in this very room fifteen years earlier on the Ripper murders. And it was from here that I was now to head my first murder investigation as senior investigating officer (SIO).

Just after 2.30 pm, two weeks into my new job and slightly shell-shocked from running the gauntlet of my first press conference with a dozen journalists, I walked back into the incident room and sensed a buzz in the air. 'It's going to be one of those investigations where there'll never be a dull moment,' I mused as a plastic bag was wafted past my eyes.

'He's written again,' an officer announced.

Again addressed to Leeds City Police, the envelope bore the words 're – JULIE DART'.

Words will never be able to express my regret that Julie Dart had to be killed, but I did warn you what would happen if anything went wrong, at the time of this letter there has been no publicity, if you do not find the body within a few days I will contact you as to the location, it will have to be moved today as it appears to be decomposing.

She was not raped or sexually abused or harmed in any way until she met her end, she was tied up and hit a few blows to the back of the head to render her unconscious and then strangled, she never saw what was to happen, never felt no pain or know anything about it.

The mistake I appear to have made is that I did not know the voice at the end of the phone, it was O.K. at Birmingham but at Leicester it appears to have been different.

I still intend to carry out this campain until I receive the monies however many people suffer. In tow weeks or so I shall demonstrate my fire bomb.

I still require the same monies as before under the same conditions if you want to avoid serious fire damage and any further prostitutes life; to contact me place an ad in the Saturdays "SUN" newspaper personal column and a phone call will be made to the box at Leicester Forest East northbound services, the box nearest the R.A.C. box. On the following Tuesday at 8.30pmThe courier to be the same W.P.C as used last time ( I presume it was her of course that was at Birmingm New Street) and when answering the phone must say "Julie speaking" she will once again be given instructions, a little clearer next time, if she misses the instructions a repaet call will be made straight away, she must not pick it up a second time if she has got it first time, as only one repeat call will be allowed. If any phone box is occupied then a call will be made as soon as available. The calls as before will be recorded, this time by a hostage picked up on the Monday evening in another cities red light district.

The ad in the Sun to read "Lets try again for Julies sake". If no message is seen in Sat 27<sup>th</sup> or Sat 3 Aug then the fire bomb will definitely be placed on Tuesday 6 August. No prostitute will be held until the message is received or until the fire bomb fails to bring any response.

The letter had to be from the killer as too many coincidental points were mentioned, the most significant being that he had strangled Julie. I rang pathologist Professor Stephen Jones in Lincolnshire and asked him to re-examine Julie's body. He now found that discoloration on her neck, which he had believed was due to post-mortem changes, was in fact a ligature mark. Coupled with this, the hyoid bone of the larynx was damaged, a fairly good indicator of strangulation. Our letter-writer was right. Who else but the killer or an accomplice would know this?

I felt increasing anger at the conceit of this person, who had taken a girl's life. Adding insult to injury, he was now trying to justify what he had done by saying it was our fault, as he said the courier should have received a message that would have taken her to Leicester – which she didn't.

The rest of the letter provided no respite from the pathetic opening paragraphs. A sick twist was his demand that the courier answer the phone with 'Julie speaking'. He had killed a young woman. To compound that, he was now using Julie Dart's name to mock us, and her death as an example of his grotesque capabilities. I wondered what sort of individual we were dealing with.

One of an SIO's jobs in a murder hunt is to construct a net system which everyone but the killer or very strong suspects should eventually be sifted through. Most murder victims die at the hands of someone they know. Stranger murders are rare, but I was working on the premise that Julie was one such victim. I decided that because of this, and the length of time she had been missing, I needed to take a more scientific approach.

Grass discoloration under Julie's body suggested she had been in the field longer than overnight. We contacted Cambridge University entomologist Dr Zakaria Erzinclioglu, who specialised in insects and would examine fly, beetle and larva samples taken from the sheet Julie's body had been encased in.

Assessing the growth of the larvae through their various stages, he thought the most mature were at least two days old by the time Julie was found and believed she had been lying in the field for over three days.

I also had to consider whether Julie was a willing party to a plot which had gone horribly wrong. Pathologist Stephen Jones detailed a series of red marks around her right ankle, indicating something tied to it, a rope maybe, which strengthened my belief she was unknown to her kidnapper.

We looked closely at Dominic Murray, Julie's boyfriend, as they had had a stormy relationship. They had fought two days before she went missing and both ended up in hospital, Julie with bruising to her face, Dominic needing a plaster cast put on his broken ankle. We eliminated builder's labourer Dominic on that basis, as he was unable to drive.

I listed what I did not know. I did not know exactly where Julie was kidnapped from or met her killer. There were sightings in Chapeltown, but of a girl wearing blue jeans and a white T-shirt. Julie had on a pink-and-black jacket, skirt, tights, shoes and handbag, all black, when she left Dominic's house. Why had she been in the red-light area anyway? She was not a prostitute.

I did not know where she was held or by whom. I assumed the motive was money, though who in their right mind would expect the police to pay up? I could not exclude the possibility that this was a man with a grudge against the police.

We had found an indented impression of handwriting on the second letter's envelope which read, 'Mavis, will not be in Tuesday, Phil'. I was sceptical, as it was so heavily indented it could virtually be seen with the naked eye. It could be a vital clue or a red herring arranged by the killer to send us down a false trail and waste our time.

Another piece of possible evidence was the green rope that had bound Julie's body. It was not of a normal type, so I set two officers on that. They would see many rope experts and visit Portugal, where, I was to learn, 90 per cent of the world's supply is made.

Prostitutes were among the few lines of enquiry we did have. Had my anonymous pen-pal been successful on his first kidnap attempt, or had there been any previous bungled efforts? The working women might have seen Julie before or on that night. He was still threatening to kidnap another prostitute from a red-light district. I knew we could not alert all prostitutes nationwide without a major press leak, and even then, how many would take much notice? I had to run the risk that he was now simply using Julie's death as a threat to me, and that no other person would be kidnapped.

My best line of enquiry, as I saw it, was to flush this person out through his demands for money. He had shown he was serious by killing Julie. He was not going to go away. I saw only two endgames. He would succeed in his quest for the money and go away, never to be heard of again. Or we would catch him.

I did not know where he was from, what he looked like, nothing. I realised we were going to have to lure this man to us. Our bait would be the £140,000. This was to be, in the true sense of the word, a 'manhunt'.

We prepared for our second run on Tuesday, 30 July 1991. After fingerprinting 900 Leeds sorting-office staff to eliminate their prints from the killer's letters, we knew they were now aware of what to look for. As a result, an employee spotted a third letter at 2 am that Tuesday.

Re Julie Dart

Seen message will phone 8.30 Tue 30 July WPC will answer 'Julie & give car make & colour + reg number she will be given name and place from where hostage (prostitute) has been picked up Sun/Mon – lets hope she has been reported missing by then – WPC will be given location of the next call – operation may be called off if young lovers car is not in lane – if 'go' then location of detector will be given – the young lovers will not be harmed provided there is no-one else at the pick-up and the detector has not detected anything – the money will be picked up by the male in the lovers car whilst female is held hostage – so a marksman shooting him would cause embarrasing headlines for the police.

After 2 hrs pondering this on the train (to post in Leeds) I am still at a loss to understand why the police are going ahead – and can only come up with the following

1)I am sucessful    (good chance)
2)Could be seen withdrawing (very long odds)
3)Could be seen phoning      (very long odds)
4)Police try to follow WPC – have second person in car – bug car – (pick up designed to block nearside doors – others observed – bug detector will detect transmitter) (long odds)
5)Police use aircraft/sattelite observation to follow – or some device

not known to me – good possibility – but escape route designed to overcome this + young female lovers & prostitute will be in car – police wont gamble with 2 lives – (therefore long odds)

6)Police set up road blocks over a wide area as not one police car was observed on m1 on the 10 July – my advantage – only i kow pick up area, escape route designed to overcome this

7)Money will be marked (odds nil can be tested)

8)Serial numbers recorded definate – money can be spent but nos deposited in banks b/s for months

9)Explosive device or marker dye in package of money – package to be opened by one of the hostages – no risk

10)Could be traced later – possible – think harder Sun/Mon/Tues

11)Could be caught committing further offence – no risk 1st & last crime.

12)Could be identified by lovers – no risk covered face

13)Could be indentified by prostitute – little risk darkness and bribe possible

14)Must be more – keep copy – think and plan hard

Game odds
Police <u>win</u>   win money back – loose receive writers female lovers prostitutes bodies

Loose   win no-one else hurt – loose £145,000
<u>bluff</u>   win loose no money loose receive 1 2 or 3 bodies

<u>Me</u> <u>win</u>   win £140,000 loose death of Julie – once game has finished will feel grief – contemplate death/suicide in RTA

<u>Loose</u>   death
<u>Bluff</u>   win ? loose?

I am tempted to ask why the bit of info released to the press has been wrong – also why no T.V. coverage when body was found?

Julie was not blugeoned to death (Jim Oldfield – D Mirror) she was rendered unconcious by 3–4 blows to the back of the head & then strangled <u>she never felt a thing</u> she wrote the letter herself wed 11pm 10 July full typed details will be available next week whatever the outcome – also how Julies body decomposed so badly

In all my then twenty-one years of policing, I had never come across anything like this. His list of odds was breathtaking in its audacity. He was trying to show what a clever person he was by detailing the techniques he thought we would use. Whichever way he looked at it, he could not lose and we could not win, as we already had one dead woman to deal with.

He moaned about Jim Oldfield, the *Daily Mirror*'s then northern correspondent, who wrote that Julie was bludgeoned to death. Our murderer did not like that at all. He wanted to be seen as a compassionate killer because he took a life in a painless manner! It would be difficult to keep the letters secret much longer, but I would try.

John O'Sullivan, my deputy SIO, went with the RCS for the second run on 30 July. We followed our man's instructions and Annette Zeknys was at the M1's northbound Leicester Forest East services to pick up the phone at 8.31 pm. Someone was speaking – the voice was tape recorded, but she could not understand what was being said, except the word 'services'. The tape's quality and background noise blocked out everything. She listened intently but could not decipher anything except that it was a male voice. The line went dead after a short time.

No message had been passed. Many officers like Annette are deployed on dangerous operations, but few are ever in the position of expecting to speak to or face a known killer. She was gutted.

And she wasn't the only one. I had to face the team and tell them what had happened. I adjourned to the police bar as I awaited John O'Sullivan's return to brief me. Searching for a record to play on the juke-box to ease my mood, I spotted 'Midnight Cowboy'. I recalled the sadness at the end of the film of that name, when Dustin Hoffman died. The haunting mouth-organ melody reflected my depressed mood. I played it four times before the other officers started to moan. But this was to become 'Julie's song', the team's anthem, and it would be played countless more times over the coming months.

When I felt upbeat I'd play another favourite, 'Always Look On The Bright Side Of Life', by Eric Idle. To this day, whenever I hear either record, I immediately recall those long, tense summer nights.

It was clear we were dealing with a complex character, so I contacted forensic psychologist Paul Britton. I was intrigued to hear what he had to say, but needed to know I could pass his observations on to my team as plausible comment.

I told Paul that the worst-case scenario for an SIO is not being able to convince your team of the credibility of what you are saying. This was my first use of an offender profiler, and I was a cynic, doubtful as to the usefulness of these people, whom I considered to be no better than professional clairvoyants. However, I was to meet Paul on many further occasions, and his quiet delivery and professional manner convinced me that a non-police perspective can be useful at times. Police officers are trained to look at matters with a certain mindset, whereas Paul would turn things around and offer a different view.

I thought it important that my management team question Paul. Most of us had started to create our own picture of the killer. Paul listed eight characteristics about him – a dislike of the police, an older man, self-taught, had technical knowledge, as shown by his reference to PIR detectors, not in a senior position, probably not killed before, working alone, and his aim was probably not to murder but to obtain the £140,000.

There was not much in what Paul said that was particularly significant, apart from him declaring to me: 'The killing of Julie Dart was no mistake. It was planned and forms part of his strategy. She was always going to be murdered!'

That point rammed itself home to me. It was difficult to see the obvious when I could not shed the feeling that Julie might have died because I had got things wrong. I knew the press would say she was killed because we screwed up. Paul's comments gave me some small comfort, but I was relying on the pathologist stating that she had died between 9 and 12 July, seven to ten days before being found, well before the first botched courier run on the sixteenth, and even before we got her letter.

Would he kill again? Paul told me that he had killed Julie purely so the police would take him seriously and he would carry on killing until he felt he had our attention. But these killings would not be his fault. They'd be ours, Paul explained, as he would consider them necessary for us to take him seriously.

We talked on after the meeting about the ploys he used – red herrings, smokescreens and the blind alleys he took us down. The killer was a games player, locked into a contest with us, and would be watching and listening to me when I held press conferences, explained Paul. As a parting shot I said, 'So I'd better be very careful what I say about him on television?'

'Oh yes,' Paul replied, 'if you upset him . . .'

I cut in: 'If I say he's a complete bloody nutcase, I might not get through Millgarth's front door for bodies the next morning.'

'Exactly,' said Paul, ignoring my black humour, though I had taken on board his serious point. I knew I was talking as much to the killer as to the public in my now thrice-weekly news briefings. Would this games strategy run throughout the inquiry? If it did it was important to interpret it right and play it right. The stakes were too high to get it wrong.

The game continued with the next letter, which arrived the morning after the last abortive run. Handwritten, it had been posted in Coventry.

> Sorry no go last night was not free Monday afternoon for make-up to get hostage Monday evening – make up takes hours
> your WPC should have been able to hear i have tried it on an extension
> Next week i will definitely be free all Monday & Tuesday so will have no problem with hostage or incendary – you will like incendary similar to one shown on TV the other night
> Still have not worked out why police would gamble with 3 lives – cannot see you providing 145000 for nothing without proof of further action by me nor can i see you providing an empty package which would result in 2 further deaths (both females – the male only used to collect money from pick up.
> still all my affairs in order – all life insurances paid up – so ill gamble
> I did say last time WPC to answer Julie speaking and then give car make & reg number. I need to see her pass me at one point before returning to drop package
> Bye ring Tuesday

Its arrival sent a buzz through the incident room. This man was still with us, becoming almost chummy in his tone. And that's just how I wanted it. The more he communicated with us, the better chance we had of tracking him down.

We prepared for our third run, this time on Tuesday, 6 August, a month since Julie was kidnapped.

I waited at Millgarth until John O'Sullivan reported back that Annette was at the phone box, but she received no call. I was gutted beyond imagination. What was the problem this time? If it were not for the fact that I knew he had already killed, I would not be doing this. John returned to discuss it with me, but there was little to say. I knew it all – nothing had happened. 'He'll come,' reassured John. 'Midnight Cowboy' got another few plays in the bar that night.

Faces were glum at next morning's briefing. I had little to offer that was positive. 'We still have lines of enquiry being pursued. We all knew it was never going to be easy. The type of person we are dealing with is a complex killer,' I said as I struggled to lift morale with some gem of wisdom. Nothing came to mind.

Then suddenly I burst into song and belted out my best version of 'Always Look On The Bright Side Of Life'. It was unconventional, not the sort of advice given in training books or police colleges, but it gave everyone a laugh, broke the tension and raised their fighting spirits.

As was the pattern of this case, it was not long before something else happened. Waiting for me when I arrived at work on Friday, 9 August, was another letter.

It made me feel as if I'd won the lottery.

Leeds City Police
Headquaters
LEEDS.

Re Julie
Could not make it Tuesday evening due to the fact that there was no suitable hostage in the Huddersfield red light area on Monday evening, also our young lovers are not down the lane on Tuesday evenings, the latter are more important than the prostitute, as a prostitute can be eliminated any time should the police not co-operate.

But another suitable couple have been located but the day will have to be changed to Wednesday. This being the case a phone call will be made to the usual box on Wednesday 14 August at 8.15pm (not 8.30pm), the extra 15 min being needed due to the location change.

Also this time your W.P.C. will need a Stanley type knife. With a sharpe blade, she will not now be traveling to the box where there is one located,

... should anything go wrong then you will not be given the location of the incendary device or the location of the prostitutes body, mind you, you found Julies in 24 hours, I did think of hiding her body till it was all over but felt sorry for her, she was only killed because she saw where she was, but this time the second prostitute will only be needed to be kept for 24 hours so there should be no problem if nothing goes wrong,

I will also need to know the phone number of where you want to be told the location of the incendary device, this phone number must be given at the second box not the first at Leicester.

I was elated, as I felt this letter was much more positive than the last ones. For once, he had written more directly and given us some interesting clues.

I believed the letter displayed the hallmarks of final preparation. Wednesday, 14 August would be our fourth run, but I hoped it would be the day he'd go for gold and try to get the money. We had four days to wait for the game to end.

I visited Lynn Dart on the Monday. This was an unusual investigation, and none of her family had uttered a word to the press about matters we did not want revealed, such as the letters. They had put their trust in me, and I felt it was right that they should understand what we were doing and why we were doing it. Experience had taught me that as soon as you can be satisfied that no family member is a party to the crime then you need good reasons to keep things from them.

I sat with Lynn and her parents, Harvey and Margaret Atkin, in their lounge. 'I have not given up hope of catching this man, and I know you will not give up hope in me,' I said.

'We know you will get him, Mr Taylor,' said Harvey. 'You've got our support all the way.' They were decent people, and I admired how they were coping with the ordeal. I was also touched by their trust.

As usual, John set off with the RCS team while I waited at Millgarth. At the crucial time, 8.15 pm, there was a migration into the incident room of off-duty officers and others waiting to spring into action to deal with any prisoner searches or statements.

Ninety-eight miles away, at the M1 Leicester Forest East services, Annette Zeknys sprang into action when the phone rang at 8.16 pm.

Taking a deep breath, she picked it up and declared: 'Julie speaking.'

A man replied: 'I am going to have to tell you where to go because my tape recorder is broken.'

Annette was startled. She didn't expect to be speaking directly to the man she assumed was the killer.

'Walkman Gardens,' he said. 'I abducted her last night. Take the M1 northbound to Junction Forty, not Thirty-nine. Take the A638 to Wakefield, go an eighth of a mile, and on your right-hand side there's a telephone box, by a bus stop with a green.'

Annette bravely quizzed him about his new hostage. 'Sarah Davis. She lives at Walkman Gardens, or something like that, I'm not quite sure, in Ipswich,' he informed her. 'You will receive the next call at nine forty-five pm.' The call ended as abruptly as it had started. Annette had the best part of ninety miles to do in under ninety minutes.

The information about Sarah Davis was phoned straight to me. I did not have time to think about what had happened. He was running with us – this was not a time for contemplation, and we all sprang into action. Almost unbelievably, he was bringing her to us, to Wakefield – just ten miles away from where I was waiting for him. He could play his game anywhere in the country, but to venture onto our home turf displayed astonishing arrogance.

I got on to Ipswich Police straight away. I asked them to check and trace all prostitutes called Sarah Davis, or anything similar sounding. I knew I wouldn't get much of a result in the seventy-five minutes left to the next call, and I had no doubt our man also knew that. British Telecom confirmed that Walkman Gardens did not exist, unless it was a street where no one had a phone.

By 9.35 pm, Annette was in Wakefield. She knew the city well, having been there many times before, although not in these circumstances – looking for a kiosk at which to take a call from a killer. Following his directions, at one-eighth of a mile she looked for the phone box but could not see one, or a bus stop by a green. The first phone booth she saw was a half-mile farther down the road at Broadway. She decided this must be the one.

George Newbold, running the operation for RCS, was informed that there was a telephone box at Eden Avenue. It was nearly a mile along the road but, apart from that, it met all the requirements. Annette could not be at two phones at once, so a second female officer was asked to answer that phone if it rang and take a message.

He rang at 9.56 pm. As 'Sod's law' would have it, it was to the Eden Avenue kiosk, where the other officer was. She had difficulty answering as the handset cradle seemed faulty.

She heard a male voice: 'Is that Julie?' She responded, 'Julie speaking.'

The caller said, 'Hello, it's me again. Problems. I'll have to ring you back in half an hour.' She confirmed he would ring back at that number and the conversation ended.

Annette dashed to the right phone box and waited for the call. At 10.35 pm she picked up the ringing phone. Only it carried on ringing. She saw that the phone cradle was stuck down. By the time she had freed it, the line was dead. She waited a further thirty minutes for another call but none came.

The news was relayed to me at Millgarth. I took it with a mixture of disappointment and elation because although I had not caught my killer he had gone much further than ever before in taking the bait. I turned to office manager DCI Eddie Hemsley and shook my head. 'I thought it was going all the way tonight, Eddie. He certainly seemed up for it.' I jumped in my car and travelled to Wakefield for the debrief. I needed to know what went wrong. What would become of Sarah Davis now? Would she be killed? Did she exist at all? I wondered.

It was past midnight when I met the RCS chiefs and discussed the evening's events. We agreed the phone should not have been a problem as he could have rung back. I returned to Millgarth at 1 am to find a number of staff still there. Eddie opened the bottle of Scotch he had bought to toast our night of success. It turned into one of commiseration. 'We need to be prepared for Sarah Davis's body to turn up with a note pinned to it saying, "I told you what would happen if anything went wrong,"' I glumly warned the team.

The following morning a strange discovery was made on the southbound hard shoulder of the M1 at Barnsley. Below a bridge carrying a disused railway line, now a nature walk known as the Dove Valley Trail, was a brown envelope attached to a white-painted brick. Next to it was a small grey container with two red lights and a piece of coiled wire coming out of the top.

The envelope had a number 3 stencilled in the corner. Inside it was a written message.

MESSAGE NEXT
BRIDGE 400 metres
2 <u>MIN ALLOW</u>
DETECTOR ON
<u>PANEL</u>
CARRY MONEY

The next bridge was a footbridge. Underneath it, on the hard shoulder, was another white-painted brick, but no message. We retrieved the items and tests revealed indented writing on the message: 'J37 Barnsley – 2 boxes 1ML RHS – 15½ ML 20 ALLOW'.

This had to be a message in the chain. We had message three; this couldn't be message two as it didn't lead to the bridge. It must be message one, and directions would take the courier from the last phone box to the next, where we found remnants of an envelope that had been stuck there, although the note was missing.

If the directions were followed from the Wakefield phone box, where the courier last spoke to the kidnapper, to the M1, down to Junction 37 and then onto the A628 towards Barnsley they would lead to a phone box outside Peanos Restaurant. There a further envelope was found stuck with double-sided tape underneath the kiosk shelf. The envelope was marked with the number 2 and contained a note and a Stanley knife blade. The note read:

SOUTH ON M1
    EXACTLY 2.1 miles FROM THIS BOX MESSAGE UNDER RAILWAY BRIDGE. UNDER WHITE BRICK BEHIND CRASH BARRIER
    PICK UP SMALL PLASTIC BOX WITH ILLUMINATED L.E.D. AND PLACE ON DASH BOARD.
    ALWAYS CARRY MONEY WITH YOU TO ALL PLACES.
    P.S. RAILWAY BRIDGE IS THE THIRD BRIDGE AFTER JOINING M1 OR FIRST AFTER "SERVICES 22 MILES" sign.
    TIME ALLOWED 5MIN

Clearly his plan was for the courier to stop at the first bridge, put the illuminated device on the car dashboard and drive 400 yards to the footbridge, where he would be waiting to drop down a rope and haul the money up. He was intent on getting the money that night, but what had gone wrong?

I decided the time was right to approach BBC's *Crimewatch*, and I knew I'd have to reveal the whole picture – the kidnapping, the extortion demands and some detail of the runs.

Suggestions came in fast and furious and were discussed at my briefings. A crime squad source made an interesting point which I put to the team. 'It has been suggested that all the places connected with this inquiry have one thing in common – they all feature in the Kellogg's Round Britain Cycle Race.' There was a pause, and then from the back of the room Detective Sergeant Paul Leach chirped up: 'Perhaps he's a cereal killer, sir.' We all fell about laughing.

Our case was on *Crimewatch* on Thursday, 12 September. It was past midnight before I got back to the hospitality room, to my officers Tim Grogan, Helen Dover and Carl Townsley. I thumbed through the messages that had been phoned in for our crime and saw nothing to set my pulse racing.

Tim did have one interesting call from a woman who blurted out: 'My ex-husband did it.' 'Which crime is it that you're putting his name forward for, madam?' asked Tim. 'All of them,' she grunted. 'Why is that?' said Tim. ''Cos he's a bastard,' she snarled before slamming down the phone.

There were hundreds of calls but only one was significant. It was from a prostitute who was with Julie and a second prostitute on the night she disappeared. They told us Julie was working as a street girl but was new to it and so they gave her advice on how to deal with punters. They also said that girls used to change and leave their clothes in bin-bags behind a health centre near where they plied their trade. This explained the accounts of different clothing seen on a woman of Julie's likeness.

But they did not see Julie being picked up by her killer. His claim that he picked her up at 11.30 pm was probably right. The problem was that Chapeltown, especially where Julie had been seen, was an inhospitable place where everyone kept themselves to themselves, so witnesses were difficult to come by.

I decided that the long summer of which I had seen little had come to an end and, needing a break, I booked a family holiday to Tenerife. I would be away from 18 October to 3 November. John O'Sullivan would run the show in my absence.

As I attempted to clear up paperwork before my trip, our man wrote again – but this time directly to Millgarth. The letter was addressed to West Yorkshire Police, Millgate Police Station, Leeds, West Yorkshire.

> Re Julie (With no hair)
> As you are no where near on my tail the time has come to collect my £140,000 from you. I do not get any bigger sentence for 2 murders and prostitutes are easy to pick up but as this time you know I mean business I don't need to pick one up until Monday & I have perfected the pick up. The money to be he same as before
> On Wed 21 Oct the same WPC will be at the phone box on platform 3 of Carlisle Station at 8pm for message at 9.15pm

He said the run was to be on Wednesday, 21 October. But Wednesday was the twenty-third and Monday the twenty-first. We'd cover both days to be sure.

I delayed the start of my holidays by a day to top and tail arrangements, but as I left my office at 7 pm that Friday I felt guilty, having been with the inquiry day and night for three months.

I knew I could not ignore what was going off in England, so by Monday night I was on the phone from my hotel. Eddie Hemsley told me it was no-go that night. There had been no call.

I had always favoured Wednesday for the run anyway, and decided I would return home early if the killer struck again or was arrested. I stretched out on my sunbed, and while my eyes were closed to the searing sun my mind raced through all that had happened since that week in July.

By Wednesday night I was back on the phone, amazed at what I was hearing. While preparing for our fifth run, George Newbold had been talking to his opposite number in the North-West RCS and to his surprise learned they were helping the London region deal with a blackmail demand on British Rail for £200,000. If it was not met an express passenger train would be derailed.

A typed demand posted in Stoke on Trent on 10 October 1991 was marked for the attention of a senior British Rail executive at Euston station, London. It was received on Tuesday, 15 October 1991.

The extortionist ordered two women couriers to be at Crewe railway station on the same day that our officer was to be at Carlisle. This could not be a coincidence.

Next Monday 21 OCT you will insert the following advert in the 'Evening Standard' personal column, "The train is ready to depart ", on Wednesday 23rd, two female employee's of B.R. (preferably two members of the transport police), must be at Crewe Station at 3pm. they must be in the car they will be using to deliver the money, the car must be a small Metro or Nova type due to the width restriction later in the journey, it must be a three door and have no ariels or phone, the rear seats must be folded up completely,

One woman must stay in the car, the other to go to the phones on platform three and await a phone call at around 7pm. The person receiving the calls must wear a skirt and shoes and heels, we want no Olympic sprinter in trainers, the two woman must have a good road atlas and have good road direction sense.

When she answers she must say "This is Amanda speaking" so that we know that we have the right person, she must then just listern,

Note. As security against police ambush we have an ace card to be played at the time the money is picked up, this you will learn later. But your females will not be harmed in any way if they attempt no heroics, there will be a firearm trained on the driver at the time of the pick up, but she will not see anyone.

WARNING
YOUR FEMALES WILL BE IN DANGER IF MONEY NOT REAL

The £200thouand to be made up as follows, exactly.
£50,000 new £50 notes packed in 4 bundles. Not consecutive numbers.
£50,000 used £50 notes packed in 4 bundles.
£40,000 new £20 notes packed in 8 bundles
£40,000 new, new type £20 notes packed in 8 bundles. Not consecutive numbers,
£20,000 used £10 notes.

The letter also included a diagram of how he would derail a train if his wishes were not granted. It had originally been passed to the British Transport Police, but they were not equipped to deal with such complex operations, so it was handed to Cheshire Constabulary as Crewe station was in its area. Cheshire gave it back on the basis that the threat was to British Rail in London and it was then passed to the Metropolitan Police.

Eventually it found its way to the desk of Pat Fleming, Regional Co-ordinator for No. 9 RCS in the Metropolitan Police area. As ordered, they placed a message in the London *Evening Standard*'s personal column. But, for reasons never explained, the RCS decided not to comply with the kidnapper's demands. I believe they thought the blackmailer was bluffing and would give up if his demands were not met. So the RCS replied: 'AMANDA. Could not make it on the 23rd could not get on the train due to your mothers illness. Please ring 0171–922–XXXX. Michael.' The decision was taken before a connection was made with the Dart inquiry. Nevertheless, it was still a serious error of judgment. I felt strongly that this man was more than capable of carrying out his threat, having shown his capabilities by killing Julie Dart.

On Monday, 21 October, a bright young detective inspector from 9 RCS arrived at Millgarth's incident room to speak to John O'Sullivan, Eddie Hemsley and Paul Maxwell about the threat. The smart, well-groomed officer came equipped with energy and enthusiasm, as well as every modern electronic device known to man – two mobile phones, a pager and an electronic organiser, for starters, all beeping every other minute from almost every orifice of his body.

He gave the impression that the big-city jack had come to town to show the country hicks in the North how things were done properly.

When Techno Man's phone went off, he would leap up, rummaging through his pockets to find out which one it was, then dash off into a corner of the room shouting down the phone, 'Hang on, guv,' or 'Now then, skip.' My staff was not sure whether it was some code or whether he had a direct line to Skippy the bush kangaroo. Of course, in Metropolitan Police jargon 'governor' is an inspector or above and a 'skipper' a sergeant. Elsewhere they are, strangely enough, called by their particular rank.

Considering he had no in-depth knowledge of the Dart case, his declaration that the BR extortion and Julie's murder were totally unconnected was a bold and somewhat foolhardy point to make; especially since Paul Maxwell had listed thirty-seven points of similarity between the two. More alarmingly, BR confirmed that the derailment plan was viable and incredibly dangerous. Senior BR managers were convinced that hundreds of lives were at risk, as well as a £2 million train.

In any event, on Wednesday, 23 October, Detective Constable Susan

Woolley from the North-West RCS was on Platform 3 at Crewe railway station when, at 7.08 pm, the phone rang. She deliberately did not use the key words 'Amanda speaking' because she was posing as a member of the public answering the phone and not intending to carry out any instructions he might give. The male caller said, 'Who's that? Who are you?' before hanging up. Nine minutes later the phone rang again, but before it was answered the caller rang off and no further calls were made. Another opportunity lost for us to find Julie Dart's killer. Cold comfort to me, but at least the London RCS now knew the letter-writer was no hoaxer.

Meanwhile, 140 miles away, our courier was at Carlisle station ready to take his call at 9.15 pm. She waited fifteen minutes but no call was made. Something strange then happened. A distant hiss grew increasingly louder and discarded paper swirled in the air as an unscheduled train thundered through the station.

'What was that?' she asked a BR official. 'Oh, it's the Transit Post Office. Since the Great Train Robbery, they don't put them on the schedules.' When I was told this, something the killer wrote in his letters came back to me: 'Letters are stamped and dropped on train.' Could he be putting the letters into the mail on the Transit Post Office?

This would be more support for our railway connection theory, which was gathering its own considerable head of steam. The first telephone contact was at Birmingham railway station, the latest at Carlisle; Julie's body was discovered at the side of a disused railway line; he had mentioned being on a train in a letter; a message was found on the M1 under a railway bridge. Now we had the link with the British Rail demand.

British Transport Police officers were attached to our inquiry so we could check whether any suspects had worked for British Rail. We were coming round to the theory that he was either an employee or ex-employee of British Rail, or a railway enthusiast.

On 28 October, the London RCS tried to regain its ground, realising the opportunity it had lost. Another message was placed in the London *Evening Standard*: 'AMANDA. We need to talk. We would like to help. Please call, Michael.' The next day British Rail HQ at Euston received a further letter. The author's arrogance was as overbearing as ever:

> Congratulations you have now qualified for retribution, but on this occasion I would like to think there might be mitigating circumstances so avoiding the full penalty, for it could have been that my fine college

[sic] indicated the wrong time for my phone call, or in fact something could have gone wrong at your end. He missed the copy of Monday's 'Standard' so could not be certain as to whether the message was in that night, but I myself saw a car parked in the designated spot in the afternoon. However, this time I will lay out the agenda and keep a copy so that there can be no dispute as to the content.

Within a week or so a small penalty will be imposed in the form of the removal of an electric locos pantagraph, and with a little luck the downing of a section of line, a suitable place has not been located, but studies are under way. This is a small demonstration I wished to perform initially to prove our determination.

Following this, we shall await a message in Monday's or Friday's 'Daily Mail' personal column within two weeks, that, "The train is now ready to depart". Failing this, then our initial threat will be carried out to the letter.

The day of the message in the daily mail your female employee will be at the two phone boxes between platforms 1 and 3 on Crewe station at 3pm for a message, everything must be ready at that time, I shall indicate the day and time she is to return, when we are once again ready to collect your offering.

No further communication will be sent, should you fail to respond to this letter then or satisfaction will have to be the considerable cost we will have incured upon yourselves, I shall be hoping this will be well over £2m by the time we call it a day.

I surmised he had expected the police to follow the instructions and that he probably never even checked the *Evening Standard*. I didn't know what a 'pantograph' was but my British Transport Police colleagues explained it was the arm on a locomotive's roof linking it with the overhead electric supply. When a train is in motion it takes its power from the electricity supply. If the arm breaks contact, power is lost.

How would he remove a pantograph from a train and bring down a section of line? I had no idea.

On Monday, 4 November, I returned from holiday to find plenty happening. A message was in the *Daily Mail*'s personal column: 'To all members of travelwise. The train is now ready to depart please contact your representative for details Michael.'

Earlier that morning debris was found on the track beneath Bridge 30 on the main West Coast line at Millmeece, Staffordshire. It had not been there five days before when it was last checked. The bridge carried an unnamed and minor country road.

The debris was a concrete block bearing the words CHIEF EXECUTIVE LONDON. There was also a sandstone block with a piece of wire bent through a hole in it, some rope and wire. They would have been attached at one end to the concrete block and at the other to the sandstone. There were scuff marks where it had been hung over the bridge parapet. The words on the concrete block, now in several pieces, were thought to have first read 'Chief Executioner'.

There was no evidence of any trains being damaged or short circuited, so I concluded that the draught of a passing train sucked the whole thing off the bridge and onto the track, where it was found.

It seemed as if our man was now holding the country to ransom and had upped the stakes in the contest.

The same afternoon, a further operation was mounted at Crewe station. Two female couriers walked to two telephone boxes on Platform 3. At 2.56 pm, one of the phones rang, but when one of the couriers answered it the line went dead. They stayed by the kiosks until 4 pm but no further calls were made.

A wet, blustery and miserable 8 November 1991 reflected everyone's mood. It was the day of Julie Dart's funeral. As I sat in St Wilfrid's Church, Leeds, I looked around and thought I probably knew more about Julie than most of the congregation. Yet I never knew her in life.

I had held many meetings with Lynn Dart at Millgarth as I talked through what we were doing and what we knew. Occasionally there was information about Julie that Lynn was unaware of. 'You probably know Julie better than I do now,' she said. 'Yes, it's strange to know so much about someone without ever having met them,' I responded.

I was slightly ill at ease at the funeral. Apart from Julie's immediate family, I didn't know anyone. I felt as if I was intruding into their personal grief, but it had to be done. The murderer may well be in the pew behind me, I thought as I scanned the church. I'd have to speak to the family to identify any strangers from the film they had agreed to let my officers discreetly take of the mourners.

Reverend David Booth conducted the service as Julie's coffin was carried in by four of her uncles. The vicar spoke about how evil could not triumph, before Julie journeyed to her final resting place at Harehills Cemetery. I stood back as she was interred and the wreaths were placed around the grave. Filming was still taking place. I remained at the grave-side until the mourners left, as I had one more task to perform.

I didn't think her killer would attend the funeral, but who could tell? This callous man may have taken pleasure in seeing Julie's burial. Likewise, as a games player, he may have sent a wreath with a cryptic message. Lynn gave us permission to collect all the cards from Julie's graveside. They'd be checked with her later to ensure the family knew who had written them.

Following our man's instructions, a further message was placed by London RCS in the *Daily Mail* on Monday, 11 November. 'To all Members of Travelwise. We can confirm that the train is now ready to depart. Your bridge message received. Representatives can be contacted on the numbers supplied, Michael.' A further operation was mounted at Crewe railway station that afternoon, but no calls were received.

There seemed little hope now that our killer would take the bait on the BR extortion. I was bitterly disappointed at how the whole operation had failed us, but one thing I was sure of – our man was out there plotting and planning his next move. We had gained a little more insight into our quarry but had missed the opportunity to capture him.

Christmas was rapidly approaching, and on 18 December 1991 I hosted a festive lunch in Millgarth's conference room. With a handful of my team, I welcomed my special guests – twelve members of Julie Dart's family, including her mother Lynn and her devoted grandparents Harvey and Margaret Atkin. We had received tremendous co-operation from the family, and it was the least we could do. Lynn joked about being a member of my team and always called me 'the boss'. And so for a few festive hours the tragic event that had brought us all together was put to the back of our minds.

I worked through December, taking Boxing Day and the following two days off. There had been no contact since the 28 October letter. I knew that, with no breakthrough in sight, I'd soon have to make staff cuts.

The coroner's inquest was at Grantham on Thursday, 16 January. As I got out of the car, I battled through the crowd of photographers baying for a picture. I felt every inch a failure. I was called to the witness box and outlined the circumstances of Julie's death and the extent of our enquiries.

The coroner returned a verdict of unlawful killing by person or persons unknown, and wished me every success with the investigation. I left not realising, as I sat deep in thought on my journey back to Leeds, that the next amazing chapter had already begun.

Our games player had already set in motion the wheels of his next criminal venture – the kidnap of an estate agent.

# chapter two

# ROOM WITHOUT A VIEW

## Monday, 20 January 1992

I turned up reluctantly at the Bramshill Police Staff College in Hampshire to attend one of its four-week command courses, designed supposedly to fine-tune a senior officer's leadership skills – all police officers seeking promotion to chief inspector are supposed to go on one. I should have attended two years earlier when I reached that rank, but successfully avoided it owing to work commitments and a lack of enthusiasm.

Apart from myself, the group was made up of chief inspectors. The only other person who was a superintendent was the course director, and I felt this unsettled him. I knew I gave the impression of being a blunt-speaking Yorkshire man, but I've never been one for going around the houses when a direct route is possible. During the week we discussed many topics, none of which I felt had anything to do with police work, but I was assured the whole process would make me a better person.

One afternoon we were asked to play 'Jim'll Fix It'. I had to explain to Chief Inspector Mung-Hung Lo from the Royal Hong Kong Police who sat next to me who 'Jim' was. The session passed in moments of fantasy as colleagues revealed their dreams. One said he'd like to hot-air-balloon across the Serengeti Plains in Africa while a female colleague announced she'd like to discover cures for untreatable illnesses, before bursting into tears. It seemed her husband had diabetes and the emotion of the moment had consumed her. I said I wanted to successfully prosecute a case in the Old Bailey as a QC. In the back of my mind, though, I was playing Bob'll Fix It, wondering what Julie's killer was doing and when, not if, we were going to catch him. Six months had passed since her death. We had been close to him but not close enough. We'd heard nothing since he tried to blackmail British Rail, but I knew he had not given up.

By Thursday afternoon, my interest had fallen to a level where I was in danger of slipping into a coma. During a discussion about what qualities were desirable for a senior police officer I suggested experience and credibility, explaining: 'I couldn't stand in front of a room full of detectives at a murder briefing and convince them of the direction I intended to take unless I had experience as a senior investigator and credibility in their eyes.' I regretted my contribution as soon as I made it as I looked at some of the group's expressions of horror.

The course director flippantly rejected my offering, effectively switching me off from that day's proceedings. It was then I was handed a note to ring Eddie Hemsley at the incident room at Leeds.

He told me that Stephanie Slater, an estate agent from Birmingham, had been kidnapped mid-morning the previous day while showing a potential client around a house. Her employers, Shipways, had received a letter earlier that morning demanding £175,000, and there was a possibility the kidnapper could also be our killer. There was a meeting in Birmingham later that day, and I told Eddie to go while I would return to Millgarth.

I was not unhappy to see the back of Bramshill. I knew I wouldn't be returning to finish my course. I went back to Leeds the following day. I didn't even call in at home but went straight to the incident room in Millgarth.

I needed updating on what had happened. West Midlands Police sent a detective inspector to our incident room and we sent Detective Inspector Paul Maxwell and Detective Sergeant Paul Leach to theirs. There was little to link the crimes at this early stage, but if it was our man I didn't want to miss him. I spent three hours with the team being briefed on the kidnap.

I first wanted to know all we had on the victim. Stephanie Slater was twenty-five, single and lived with her adoptive parents in Great Barr, Birmingham. She had worked for estate agents since 1985, latterly as a senior negotiator for Shipways at its Great Barr office.

Eddie said a man had telephoned her workplace late afternoon on Tuesday, 7 January. He gave the name of Bob Southall and said he was calling from Wakefield. That was our first link between Julie and Stephanie, Wakefield being one of the locations he sent our courier to. He had asked for details of semi-detached houses priced up to £60,000 and said he would call at Shipways the following day at 9 am to collect them.

Sylvia Baker, Stephanie's colleague, got together details of fifteen properties. They did not include the house from where Stephanie was kidnapped – 153 Turnberry Road – although it was displayed in the window. The man came in the following morning and collected them.

Ten days later, on Friday, 17 January, Shipways received a letter:

143 Wakefield Rd;
Durkar;
Wakefield.
West Yorkshire.
WF26RR

Shipways
905 Walsall Road;
Birmingham
B42 1tn

f.a.o. Mr Kevin Watts

15 January 1992

Dear Sirs;
I called into your offices last Wednesday, 8 January, and Sylvia gave me some leaflets on properties, although she was unable to tell me anything about the properties.

However there was a property at 153 Turnberry Road, for which you did not include a leaflet, this could be very suitable to myself as I am able to undertake most property repairs. could you also enquire if they are prepared to accept £47,000 for quick sale.

If the vendors will accept my offer could I please make arrangements for yourselve to show me the inside of the property on Wednesday 22 January, at about 10.30am.

As I am not on the phone at the above I shall contact you around 9.30am on Monday 20 January

Yours faithfully

Robert Southwall

I noted that, like the killer's letter to us, this was typed on a word-processor and its style was similar to the second BR letter. His first typed letter to Leeds City Police issued the threat: '... next time an employee of say the Electric/Gas /Water companies will be used, to kidnap them in the course of there work will make the company pay the ransom'. Stephanie had been kidnapped in the course of her work; the company was being made to pay the money. Could it be our man?

At 9.30 am on 20 January, the man again phoned Shipways and spoke with the manager, Kevin Watts. He wanted to know whether the vendors had accepted his offer. Kevin did not know as Stephanie was dealing with the sale, but took his phone number, passed it to Stephanie and asked her to call the client back. After a time, he rang again to say no one had phoned him back. Kevin explained there were difficulties in contacting the vendor but confirmed a viewing appointment at the house for 10.30 am on Wednesday, 22 January. Kevin was unsure whether he told the man that it would be Stephanie who'd attend, though it was certainly penned in her diary that she would go.

That Wednesday, Stephanie left at 10.30 am to meet her client, Mr Southwall. At 11.40 am, Kevin Watts and colleague Jane Cashman drove past the address and saw Stephanie's company car parked outside.

Twenty minutes later, back in Shipways office, Sylvia Baker answered the phone in the office.

'Can I speak to Mr Watts?' said the male caller.

'I'm sorry, he's not in the office.'

She noted the caller's mood change. 'Who's in charge?' he said impatiently.

'I'm here. Can I help you?' said Sylvia.

'Listen, Stephanie Slater, she's been kidnapped. There'll be a ransom in the post tomorrow. Contact the police or anybody and she'll die.'

The line then went dead.

Sylvia was shaken as she rang Kevin and told him what had happened. He was at a property just four hundred yards from the office. Jane Cashman ran back to comfort an obviously distressed Sylvia and to find out what exactly had been said. Kevin drove back, by which time Sylvia was near-hysterical, and he decided to ring his regional director.

Sylvia checked with directory enquiries for a telephone number at the address given by Robert Southwall in Wakefield. Not surprisingly, there was no R. Southwall listed in Wakefield. When she rang the number he had left on the Monday she discovered it was a call-box. We later found it was a call-box at Blyth services on the A1 in north Nottinghamshire.

Kevin Watts was by now extremely concerned. Accompanied by a male colleague, he drove to Turnberry Road in the faint hope that Stephanie might be there and that it was all a hoax. Stephanie's car was still outside. The two men went to the back of the house and entered it through the open French windows, to find it empty. As they searched the premises, they found two sets of keys on the meter in the hallway. They were Stephanie's car keys and the ones for the house.

They drove back to the office, and as they showed the keys to the other staff they noticed spots of blood on them. Kevin rang his head office and told them what had happened. He then rang nearby Walsall Road police station: 'One of our girls seems to have gone missing,' he said, before telling them of the phone call and the threat to Stephanie's life if the police were contacted, and that Shipways would be receiving a ransom demand.

Uniform officers were sent to Stephanie's offices and Turnberry Road. I winced when I was told this. The cardinal rule in kidnappings is that there should be no overt police activity. Sending uniform police to the house and office may already have sealed Stephanie Slater's fate. A search of Turnberry Road revealed bloodstains near the top of the stairs and more on the lounge wall near the kitchen door. Neither indicated excessive bleeding.

Susan Hall, manageress of another Shipways branch, was comforting her shocked colleagues when the phone rang at 3.10 pm. 'Just listen. Stephanie dropped her keys to the house in the hall, so go and lock it up,' ordered the kidnapper.

West Midlands Deputy Chief Constable Richard Adams, Assistant Chief Constable (Crime) Phil Thomas and Head of CID Detective Chief Superintendent Tom Farr had been informed and decided that a press embargo should be requested and that reporters should stay away from

Shipways and Turnberry Road. An incident room was set up at Nechells Green police station just outside Birmingham city centre. Tom Farr would be the senior investigating officer (SIO), though ACC Phil Thomas would be in overall command.

They were aware of the Julie Dart case through our circulations, and wanted to know whether there was any connection. They knew that the address on the letter sent to Shipways from Robert Southwall did not exist.

The caller had promised that a ransom letter would be in the post the following day, so a team of officers was dispatched to the sorting office at Great Barr, where at 4.55 am on Thursday it was found. It was word-processed and postmarked Stoke on Trent.

Back in Millgarth, I was handed a copy of the letter and read it slowly, looking for any obvious connections.

Your employee has been kidnapped and will be released for a ransom of £175,000. With a little luck he should be still O.K. and unharmed, to prove this fact you will in the next day or so receive a recorded message from him. He will be released on Friday the 31 January 1992, provided;

On Wednesday 29 January a ransome of £175,000 is paid and no extension to this date will be granted.

The police are not informed in any way until he has been released

On Wednesday 29th at 4pm (on line 021 358 XXXX) you will receive a short recorded message from the hostage. To prove he is still alive and O.K. he will repeat the first news item that was on the 10am, Radio 2 news. He will then give further instructions. A second and more detailed message will be given at 5.05pm the same day. Your watch must be synchronized with the 5pm pips on Radio 2. The location of the second call will be given at 4pm, so transport with a radio must be available

The money must be carried in a holdall and made up as follows, precisely;

£75,000 in used £50. £75,000 in used £20. £25,000 in used £10 packed in 31 bundles, 250 notes in each.

Kevin Watts (if not the hostage) must be the person to receive all messages and carry the money to the appointd place. However, please not that all messages will be pre-recorded, so no communications or negotiations can be made.

YOU HAVE BEEN WARNED, HIS LIFE IS IN YOUR HANDS

I guessed he typed the letter before the kidnapping so he could post it immediately afterwards with a taped message from the victim, in a town which would give no clue as to where he was going.

I was not at all convinced by his declaration that he intended to take a male victim. He wanted us to think that he had planned to take a man, but I believed a woman was always going to be his next victim, as he knew from his conversation with Kevin Watts that the viewing was in Stephanie's diary.

There was a cassette tape with the letter. John O'Sullivan pushed a copy of it into the player on the desk beside us. Eddie explained that the sound quality was poor, and so we all leaned forward to listen as the gentle hiss at the beginning of the tape came over the speaker, quickly followed by Stephanie's trembling voice.

Her audible fear made it even more difficult to understand her plea. It went through my mind that I might be listening to this woman's last words, as she could well be dead.

'This is Stephanie Slater. The time is now eleven forty-five. I can assure you I'm OK and unharmed. Providing these instructions are carried out I will be released on Friday, 31 January.

'By Wednesday you will need an Ordnance Survey map between Blackburn and Burnley. Kevin Watts must be the person that acts as courier and use his car. Sylvia or Jane may be a passenger to act as guides but only these two people must be in the car.

'The passengers must never leave the car.

'Next Wednesday at every point clear instructions will be given.

'The boot of the car must be open for thirty seconds.

'Money must not be marked in any way whatsoever or contain any device whatsoever.'

I feared for Stephanie, who was in extreme danger if she was being held captive by Julie's killer. The desperation in her voice screamed out. I played the tape several times, trying to cut through the emotion to pick out her words.

Stephanie's order that the boot be open for thirty seconds was identical to the instruction in the British Rail demand. It was not a common request, and I felt it was the first link between the Slater kidnap and the BR blackmail. We had already established a series of positive links between the Julie Dart murder and the BR extortion, and it now appeared that all three crimes were connected. Murder, blackmail and now kidnap. Our man appeared to recognise no bounds to his burgeoning criminal career.

I jotted down the similarities between the cases of Julie and Stephanie:

Instructions by tape-recorded message
Combinations of taped, verbal and typed messages
Warnings regarding devices
Wednesday for ransom delivery
Money to be specifically bundled
Promise that location of hostage to be given after receipt of the money
Spelling mistakes – especially the word 'ransome'
Use of term 'With a little Luck' – this was also used in the 'BR congratulations' letter.

The letter was overegged with instructions, seemingly trying to impress the reader with the author's intellect, but his poor spelling and grammar let him down, and the impression he tried to create was wasted on me.

Here we had a kidnapper who, while laying out intricate and clever plans, unfortunately for him could not spell the word 'ransom'. It would have appealed to my black sense of humour had the situation not been so serious.

As Friday night's briefing drew to a close, I sat in Millgarth's incident room, feeling tense but excited. I obviously feared for Stephanie's life – but I also knew the game was back on. 'If the kidnapper of Stephanie Slater is found, we have the killer of Julie Dart,' I mused aloud to John O'Sullivan and Eddie Hemlsey. Not that I needed to make the point – they were already convinced of it too.

I wrestled with the awful odds of Stephanie surviving. Not great, I considered. I tried to be positive and think of reasons why he should release her unharmed.

We now had to play a waiting game. With the Wednesday deadline looming, I travelled to the West Midlands on Sunday. John O'Sullivan and I arrived at Nechells police station just after 11.30 am to meet ACC Phil Thomas, a big man who looked every inch the hardened detective, with a voice so deep and rasping it could probably cut granite. We went over the facts as we knew them. There was no forensic evidence or fingerprints to link the two crimes, but my gut feeling was this was our chap. Phil was a wise man and certainly did not dismiss my thoughts.

It was the fourth day of her kidnapping ordeal, and Stephanie might already have been dead, but his letter gave me hope. If she was able to repeat the first item of news on the coming Wednesday we'd know she was still alive. I had a long conversation with Detective Chief Superintendent Mick Foster, co-ordinator of No. 4 Regional Crime Squad (RCS), who'd be running Operation Kaftan to bring Stephanie home alive. He was notably interested in whether or not I believed Stephanie's kidnapper was Julie's killer, as this would affect what actions he would take – they'd clearly be different if he thought they were dealing with someone who had already killed. Mick was a sensible and likable person and he took in all the information thrown at him.

You can always sense when something happens on a big job as the activity all around steps up a gear. As I sat in the Nechells incident room, I picked up a buzz about the place and quickly learnt why. A short time before, our man had rung Stephanie's home. His confidence appeared undiminished as he spoke to her father, Warren, who was obviously taken aback, as the last person he expected to be conversing with was his daughter's kidnapper.

'Mr Slater?'

'Who is it please?' asked Warren.

'Is that Mr Slater?' the man persisted.

'It is.'

'Just listen,' the man ordered, before explaining that the next voice he heard would be Stephanie's. It was clearly a tape-recorded message.

'Hello, Stephanie here. They've allowed me to make a message to you just to let you know that I'm all right and unharmed. West Bromwich Albion lost yesterday to Swansea three–two. I want you to know I love you and not to say too much. Whatever the outcome, I will always love you. Look after the cat for me.'

The line then went dead.

Officers were at the Slaters' home and would be there until this was all over – whatever the outcome, to quote their only child. At least she was alive up to 5 pm yesterday when Saturday's football scores were announced, I thought. The clock was ticking away, and the number of officers on the case was growing by the day. No. 4 RCS was girding its loins for the operation just seventy-two hours away.

John and I stayed down there overnight as I had arranged to see a West Midlands Police crime analyst on Monday to formalise the list of links between the Dart and Slater inquiries. After our meeting with him, I dwelt on the scepticism I felt emanating from some of their detectives to the effect that the crimes were not linked at all.

I knew we'd be the least welcome faces to some Birmingham officers because West Yorkshire Police had investigated the West Midlands Serious Crime Squad over corruption allegations a few years earlier. One Midlands detective told me: 'Your lot came to investigate corruption and ended up looking at our expenses and girlfriends.' The fact that none of my team was involved seemed irrelevant to them.

Meanwhile, Kevin Watts was undergoing training to act as a courier. The kidnapper had been in Shipways and he might have seen all the staff, Kevin included, so a substitute courier was out of the question. Kevin, thirty-three and married with three young daughters, volunteered as he felt it was the least he could do for Stephanie. He would need to be trained on how to act – Stephanie's life could depend upon him.

Like our courier Annette, Kevin had been given psychological counselling to help him get through the ordeal he faced. He was also given more practical aid in the form of a bullet-proof vest and a hidden microphone in the car into which he could give us a running commentary as events unfolded.

Just before 5 pm on Tuesday, Jane Cashman took a phone call at Shipways. 'I want to speak to Kevin Watts, quickly,' the male speaker said.

'Who's calling, please?'

'Never mind,' he tersely responded.

She put the call through.

'Kevin Watts?' the caller said.

'Speaking.'

'Have you got the money?'

'For tomorrow?' said Kevin.

'Yes.'

'I'm getting it.'

'You'll get a message at three o'clock,' said the man impatiently.

'A message at three o'clock tomorrow,' replied Kevin, remembering he had been told to repeat everything for the sake of accuracy.

'Yes. Do you want a password? If you give me a word I'll get her to repeat it to say she's all right.'

'Yes. Could I have her parents' Christian names, please?' said Kevin.

'OK. Three o'clock tomorrow.'

The call had lasted one minute. Game on at 3 pm tomorrow. That was fine by me. I had been through this before.

On Wednesday, I felt as if we were about to finally confront the man I had been hunting for six months. Norman Mould, the No. 3 RCS co-ordinator, would relay what was happening from their Leeds office to me at Millgarth. This was a West Midlands RCS show, and we had to take a back seat. At 3.45 pm, it was confirmed that a call had gone into Shipways. The game was under way.

Jane Cashman took the call at 3.25 pm.

'Kevin Watts, please.'

Jane recognised the caller's voice. 'Who's calling, please?'

'Never mind,' came the reply.

Jane put him through to Kevin.

'Hello, Kevin Watts?'

Kevin: 'Speaking.'

'Have you got it?'

Kevin: 'Yes, I have.'

'Her mother's and father's names are Betty and Warren and after the end of this message I will play you a tape in which she mentions it, right?'

Kevin: 'OK.'

'You go to Glossop station ...'

Kevin: 'Glossop?'

'Glossop station.'

Kevin: 'Could you spell that?'

'G-L-O-double-S-O-P.'

Kevin: 'G-L-O ...'

The caller interrupted, and finished the sentence for him. '... double-S-O-P.'

Kevin: 'OK.'

'West of Manchester,' explained the caller.

Kevin: 'West of Manchester.'

'There's a phone box inside the entrance hall, there's only one, and there'll be a further message at seven pm.'

Kevin: 'Seven pm?'

'Yes. It's an hour and a half's journey. I'm in Glossop now and it's sunny. If anything goes wrong, you ring your office.'

Kevin: 'Ring my office here?'

'Yes.'

Kevin: 'But there won't be anybody here, so I'll have to have somebody here.'

'Well, they won't know what's happened unless you get there at seven o'clock. Who's coming with you?'

Kevin: 'I'll be on my own. I can't take anybody with me. Is Steph OK?'

'Definitely OK. She'll be released tomorrow night just after twelve o'clock.'

The caller then played a tape recording of Stephanie speaking down the phone. The quality was poor and her words were barely understandable: 'My parents' names are Betty and Warren Slater. I am frightened but unharmed,' she tearfully mumbled.

'Did you get that?' the man said.

Kevin: 'Yes. Wasn't very clear.'

'Seven o'clock.'

The call lasted two minutes.

I was elated when I was told that Kevin had set off in his Rover with the £175,000 in a holdall on the back seat to his rendezvous at the phone booth. He headed north, albeit to the wrong side of the Pennines from my Yorkshire base. The kidnapper had said Glossop was west of Manchester. In fact it was east of the city. Was that a slip of the tongue or did it indicate he did not know the area?

I arrived at the RCS Leeds office at 6.30 pm as Kevin Watts was driving to Glossop. I needed to be as close to the action as I could, and sat drinking tea to pass the time. All the phones in the office bar one were permanently staffed with open lines. I was getting regular updates with messages being repeated verbatim as they were passed across the country. It meant we all seemed to share a sense of the tension that Kevin, a brave, ordinary man hurled into this remarkable drama, must have been enduring.

But as the clock neared 7 pm, no word was passed of Kevin's arrival at Glossop. With just two minutes to go, it was confirmed he was there. 'Cut that bugger a bit fine,' someone quipped as the message was relayed. Nervous laughter and collective relief swept through the room.

For us in Yorkshire, this was all familiar territory. We had endured five courier runs with all our hopes and planning brushed aside by this man, who yet again appeared to be destroying innocent people's lives – and almost seemed to enjoy doing it. As I pondered this, it was relayed to me that the phone had rung at 7.04 pm and Kevin had answered it.

The caller asked for Kevin's car registration number but he could not recall it.

'Parked outside the station?'

Kevin: 'Yes.'

'Go out of the station, turn right down the hill towards the town centre and go past the Norfolk Arms public house. You will see two phone boxes. The first, a phone card box, under the shelf, you'll find a message.'

The call was terminated.

Out came the map in the office as we calculated how far he would walk. It seemed like an age before we were told the details of the message. A brown envelope marked with an 'A' was under the shelf in the phone box. The typed instructions read:

Take B6105, (Which is the road outside that station) uphill and continue until joining A628.

Right on A628 to Barnsley.

At junction of A628 & A629 turn right at roundabout. to Sheffield. Phone box 1.6mls from roundabout on left hand side. Just past cross roads.

Stay in car and enter box at 7.40pm, if phone is not ringing there is a message taped under the small black shelf. Open boot before going in box and leave open until returning.

Warning. Enter boxes only at times given. At sometime you will be observed.

I checked another map and worked out he was being directed to a phone box at a junction in Oxspring near Sheffield. Using my finger, I traced on the map the route of the A628 as it snaked across the Pennines, towards Junction 37 of the M1. It was 3.5 miles from where I reckoned he was due to collect the Dart ransom from our courier Annette on our fourth run of 14 August. I was amazed. Surely he wasn't going to use the same place?

I knew we faced a long wait, as the thick fog would mean Kevin's journey over the A628 would take longer than normal. This would not be to our advantage, but it would help the kidnapper as a cover. I asked for aerial photographs of the area to be brought up.

Norman Mould contacted West Midlands RCS control room, which had been set up at Bournville Road police station, to let them know Kevin was being sent to within a few miles of the Dart drop point. Did they want to deploy our local crime squad officers who, though not involved in the operation at this stage, were on stand-by close to the area? They knew this patch well, having been there on the Dart operation. With their superior knowledge, they'd be crucial to cover observations there. The reply came back – an emphatic no. I found out later that when they did decide to try to deploy some officers at the Dart drop point, West Midlands gave them the wrong map reference, so they were covertly observing nothing as they were in totally the wrong place.

The fog was now creating serious problems. Kevin would not be able to meet the kidnapper's tight deadline. He was to be at the phone box at Four Lane Ends in Oxspring by 7.40 pm. That came and passed and he seemed to be nowhere near. I couldn't believe that Stephanie's life might depend on the weather. It was just after 8.15 pm when Kevin eventually got there. Visibility was now down to five to ten yards.

Kevin's next message came over to us. I doubted that he realised hundreds of officers from a dozen forces were hanging on to every word he spoke.

> THIS ROUTE WILL SHOW IF YOU ARE BEING FOLLOWED
> BACK TO CROSS ROADS. (50yds)
> RIGHT UP HILL (B 6449 TO DODWORTH)
> LEFT 100yds (signposted public bridleway) This is a small lane on LHS before main B6449 bears right.
> Take care to turn right 100yds down lane.
> LEFT FORK BY FARM HOUSE. (Down the hill)
> 150yds DOWN LANE IS A SMALL BUILDING ON LHS.
> PICK UP BLACK BAG BY RED/WHITE CONE.
> TRANSFER ALL THE MONEY FROM YOUR HOLDALL TO INTO THIS BAG.
> 2 MINS ALLOWED FOR THIS.
> DO NOT MOVE OFF UNTIL YOU HAVE DONE THIS.
> MOVE OFF AT EXACTLY 7.47pm.
> TAKE MONEY AND BAG WITH YOU.
> FURTHER MESSAGE IN BAG.

I was concerned that Kevin was up to forty minutes behind schedule. It was now 8.40 pm and he had not reached the point where the kidnapper's money bag was. The money transfer from one bag to another worried me owing to the rural nature of his location and the fog, because while he did this he was at great risk the kidnapper could attack him.

Again, I waited. I sensed that the kidnapper was not far away. It should take only minutes for Kevin to travel to the next specified point. You get a feeling on these jobs when things start to go wrong as communications slow down, eventually grinding to a stop. I pictured frantic messages being relayed from the West Midlands control room trying to find out what was happening, but until they were in the picture I knew we'd hear nothing.

Suddenly the phones burst into life. 'He's arrived at a small building,' shouted one. 'He's found a wooden stake in the ground. There's an arrow-shaped piece of card on it with Shipways written on. There's a red-and-white cone in the middle of the track. He's transferred the money into the other bag and there was a message in it.' I listened further. 'He's gone back to the car and has read the message.' Kevin was still speaking out loud and everyone in the room was listening intently to what he said. One person noted down his every word.

```
GO TO END OF LANE. TURN
LEFT BACK TO ROUNDABOUT
(A628/9 TURN RIGHT > PHONE
BOX 3.5 mls LHS MESSAGE
TAPED UNDER SHELF
15 mins ALLOWED
```

I knew, now we'd reached the point where the money had gone into the kidnapper's bag, that the game must be nearing its end. I looked at the map book again and was struck by two things. Whatever lane Kevin was in, it was not in our book, and neither was the Dove Valley Trail, which I knew was very close to where he must now be. The maps lacked fine detail. It was to be of no help to us now, but after this operation new, more detailed ones were issued nationally.

A message was passed to the operational command to the effect that the Dove Valley Trail passed through where they were, but we were told the bag was under observation in a hedge bottom somewhere. No one seemed to know where Kevin was, and my concern was growing.

I could not work it out. He must have had instructions as to where to leave the bag. I even wondered whether he had come across a device which would explode if he passed on any message. More to the point, if they did not know where Kevin was, how did we know the kidnapper was not driving him away in his vehicle? One of the operation's objectives was to safe-guard Kevin, which could prove difficult when no one apparently knew where he was.

The tension was unbearable. It was like being an expectant father wait-ing outside the maternity unit with everybody rushing about and nobody telling you what was going on. I could not understand why they did not know where Kevin or the money were.

It was over an hour before it was established that whatever it was that was 'under observation in a hedge bottom somewhere', it certainly was not the bag of money. Kevin Watts had been found. Following his further instructions, he had put the money in a tray and driven off to find the next phone box – only it didn't exist. At 12.30 am, I went with John O'Sullivan to meet the crime squads who had been involved in the opera-tion for a debrief on the night's disastrous events. I was annoyed that our RCS had not been deployed during the operation when it came on to our patch. We had no murderer, no kidnapper, no money. Nothing.

It was the worst possible outcome for me as he had slipped through the net once more, and if he had the money he might now disappear for ever. I was frustrated and disappointed, though not as much as I would have been if I had known the well-kept secret that most of the Midlands RCS were not even trained to do kidnap operations, but bullishly went ahead with it rather than allow the hugely more experienced northern RCS to take on the job.

At the meeting, I learnt of Kevin's ordeal. As instructed he put the money into the other bag. He drove to the end of the lane towards the phone box but after a short distance encountered another traffic cone in the middle of the lane. He described the lane as more of a track, and doubted that two vehicles could pass at most points. He was terrified, as he expected to be confronted by the kidnapper's vehicle blocking his way. He stopped his car at the cone, which he thought was on a river bridge. Pinned to it was a sign, which read:

```
STOP. 60 SECS ALLOWED
ON WALL BY (4) SIGN > WOOD
TRAY > DO NOT MOVE TRAY
SENSOR INSIDE > PUT MONEY &
BAG ON TRAY > IF BUZZER DOES
NOT SOUND LEAVE MONEY
```

THERE > REMOVE CONE IN
FRONT OF CAR AND GO >
MONEY WILL NOT BE
COLLECTED UNTIL YOU
HAVE LEFT

Kevin followed the instructions, petrified of what would happen if the buzzer went off as he placed the money in the tray. He was driving on, looking for the next telephone box, when the local RCS officers found him.

As we took in the whole saga, Norman Mould answered a call from West Midlands at 1.10 am. He turned to us and, with an amazed expression on his face, announced: 'Stephanie has been released. She's safe and at home.' I was stunned into silence, as I'd rated her chances of survival as barely above zero. It was great news, though it hardly dispelled the sense of failure shrouding the crime squad teams. The news lifted me, as I saw another door opening in my hunt for Julie's killer. Stephanie might have information which could be vital to us.

Kevin Watts had done an excellent job, but even though it had been a long day he had one last task to do on the way back to Birmingham – to show officers the exact spot where he had left the money. They found the bridge on Blacker Green Lane where it crossed over the disused railway line of the Dove Valley Trail at Silkstone Common, South Yorkshire. It was then Kevin realised that it was not a bridge over a river as he had thought. The Dove Valley Trail snaked east through the cutting for three miles to where it crossed over the M1 at the Dart money drop point. On top of the bridge wall was a patch of sand. Under the bridge they found a drawer with a cigar tube and a light bulb box fastened together, both painted the same silver colour as the M1 device, which he intended Kevin Watts to think was an explosive anti-tamper transmitter detection device.

The kidnapper must have been waiting on the trail, just sixty feet below Kevin. He would have heard him place the money on the tray and drive off. He then simply pulled the line attached to the tray and the money came tumbling down. It was a simple but effective plan which had made him £175,000 richer.

I arrived back at Millgarth at 2.15 am and immediately debriefed our team. I knew the case had now fallen into the lap of Mick Williams at

Nechells. By 3 am I was on my way home, but would be back at my desk five hours later. I couldn't wait to see how the media would carve us up on this one.

But not a word was printed in the morning papers. I discovered that the embargo was still in place at 6 am. In the euphoria of Stephanie's release no one had lifted it or told the media. Naturally, they were furious. This was a big story and their co-operation had not been rewarded. They had last been briefed at 6 pm the previous night when ACC Phil Thomas announced: 'At three thirty pm today, as a result of a call received at Shipways, a pre-planned operation to bring home Stephanie and arrest the kidnapper was launched. This operation involves more than a thousand detectives from six forces who are now on station. The courier is now, as we speak, following instructions from the kidnapper.'

A press embargo is a voluntary agreement between editors who, on receipt of a written request from a chief constable in a life-and-death situation, agree to a news blackout. The police obligation as part of the agreement is to inform the media as soon as those circumstances change. At 1 am, when Stephanie was released, the West Midlands Police press office should have ended the embargo.

Someone had to take the blame. TV, radio and the regional evening papers cleaned up on the story. The national papers came in last, having to wait until Friday morning to go into print. The penalty was exceptionally bad press for West Midlands Police and ridicule for all.

More bad news for us followed. The places where the kidnapper had been were not secured by West Midlands police for examination. Vital evidence – footprints, tyre tracks, fibres, maybe cigarette ends with his DNA for us to examine – was lost. Following Stephanie's release, crime squad officers simply picked up all the signs the kidnapper had put out for Kevin Watts, threw them in a car boot and took them back to Birmingham. The places and phone booths the kidnapper had visited should have been examined. In my view it seems like an astonishing lack of professionalism that those in command at West Midlands should have botched such a basic crime investigation procedure.

To compound the situation, I turned on the TV and saw South Yorkshire Police staging a press conference at the very bridge where the drop had happened. There was now a very real risk that the crime scene was now lost through contamination. There was little I could do as it was West Midlands' show but I had expected better than this.

I still did not know how things had gone so farcically wrong. Why was a bag that wasn't a bag being watched? Our presumption that an officer could see the money bag and was waiting for the kidnapper to pick it up was wrong. He was not watching the bag because he was at the wrong place. Why didn't they know when Kevin had put the money in the tray? The Midlands RCS said Kevin had not passed on the vital message when he deposited the money, but the truth was that crime squad communications had failed. Kevin had also, understandably in the darkness, missed a letter placed in the tray where he deposited the money. It was marked with a 'D' in the corner and read:

IGNORE LAST LETTER IN BAG.
Continue to end of lane turn right onto A628 Barnsley.
Continue to M1 and join Southward.
Continue to J23A – A42 & M42 to Birmingham.
Return to you office on Walsall Road where a phone call will be made at 11pm to 11.15pm indicating the whereabouts of Stephanie. Dead if no money, alive if all is correct.

It was a chilling reminder of what this person was capable of, yet he had still released Stephanie unharmed. She was taken to Birmingham's Priory Hospital. The inquiry urgently needed information from her and, while respecting her need for medical supervision, she needed to be debriefed. Armed officers were also posted outside her room for her protection.

Shipways appointed employee Melvyn Measure to deal with the media offers flooding in to buy Stephanie's story. She had suddenly become a celebrity, a sellable valuable commodity, and that seemed at times to overshadow her role as a witness who had information vital to efforts to catch not only her kidnapper but maybe a murderer as well.

Her kidnap and the Dart murder were still separate inquiries, run by different forces and from different locations. The two chief constables, Ron Hadfield of West Midlands and West Yorkshire's Peter Nobes, would decide the way forward.

Ron Hadfield was a larger-than-life character and was unfazed by the attention his position brought him, while Peter Nobes was quietly efficient. A meeting was arranged for Friday. I accompanied ACC Tom Cook and the Chief to Birmingham and *en route* briefed Mr Nobes on the investigations and why I thought they were connected.

Mr Nobes turned to me. 'Bob, on a scale of one to a hundred, what figure would you put on the likelihood of it being the same man?' I thought a moment. While pretty sure it was the same man, I had to have some doubt, however small. 'I could go no higher than ninety-five per cent.' 'Very wise,' said Mr Nobes. 'You could never go a hundred per cent without some forensic evidence or fingerprints.'

The two chiefs agreed to run Dart and Slater as a linked inquiry. The problem was who would be in overall command and which computer system would we use.

In its wisdom, the national police service had ended up with a number of suppliers when it put out to tender the contracts for the Holmes computer system (Home Office Large Major Enquiry System). West Yorkshire was on the MacDonald Douglas version and West Midlands on the Honeywell Bull version. The theory was that any two forces could be linked together if they had a Holmes system from one of the approved suppliers. Not so, as these two systems would show.

We had ten times more information than West Midlands so we agreed to give them some of our MacDonald Douglas computers to use to transfer data. As it would take some time to get up and running, we arranged a tape transfer from their database to be loaded onto our system. When the tape arrived two days later and was put in our computer, the information was for a completely different investigation.

To Tom Cook's surprise, he was put in charge of both inquiries. I had not anticipated this as I thought Ron Hadfield wanted the job and was the obvious frontrunner. I learnt from Tom that this was not part of Mr Hadfield's plan. If West Yorkshire ran the linked inquiry and if no one was caught or there were further kidnaps and it all went horribly wrong, the beleaguered West Midlands Police would not be savaged by the media. This might have been a shrewd political move by Ron Hadfield, but I didn't care. I knew my team would be happy with Tom Cook in overall command. However, he likened the moment to being handed a poison chalice as, if it all went wrong, it would now be West Yorkshire's fault.

On the following Monday, 3 February, Tom Cook, flanked by Mick Williams and myself, faced the press in Birmingham as a united front, though behind the scenes it was a different matter. West Midlands and West Yorkshire forces ranked first and third in size after the Metropolitan Police. The underlying tension of the inquiry our force had undertaken on their Serious Crime Squad remained tangible.

A doctor examined Stephanie after her release. She had no significant physical injuries, though she was disorientated and light sensitive – not surprising since she'd been blindfolded for eight days.

She was being interviewed under medical supervision, and information was slow to filter through. The immediate focus seemed to be on what sort of container she was kept in. The first suggestion was a green plastic bottle bank. Stephanie was not as co-operative as she could have been; this was understandable, as we thought she was suffering from Stockholm Syndrome, where victims become psychologically dependent on their captors. It is named after a 1973 incident in which four hostages were taken in a botched bank robbery in Stockholm, Sweden. Six days later they actively resisted rescue. They refused to testify against their captors and even raised money for their legal defence. One hostage eventually became engaged to one of her jailed captors.

It typically takes about three or four days for the psychological shift to take hold. It is typified by a strategy of the victim trying to keep his or her captor happy in order to stay alive and developing an obsessive identification with the abductor's likes and dislikes, eventually warping their psyche so they come to sympathise with their tormentor. In time, Stephanie's feelings were to turn to hatred.

During the ten days over which she was debriefed, information was passed to us on a regular basis. She first noticed her client at the front door of the house, and he confirmed he was Bob Southwall. She said he was aged between forty and fifty-five, with a dark, almost dirty complexion, of medium to stocky build and about five foot eight inches tall. His dark hair was brushed back off his face and he wore heavy rimmed glasses, like those worn by film star Michael Caine. His clothes had a tattered look and he had a faint smell of grease about him. He had a train badge on his duffel coat.

He gave no hint of his ultimate intentions as he wandered around the ground floor of the house, but when they went upstairs she sensed he did not really seem interested. They had been in the bathroom already but he suddenly called her back in, pointing at the corner and saying, 'What's that up there?' She leant over the bath and was about to tell him it was just a little hook when Bob came up behind her.

His mood changed and he spoke in a harsh voice, threatening her with a knife. He was now wearing gardening gloves, but she bravely made a grab for the knife, cutting her right hand in the process. He overpowered her, forced her into the bath, ordered her to lie still and said he was not going to harm her.

She lay terrified as he bound her hands together with a length of washing line, put sunglasses over her eyes and a rope around her neck. He then told her to get out of the bath and guided her down the stairs.

At the bottom, he tied a gag around her face. He loosely tied her legs together, leaving her able to shuffle, and then guided her out of the French windows into the back garden. As she walked towards the garage she knew, from previous visits to the house, where she was. Only this time there was a car in the garage and he placed her in its already reclining front passenger seat. He tied her to it with a piece of rope and fastened her in with the seat belt, threatening her with the knife if she did not lie still.

Stephanie reckoned it was about 11 am when they left the house and thirty minutes later when he stopped the car.

'What's your name?' he asked, and she told him. 'You can call me Bob. It's not my real name but it will do for now. He held a tape recorder to her lips and said he wanted her to tape a message. As he dictated it, Stephanie followed his orders. They must have been near Stoke on Trent at this point, as he then went and posted the cassette tape and first demand letter to Shipways.

He stopped again after an hour-long drive and they sat in the car as he casually ate ham sandwiches he had brought with him, almost as if he were on a day jaunt to the countryside. Stephanie declined his offer of food. He said they needed to kill some time as he did not want to arrive at their destination before 6 pm. They were near a railway line, as she could hear trains going by. He let her get out of the car on one occasion to go to the toilet but quickly ushered her back in when a train approached.

After another hour-long drive they parked up for a further forty-five minutes until it got dark, then he drove the final leg of their journey to her prison. He had been quite clever, as she had no inkling how far he had taken her. It was possible he had driven round in circles and had not actually gone very far at all. For most of the journey, he played a Beach Boys tape and Radio 2.

'Right, we're here. When you get out, remember, no screaming. Not that anybody's going to hear you out here,' he warned.

Stephanie lay perfectly still. 'I strained my ears but couldn't hear a thing. Then through the darkness there was a grating, scraping sound of metal against metal as if a large iron door was being pulled open along iron runners. "Swing your legs out and stand up," he ordered. Standing behind me with his hands on my shoulders, he propelled me slowly forward. It was only a few steps but he seemed to rush me inside the building. I couldn't understand why: the place gave me the impression of being totally deserted.

'He helped me shuffle inside. "Come on, you're all right. Keep walking," he kept saying. He turned me to face the left. "That's far enough. There's a chair behind you." I sat down gingerly on a hard wooden chair. Immediately he secured handcuffs around my wrists and ankles and tied my arms and body to a straight-backed chair with a length of rope.'

He left Stephanie there while he went to buy fish and chips for her. She knew she had been kidnapped for a ransom from her employers, and he had told her on the journey she would be held for eight days.

After managing to eat a handful of chips, Stephanie had to be secured for the night. 'He said, "I want you to lie down on the mattress and shuffle forward towards the box that's at the end of it, as if you were getting into a sleeping bag." I had no idea what I was supposed to be shuffling into but I did as he asked. I continued to shuffle down until my hips wedged against the sides and I told him I could go no farther. "You should be able to. I can get down it," he said.

'As soon as I was in, he took hold of my wrists by the handcuff chain and tied them above my head to what felt like a metal bar. "Feel this," he said, stretching one of my fingers. I touched what felt like stone. "Don't pull on the bar because there are boulders above you. Can you feel them?" I nodded. "If you pull on the bar, you'll pull them down and crush yourself. No shouting, no screaming, don't make a sound. When I open this door in the morning, I want to see the gag and blindfold still on you. Have you got that?"'

He also said there was a length of wire in the box which he'd attached to electrodes, and if she moved she'd get an electric shock. As I read Stephanie's statement, I recalled the 11 July 1991 letter to Leeds City Police: 'The hostage will be guarded 24hrs a day by P.I.R detectors connected directly to the mains. BEFORE ENTERING HOUSE THE ELECTRICITY MUST BE SWITCHED OF FROM OUTSIDE before opening the door or any movement will activate the detectors.' I knew this was a further link between the two crimes. Stephanie had seen Julie's killer when she arrived at Turnberry Road. Through her, I would find him.

Undoubtedly, Stephanie's week in captivity was a horrific ordeal. After spending most of her first day trussed up, he made her take off her own clothes and wear some of his old ones. She then had to endure the pain of lying still and blindfolded and half suffocating with the gags, in a bitterly cold box with her arms above her head.

But in that confined space, Stephanie absorbed everything, by sound, sight and touch. She even peeked out over her blindfold. We expected some of what he told her to be disinformation, but he could also have slipped up and told her something factual about himself. The list she made was endless.

Radio 2 played all day. He told her he had a six-month-old Alsatian bitch. When he had gone for the fish and chips, he was only away fifteen minutes. There was a microwave on the premises which she heard ping. The phone had an old-style ring. There was an old-fashioned cash register as she heard that ringing sound when the drawer was opened.

She heard trains in the distance and thought he had a motorbike as she heard it one time. He talked often of his mate, though she never saw him. He described him as a 'nasty piece of work' but also spoke of him with admiration and affection.

She used cat litter trays as a toilet as he said there was electricity but no running water on the premises. She could feel that the building's walls were of stone, rough and unfinished. When she peeped through the blindfold, she saw that the high ceiling above had a wooden beam stretching across it.

Stephanie recalled: 'As we chatted one day, he announced, "I'll have to get rid of that bin now." "Which bin is that?" I said. "There's a plastic wheelie bin in the corner over there. I was going to wheel your body out in it." I imagined he was referring to the plastic bin I had been forced to sleep in. Now it seemed that all the time I had spent in the workshop, all those tedious, awful hours, had been spent in the same room as the bin he had intended to use to get rid of me. "My body?" I croaked. "Yes, we planned to wheel you out in that plastic bin and then get rid of your body," he sniggered. "You're not going to kill me, are you, Bob?" He said, "No, I've just told you, haven't I? I'm going to get rid of the bin, Of course I'm not going to kill you!"'

Our killer had written that Julie Dart '... was kept in a wheely bin in a greenhouse for two very hot days ... It was used to transport the body to where you found her.'

He also let slip personal details, telling Stephanie he lived in a big white house with a greenhouse and that he'd bought a new computer. I had guessed that from some of the letters we had received, as they had been typed on a word-processor, but he did not always use the spell check as they were littered with errors. They seemed also to have a mutual interest in astronomy, as he spoke to Stephanie of star constellations. I hoped he'd soon be star-gazing through the bars of a prison cell. He even chatted about *Coronation Street* to her.

Six days after she was kidnapped, he told Stephanie he had to ring Kevin Watts, and if everything went to plan she would be going home on Wednesday. He told her this would be the last time she would sleep in the box. On the Tuesday night he stayed with her and allowed her to remove her blindfold once the light was turned off. She noticed a red flickering light on a beam above her head.

As I read Stephanie's account of that last night, I felt there was a strange scarcity of detail about it. Generally, she had given us a minute-by-minute account of what happened and the detail was fantastic, but that relating to the last night, when she slept on the mattress next to him, was vague. I asked Ellie Baker, the inspector in charge of her debriefing, what she thought. I suspected Sams had raped her. Did he do it on that final night? Ellie said she thought the kidnapper did have sex with Stephanie but she had denied it. It was only when Stephanie wrote a book about her ordeal that she felt able to admit he had raped her, but on her first night of captivity, not her last.

We went through in detail what was said and happened on the last day. She had porridge for breakfast and he told her that as he had a lot to do she would have to spend most of the day in the box. He also sat her in the chair took her blindfold off, and photographed her – a bizarre thing to do by anyone's standards. 'I was thinking it'd be nice to have a photograph of you, something to remember you by,' he said. Stephanie did not realise that her kidnapper had, in his own twisted way, fallen in love with her and wanted a keepsake of their week together.

He gave her five small KitKats and a can of lemonade, and told her he would not be back until nine o'clock. It was early afternoon when he left. He said his mate had come to pick him up and they were going to get the money. He had to be back for 9 pm for a phone call, after which he would take her home.

Because Radio 2 was on all day, Stephanie knew minute by agonising minute exactly what time it was. He told her he had a note in his wallet explaining where she could be found if anything went wrong, but that did not stop her worrying when 9 pm passed without his return. What Stephanie was unaware of was the part the fog was playing in the night's drama.

It was long after the 10 pm news when he returned to find her panic stricken. He helped her out of the box and gave her back her own clothes. They had been cleaned and ironed. Still blindfolded, she was led out of her jail to his car and put in the front passenger seat, this time without ropes or handcuffs and with just a cardigan over her head.

She tried to track the journey back from where she had been kept. At one stage, he stopped and said he wanted Stephanie to ring her father. Elated that he had the ransom money, he wanted to let her family know she was OK. He guided her to a kiosk but the phone was out of order.

As they drove on, he made comments about approaching Birmingham, reading aloud the road signs and distances to the city. He said they were going over Spaghetti Junction and passing a turn-off for Castle Bromwich. From that point, he announced every turn he took, every set of traffic lights he came to, and named some of the shops they were passing. If these were right they would maybe help us map out where he came from and what sort of distance he had driven her. Stephanie knew where she was and, although still blindfolded, directed him to the end of her street, where he stopped the car.

Making a final farewell to his hostage, he meekly requested: 'Give me a kiss, then. I'm sorry it had to be you.' Stephanie obeyed his final order before he removed her blindfold and told her to keep her eyes shut until he had driven away.

As she stumbled out of the car, a neighbour saw her take her first unsteady steps to freedom. Purvis Barnaby was to be a vital witness. It was about 1 am, and Purvis was in bed watching the end of a film when he heard a car engine outside his home. He looked out of the window and saw Stephanie walk awkwardly from the car.

His fifteen years' experience as a car sprayer were an unexpected piece of luck for us, as not only did he know the vehicle's exact make but its colour and shade as well – a vermilion British Leyland Austin Metro.

The kidnapper drove her right into the area in which at least a dozen armed police officers had been guarding her home. But just two hours before they entered this so-called ring of steel, all the officers were withdrawn. I was never told why but I assumed the decision was based on cost. Stephanie was dropped off in the street next to where she lived, probably no more than two hundred yards from her home. It seemed the kidnapper even had time on his side.

We eventually got up and running with the linked computer system, which gave both Leeds and Birmingham access to the entire database. Except it wasn't working like that. We at Leeds could not get to see vital briefing documents which West Midlands were placing on the system. It meant we knew little of what was happening. I knew they had sought the services of mathematicians from Birmingham's Aston University, who were supplied with the details of Stephanie's journeys.

West Midlands believed they had worked out the area where she was held hostage. The 'Golden Triangle', as it was known, was the area inside where the A46, the A606 and the A52 formed this shape. It was south-east of Nottingham, measuring roughly seven by five by six miles. The top of the triangle was fifteen miles south of Newark upon Trent, fourteen miles west of Grantham, and the southerly tip twenty miles north of Leicester.

It felt like competitiveness on the part of West Midlands was such that this information was not making its way to my side of the inquiry. I felt it was because they wanted to get the arrest. The triangle theory was kept exclusive to a select team of their own officers operating from RAF Newton near Radcliffe, a secret location chosen because it was in the 'Golden Triangle' and away from Nechells incident room. Both secrets were kept from me – one of the two senior investigating officers.

Knowing I was being kept in the dark, I sent one of my detectives to Birmingham; his brief was to find out as much as he could. There were now 170 West Midlands officers on the inquiry, and they could not all be briefed at one go, so he found it fairly easy to slip into some of their meetings. I was unhappy at being out of the loop, as we could easily stumble into whatever they were doing without knowing it and spoil things. I somehow got the feeling they wanted to steal the show, only so far as I was concerned there was no show to steal. I was searching for a killer.

Territorial areas of operation were set when a meeting of our office managers took place. However, South Yorkshire decided to get in on the act and, much to my irritation, opened their own incident room without consulting us. We could now not operate within thirty miles of Barnsley, which actually put our own incident room in Leeds out of bounds to us, as it was only twenty miles away! We had Lincolnshire, where Julie's body was found, and my team joked that we also had the Orkneys and the Outer Hebrides, while West Midlands had the rest of the country, apart from South Yorkshire.

An artist's impression of the kidnapper was released on Tuesday, 4 February, showing him wearing the Michael Caine-style glasses. The media continued to be hostile towards West Midlands Police when it was leaked that even if the money were found it would be unlikely that any notes could be identified as the video was out of focus when the police filmed the cash being placed in the bag, thus making the serial numbers unreadable.

A battle developed between Tom Cook, who wanted more time to debrief Stephanie, and the media who were bidding against each other for her story. The *Sun* put in a substantial bid, believed to be around £100,000. They even threatened to reduce it on a daily basis until she was handed over to them, putting considerable pressure on Tom as he tried to balance the investigation's needs in completing her debrief against the obvious and considerable financial benefits to Stephanie.

She had been through 20 tape-recorded debriefing sessions since Thursday, 30 January, amounting to 13 hours of interviews, covering 537 pages and consisting of around 150,000 words. After being typed up, checked and double checked, a 70-page statement was distilled from them. Stephanie arrived home at 5.30 pm on Saturday, 8 February.

The *Sun* won the bidding war, reputedly paying between £80,000 and £85,000 for Stephanie's story. Good luck to her, I thought. It was small compensation for being held captive for a week, not knowing whether you would get out alive. The *News of the World* had made a more curious public gesture, offering £175,000, the amount of the ransom money, for information leading to the kidnapper's arrest.

On Thursday, 6 February, a letter arrived at Millgarth. Like one other letter, it was incorrectly addressed to Millgate police station. I was aware that copies were also sent to West Midlands Police, Shipways' Melvin Measure, the media – and Lynn Dart.

Entitled 'The Facts', it read:

I, being the kidnapper of Stephanie Slater, am not he killer of Julie Dart. It is impossible that there can be any positive connection between the two cases.

I am also not the person who idiotically tried to blackmail B.R. The idear was a variation of an idear I had discussed with another, I now believe that he may have used my word processor to make demands. The reason for the sudden cessation of communication between B.R. and the other, was my intervention when I learned with horror that he was to use my idears about picking up the ransom monies.

It could have been to my advantage to allow the police to continue to believe that the cases are all connected, but my concerns are for Stephanie and her parents, and how they must be feeling after the reports. I promised and gave my word to Stephanie on a few things, and with only one exception I kept them. Some of the promises were; a) I had not killed before, b) Provided she did not remove her blindfold she would be released and not harmed in any way, both at that time and any time in the future.

The only time I ever broke my promise to Stephanie was on the Wednesday when she was released. In the morning I knew she was getting very nervous about me not returning, so I gave her my word that I would be back at 9.30pm at the latest and she would be home by midnight. But a slight delay, probably deliberately caused by the police, meant that Kevin Watts did not arrive at the spot until 8.30pm and not 7.49pm as planned. Many times during this 40 minute delay my thoughts were for Stephanie, but the presence of the police helicopter hovering overhead indicated that they were still going ahead with the drop. Incidentally this was not the first time I suspected the presence of police, for on the Tuesday at 5pm I unexpectedly phoned Kevin watts, he panicked for 4/5 secs and this confirmed what I suspected, that the police had been called in immediately and that all calls would be taped.

I arrived back to Stephanie's hide at 10.30pm. I informed her that everything was O.K. and she was going home. It was the first time I had seen her cry, she virtually collapsed in my arms with relief. Fortunately she had her blindfold on and could not see my tears for her, streaming down my face.

Dropping Stephanie off near her home was not part of any game, it never entered my head that the police surveillance would extend beyond the fence of her parents house. Initially it was discussed with Stephanie about dropping her off a Uttoxeter police station, but this was abandoned as I was worried that they would delay her return to her parents, the second option was Uttoxeter hospital, where I knew doctors would have kept her away from police for a while, but this again delayed her return to her parents, for during the long chats we had her love for her parents was uppermost in her mind, it was not my bravado on my part as I was terrified, not about the car being spotted, but I knew the police could win any ensuing chase.

No blame can be attached to the West Midlands police for any of there actions, they did not know which direction they were heading, let alone into South Yorkshire Territory, they did not know or could not have known where the money was to have been dropped until at least 30 secs after it had been. They were not expecting her release until Friday.

There was no way they could have made any arrest that evening, unless by accident, I had been stopped and searched for any traffic offence or accident, for in my car and pocket were letters informing the finder the whereabouts of Stephanie, I did not want Stephanie starving to death had anything happened to me, for her location could have remained a secret for weeks.

The fact that I knew, could, and did carry out the crime extremely successfully is my only satisfaction, I am ashamed upset and thoroughly disgusted at my treatment of Stephanie and the suffering I must have caused to her parents, Stephanie will most likely insist she was well looked after, but during the time we talked and I tried to make her laugh and smile, the sudden change of her smiling face to one taught and terrified was heartbreaking, and I knew I was doing that to her. Even now my eyes are all filled with tears, I wake up during the night actually crying, with a little luck Stephanie will get over it shortly. Myself? I do not think I ever will.

Sorry Stephanie. Sorry Mr & Mrs Slater.

Before I destroy the last bit of forensic evidence, this W/P, I shall put onto paper a full and detailed account of everything from June 1991 to date, this will be given F.O.C. to any paper or periodical who thinks that Stephanie's exclusive story could be of use to them, this, in my own little way, seems to be the only way I can hope to offer any repayment for what I did to her. This case will never come to court as I have contingency plans should the police be two steps behind.

I was appalled by this latest publicity stunt. It showed callous disregard for Lynn Dart, who had endured months of suffering. I also felt this missive was about the perpetrator preparing his defence should he be caught. He denied Julie's murder and the BR extortion, yet the wording and spelling errors in this letter, and the fact that it was addressed to Millgate police station, actually provided us with more evidence of links. He was now putting this other person centre-stage by blaming him for the crimes that I was certain he alone had committed.

The letter was full of self-gratification and pathetic pleas about how he cared for Stephanie and how upset he was by what had happened. It was a sickening attempt on his part to put himself forward as a victim. His self-pity was laughable, but I also found it pathetic and distasteful.

Why send the letter? While Lynn received one, Stephanie didn't – even though it was very much an apology to her and her parents. It was as if he were issuing a trailer to her story, which was about to be published.

By 18 February, the media knew of our plan to go to *Crimewatch* with the Slater kidnap. It would feature the links between that, the Dart murder and the BR extortion, but would mainly concentrate on Stephanie's case. There were four main points of appeal: the voice – when calls had been made to Shipways, they were recorded; the artist's impression; the vermilion Austin Metro; and the railway connection, with a picture of the train badge on the duffel coat the kidnapper wore at Turnberry Road.

The media already knew some of these details but by presenting them as one package in a public appeal we hoped to hit as wide an audience as possible. One newspaper ran an artist's impression of its own of what it thought the kidnapper looked like, causing tremendous confusion both for us and for the public, who were phoning in with suggestions. The *Mirror*, *Daily Star* and *Daily Express* reported that the kidnapper's vehicle was a vermilion Metro.

Only the voice had so far not been released. Experts on accent decided it originated from the border of Lancashire and Yorkshire, but my experiences on the Yorkshire Ripper case with the hoax 'I'm Jack' tape made me sceptical. When the press discovered that the kidnapper's phone call was to be given exclusively to *Crimewatch*, certain newspapers turned nasty to the point that some refused to print the show's phone number in their articles.

At 3.15 pm on Wednesday, 19 February, the day before *Crimewatch* was aired, the kidnapper rang Shipways one last time.

'Can I speak to Sylvia?'

Jane Cashman recognised the voice. 'Who's calling?'

'It's a friend of hers.'

Jane passed the phone to Sylvia Baker, and said: 'You'll never guess who this sounds like. It's him.'

Sylvia picked her phone up and listened.

'I just want to speak to you for five minutes and then I won't speak to you again. I'm the man that kidnapped Stephanie. You and her are the only people who can identify me and Stephanie won't because she knows what will happen. Do you understand? If I'm not caught I've got enough money to look after you. I know where you live and I know about your family, do you understand?'

Sylvia burst into tears as the line went dead. She understood all too well.

The threat was unmistakable – he was obviously concerned about the growing publicity. I would watch the programme at Millgarth, where the flow of information was still poor and we had a sense of being left in the dark. I put some of my team on through the night just in case we needed to respond to anything from the appeal.

I knew that where Stephanie had been held captive was likely to be the same place in which he had kept Julie Dart, and the forensic scientists would find the evidence to prove it – if it was there to be found. West Midlands had a lot going for them if the man was identified, as they could connect him to the Slater kidnap by his voice and possibly by identification. We had a lot of evidence, like the letters, the rope and the sheet, but no one had seen Julie's killer, nor had we any record of his voice, any DNA or fingerprints. I reassured myself with the thought that forensic scientists from the labs at Wetherby near Leeds and Birmingham would work together if a crime scene was found.

Calls from the *Crimewatch* appeal would be taken at its London studios and the Nechells incident room. It was agreed they would be prioritised so that if a caller named a suspect who corresponded with all four points of appeal and lived in the 'Golden Triangle' he would be ranked highest on a scale of one to seven. I expected few calls to come into Millgarth.

As the TV set was wheeled into the incident room, I knew we'd reached another significant milestone. I watched Nick Ross interview Tom Cook and heard once again the kidnapper's reedy, flat tones. I could recite verbatim his conversation as I heard him say: 'Kevin Watts. Have you got the money?' in that mocking voice.

As the shutters came down on the Millgarth bar at 11.15 pm, I was discussing that day's events with DS Tim Grogan when DC Wayne Greenwood came looking for me. He'd just taken a call from a Susan Oake of Keighley, West Yorkshire. He said she was in a bit of a state as she'd taped *Crimewatch* and had just watched it, on her return from an evening out. Susan was adamant that the kidnapper was her ex-husband, said Wayne. Remembering the call he had taken at *Crimewatch* on the Dart inquiry, Tim quipped: 'Ex-husband. Is it 'cos he's a bastard?'

Wayne convinced me she was genuine, so I sent DCs Helen Dover and Steve Newboult to see her. I knew they would not be back before 2 am and told them to ring me at home if he was a red-hot suspect, otherwise they could brief me in the morning.

## chapter three

# I'VE BEEN EXPECTING YOU

Friday should have been my day off, but I was in my office at 8 am to see what had come in from *Crimewatch*. There had been over a thousand calls. We took thirty at Millgarth, including the one from Susan Oake, who was absolutely certain her ex-husband, Michael Sams, a tool repairer, was the kidnapper.

I presumed her call had come to nothing until I saw Tim, Helen and Wayne huddled in a corner of the incident room. Tim beckoned me over. 'It looks good,' Wayne said, 'but he's only got one leg.' Tim immediately dismissed that problem: 'The best burglar I know in Leeds has no legs at all!'

'Where does Sams live?' I asked.

'Susan doesn't know his address. We just have an ex-directory number,' said Helen. 'She saw him last week at his stepfather Ernest Walker's funeral. He was driving a red Metro. She is adamant on the voice, he looks a bit like the artist's impression and he's a real railway fanatic.'

I looked across at the West Midlands inspector and sergeant who'd been attached to us from day one and asked whether they knew about this. 'Yes,' said Tim. 'They had the same call from Sams's son, Charles. He rang *Crimewatch* but they gave Sams a low priority because of his one leg.' After speaking to a contact, Wayne came back with an address – Eaves Cottage, Barrel Hill Lane, Sutton on Trent.

Tim rang the Criminal Records Office and asked them to fax us a photo of Sams. He'd been convicted of dishonesty in 1978 at Bradford Crown Court and was jailed for nine months. I watched the fax as it slowly spooled through. Stephanie had talked of the kidnapper having a snouty nose and a furrowed brow. I saw both features, but when I looked at the full face it just wasn't what I thought our killer would look like. But as it was the only half-decent call we'd taken, I told Tim to get it sorted.

Within seconds, he was on his way with Helen, Wayne and DS Paul Leach. At 9 am, I briefed the teams on the response to *Crimewatch*. I didn't mention Sams for no other reason than I did not think it was important enough.

Two hours later, I took a call from Helen Dover. 'Boss, it's him,' she announced. I had no doubts about what she was suggesting, but my over-riding instinct told me it could not be right. After all these months, this was too easy.

Every senior detective had told me that, like the Yorkshire Ripper, our man would be in the system. Sams wasn't. My mind was telling me to reject Helen's declaration. 'Stop pissing about, Helen, I'm busy. Get Tim to call me.' Helen was known for winding people up and I'd wait for Tim, as team leader, to ring. That morning I had started to feel a sharp pain in my right knee joint, so I was limping grumpily around the office because of that and because I did not know what West Midlands were doing. It was a busy day and I was in no mood for practical jokes.

The phone rang again. 'It's Tim Grogan,' somebody shouted. As I walked to the phone, I was thinking that Tim was ten times more of a practical joker than Helen ever was – but not on this, he wouldn't dare.

'It's him,' said Tim.

'How do you know?'

'It's all here. I'm ringing from next door to his workshop,' Tim told me.

He then reeled off a list of points that we knew from Stephanie were the linking factors. 'The Metro, voice, artist's impression, wheelie bin, British Rail signs all over his house. Word-processor, till, Radio Two play-ing, wooden beam, microwave oven, the gardening gloves, and there are sliding doors at the entrance to his workshop.' It was the best shopping list I'd ever heard.

I urged him, my heart pounding, to tell me what had happened. 'We got to Eaves Cottage. It's fifty yards from the main East Coast line. By the door was a green wheelie bin and a concrete block like the one used at Millmeece. His wife invited us in.'

'I take it he wasn't there,' I said.

'No. But as soon as we got into the house, we saw two motorcycles, seed trays like Stephanie had described, railway signs all over the walls.'

The pitch of Tim's voice was rising all the time. He was like a football commentator describing a run towards goal, getting nearer and nearer. I was hoping this shot was not going over the bar. I tried to visualise the scene. Excitement rushed through my body like a flush of embarrassment. I turned to look at the incident room; my knee was throbbing like hell, but all else in the room was blocked out as if everything were happening in slow motion. No one was aware of the conversation.

'Go on, Tim,' I urged.

'We went into the lounge. Again a big railway sign over the fireplace. Just off the lounge was another room, with a word-processor.

'And get this. She said they'd watched the Slater case on *Crimewatch* and her husband had told her they could expect a visit from the police as they had a car like the one shown in the programme! She said he was at work, at T&M Tools, the Swan and Salmon Yard in Newark.'

'How far is that?'

'About a ten-minute drive. So as not to alert him, we told her we would not bother him at work but would call back at five pm.

'We drove into Newark, and as we turned into the yard, it was like a football player driving into Wembley to play in the Cup Final and get a winner's medal. Everything was as Stephanie had described.

'We walked into the shop and he came from the back, dragging his leg. I told him who we were, and he just said, "I've been expecting you." I walked through to the back and saw the wooden beam Stephanie described. Paul Leach pointed out the old-fashioned phone and Wayne clocked the stencils. There was an old radio playing music. Helen asked him what station it was tuned to. "Radio Two. I have it on all day," he said.'

I was now convinced this was something special. I had been jotting down the key points on a memo pad and had the feeling I would be repeating this story many times. 'What happened then, Tim?'

'Arrested him for Julie's murder and kidnapping Stephanie. Wayne found the gardening gloves in the car and a Beach Boys tape still in its cassette player.'

My mind was racing as he was talking. I was thinking it couldn't be right, but the more Tim told me the more I realised that it was.

'Has Newark got a police station?'

'No idea. He says there is and will direct us,' said Tim. How helpful of Mr Sams, I thought. I called over John O'Sullivan, Eddie Hemsley and Paul Maxwell and ran through what had been said.

There was a lot of work to be done. It was time to test our theory that Stephanie's kidnapper was also Julie's killer. I gathered my thoughts, waiting for the next phone call when they got to the police station in Newark. I would not send the balloon up yet. I would wait to see what else happened.

At noon, the phone rang again. It was Tim. 'Right, what's the score?' I said.

'He's coughed Slater,' he said.

'What? What's he said?' I spluttered.

'While he was being booked in, he declared: "I kidnapped Stephanie Slater but I did not murder Julie Dart. You'll find nineteen thousand pounds at the workshop with my confession."'

'Right, I'll let Tom Cook and Mick Williams know. If we can interview him to get the confession on tape, fine. Paul Maxwell is coming down,' I barked.

I got Mick Williams first and told him the news. His first reaction was total disbelief. Shortly after I rang, Birmingham found Sams's son's call to *Crimewatch*. Strangely it now went from the lowest to the highest priority.

I still cannot decide whether it was weakness or common sense on my part that prevented me from ordering my team to bring Sams back to Leeds. I sensed West Midlands manoeuvring as they lobbied Tom Cook for Sams to be handed over to them and taken to Birmingham.

My problem was that he was admitting involvement with Stephanie but not Julie, and we had no evidence to put to him. I needed time for forensics to get me that, assuming he had held Julie in his workshop or his home.

I dispatched John O'Sullivan to Newark to ensure that what we needed for our inquiry was being carried out. At teatime the Chief Constable of West Midlands turned up at Newark police station, some seventy-five miles from his office. We were told he was just passing by and had popped in as he used to be a sergeant there.

Susan Oake was brought to Millgarth. She would stay in the VIP suite, a misnomer if ever there was one, as it was smaller than a room at a Travelodge. But Princess Michael of Kent had used it when she visited Leeds as part of her duties as the city university's chancellor. She was once disturbed while resting with a migraine in the suite by a tramp called Billy McHale, an ex-boxer. He was the best-dressed tramp in Leeds as officers used to give him their old clothes. He slept under a market stall across the road and was in evidence every day outside the entrance of the nick, shouting, 'Get the lot. They're all dossers,' and when he saw a police officer, 'He'll get 'em. The boiled beef [chief] will get them.' Owing to Princess Michael's complaint of disturbance, Billy was moved on for a couple of hours.

I spoke to Susan, who had no doubts that her ex-husband Mike, as she called him, was Stephanie's kidnapper. She was even more convinced when she looked at the handwritten letters. She did not know when she unequivocally identified the writing as that of Sams that they were the Dart letters she was looking at. She assumed they were to do with the Slater case.

When I told her they were letters written by Julie's murderer, she was visibly stunned. She could not believe that the man she was once wed to and had two fine sons by was a killer. I arranged for two officers to interview Susan, but it was too early to know what might be relevant. They'd have to go through every aspect of her life with Sams, from the moment they met in 1964, when he was working installing a lift at her workplace, to the present. Every intimate detail would have to be revealed. Susan cooperated brilliantly and was a great help to the inquiry.

I was concerned that Sams had been married three times and we only knew where two of his wives were. The second, Jane Marks, had mysteriously disappeared one night, leaving her clothes behind. I always had it in my mind that he might have killed more than one person, so I dispatched two officers to find Jane, a teacher. In a matter of hours she was traced. She had remarried. She too would spend many hours with detectives going over the three years she was with Michael Sams.

At 9 pm, Tom Cook appeared on Newark police station's steps and read a short statement: 'At eleven twenty-five am today a fifty-year-old man was arrested in Newark, Nottingham, and is being held in connection with the kidnapping of Stephanie Slater. He was arrested by detectives investigating information received in telephone calls to police following the *Crimewatch* appeal. The man will later be transferred to the

West Midlands Police area. He is expected to be charged in the near future.'

Tom indicated that no questions would be answered as he had to be careful not to say anything that might deny Sams a fair trial by implying any guilt. I watched the news in Millgarth's TV room. I felt let down that police politics had prevented even a mention of the fact that my team had made the arrest. We had been chasing him a long time. Neither was there any mention of the Julie Dart murder. One thing I did know was that at 8 pm Sams had gone to Birmingham, handed over to West Midlands officers. The arresting officers, Tim, Helen and Wayne, did not have the pleasure of escorting him there.

However, disappointment was tempered by elation, as we were much closer to our killer than we had been twenty-four hours earlier, even if it was on the back of the Slater inquiry. We couldn't complain too much, as long as we were allowed to be part of the inquiry and were not cut out by West Midlands.

But things ran far from smoothly. A crime scene manager who was only weeks off retiring was appointed a West Midlands chief inspector. He would oversee the examinations at both T&M Tools and Eaves Cottage. Forensic scientists were there within hours of Sams's arrest, but the crime scene manager would not let them enter the workshop as he was waiting for a dog specially trained to sniff out dead bodies to arrive from West Midlands.

I was unaware of this but furious when told. It was seven months since Julie had been in the workshop, if she'd been there at all. We knew were Stephanie had been held, so putting a dog in first was of no great benefit and, in fact, could have contaminated the scene.

The scientists, costing about £300 an hour, were kept waiting for Rover to put in an appearance. When the dog arrived, it had been rocking about in the back of the van and was feeling sick, so it needed to rest before it could get sniffing. The scientists were tearing their hair out. Dave Loxley, co-ordinating the scientific examination, memorably described to me what happened when the hound finally made his appearance: 'The dog went into the workshop, farted, barked in the back, came out and had a pee against the wall.'

Sams was being held at Belgrave Road police station. He had been interviewed initially at Newark and further interviews took place when he arrived at Birmingham. All were conducted in the presence of his lawyer,

David Payne, a past Lord Mayor of Newark and a highly respected local figure. He would spend many months on this case.

When the Midlands interviewing team concluded their interviews, they had surprisingly not physically recovered the outstanding ransom money of £156,000. They claimed Sams had said he would show them where it was. But they did not follow it up. This was to be a costly error, as he later denied that he knew where it was buried.

Paul Maxwell and Tim Grogan would interview Sams about the Julie Dart murder. They began questioning him on the Saturday afternoon. It soon became clear that he was not going to admit to the murder, as he denied knowing Julie and that his premises were connected to her kidnap or murder in any way.

He also denied having discussed with anyone else an attempt to blackmail West Yorkshire Police for £140,000, or being involved in the planning or preparation of it. It was then he introduced us for the first time to the other man, or, as I liked to call him, the Absent Protagonist. He stated that he had discussed Stephanie's kidnap with another man whom he refused to name or identify in any way, saying he was protecting her life with his silence.

He then dropped a bombshell and announced that the other man had killed Julie Dart, by this linking himself directly to the murder: 'I did not know anything about the death of Julie Dart until I heard it on TV. I might have discussed it afterwards, somebody might have been bragging that he killed her.' Sams later went on to tell the officers what the other man had done or told him, such as the fact that Julie was murdered on the night she was kidnapped, claiming that if Julie had been kept in the den – his preferred word for the coffin-like container that Stephanie was kept in – there would be forensic evidence in it, though he said he had got rid of the one used for Stephanie.

I was disappointed that he didn't admit to killing Julie Dart, but I hadn't really expected him to. He'd played games with us for months; why should he stop now? But he was talking, and had linked himself to the killing through the other man. He was confident when being interviewed, verging on arrogant.

That had not been the case when he was first taken to Newark police station – his face was ashen and drawn and he was at his lowest ebb. It would have made good sense to have interviewed him straight away before he regained his composure – he might have admitted his guilt then much more readily. But political wrangling prevented this. West Midlands were the first to interview him but unfortunately another opportunity was lost.

I had been to Nechells incident room the day before on the Friday, and weathered the storm of questions over why my officers had arrested Sams in a part of the country that was allocated to West Midlands. I pointed to the fact that they had the same information as us – a call from Sams's family – but did not act upon it. 'He who hesitates comes second,' I stated. I felt that, as things stood, my officers had run the marathon and come first but the gold medal had been awarded to West Midlands.

Word was coming back to me that the West Midlands team was preventing our officers going into either Sams's workshop or the house. Mick Williams denied this was happening. I went to the Swan and Salmon Yard at Newark to see the place where I believed Julie Dart was kept and murdered. On the way, I quizzed Tom Cook as to why Sams had been taken to Birmingham instead of Leeds. 'Their need was greater than ours,' he said. I took this to mean it was a political rather than an operational decision.

Just as a golfer will walk a course before playing it, a detective will visit the scenes and read all the statements before starting an interview. Although I would not be interviewing Sams, I needed that same knowledge. As I stepped into the dark workshop, I knew these were the final few yards of Julie Dart's last journey in life. To my left was the big black sliding door with its stencilled sign, 'T & M Tools. Closed Wednesdays.' So that was the reason for activity being concentrated on Wednesdays.

We drove to Eaves Cottage, where Wayne Greenwood confirmed what I had been told. My officers were not being allowed access. Hearing this, Tom Cook asked the West Midlands detective sergeant at the front door whether the scene was being jointly searched. He said it was.

On Sunday morning, I arrived at Millgarth at 7.30 am to brief Paul Maxwell and Tim Grogan before they went to Birmingham to interview Sams later that day.

Tom Cook arrived just after 9 am and took a call from one of Mick Williams's leg-men. It seems from the side of the conversation I could hear that West Midlands wanted to interview Sams about the Julie Dart murder. I thought that this was optimistic as they had already failed to get information from Sams as to where the money was.

Tom put the phone to his chest and the proposition to me. Clearly missing the thunder in my eyes, he said, 'Their staff are getting on really well with him.' Rage was welling up inside me. Getting on well with him

– it was a murder inquiry, not a vicar's tea party. I was having none of it.

'They're a set of wankers,' I snarled through gritted teeth. 'They know nothing about the Julie Dart murder.'

'Now that's a good reason, but not the first,' Tom said.

I felt a serious need to get Sams back to Leeds after he appeared at Birmingham magistrates' court on Monday morning.

Officers were going into Sams's cell during the night to ask him unofficially where the money was, telling him how he had ruined Stephanie's life. Sams was no fool, and waved a copy of the *Sun* showing Stephanie drinking champagne. 'I do not think so,' he retorted.

It was vital that Sams come to us so we could control our own interviews. I told Paul and Tim to sound out his solicitor about agreeing to a three-day remand to Millgarth police cells after his court appearance. I asked them to point out that Iris Walker, his mother, who lived in Keighley, could visit him here without much inconvenience. I knew they were close, and that he had not seen her since his arrest.

Sams had no cast-iron alibi for any of the relevant dates. He was relying on his wife Teena to alibi him for the night on which Julie was kidnapped. Sams said he would have been at home, but on either a Tuesday or Wednesday evening in the summer he collected rent from Lennie MacDonald, tenant of a house they owned in Peterborough.

Teena Sams was in a state of deep shock from her husband's confession and the fact that he was being accused of murder. She was no use at all to us as a witness. Her diary gave no indication that Sams was away from home on the night of Tuesday, 9 July 1991, let alone on any of the other key dates. Teena was sure she would have marked it if he had been away.

Sams's interview strategy was to enter into banter with his inquisitors on minor points, ignoring the more important ones and hoping to divert their attention. He also employed a tactic of deny and confess, whereby he would deny something when confronted with it, only to confess at a later stage when he had had time to think of an answer that suited him.

His answers were designed to please himself. It seemed he believed that anything he said must be right because he had said it. He would also feign ignorance when faced with hard evidence, or introduce another topic in an attempt to cloud the issue.

Linking factors between the Dart, Slater and British Rail inquiries were put to him. Having previously vehemently denied they were connected, he now accepted they were, because as he said: 'I have linked them, not the police.' His logic was difficult to follow at times.

He accepted that he had introduced the other man only after Stephanie was released. He tried to taunt his interviewers, saying, 'The other man has the missing £140,000,' and claimed he had assisted him in the Slater case, saying, 'The other person was using my ideas.' He did admit that the other person involved in the British Rail blackmail was also the person who had murdered Julie Dart.

Sams was aware what was happening at his home and the workshop, and was obviously thinking about what we might find. In an attempt to deflect any forensic evidence away from him, he declared that the other man had had his workshop keys for a month, and Julie Dart could have been kidnapped during this time. He later added that the other man had coincidentally had the keys at the time of the Slater kidnap.

The first forensic information came in on Sunday from Val Tomlinson, a scientist at the Wetherby laboratory. She had been sifting through fibres found on the workshop's cobbled floor to try to match them to the brown carpet fibres found on the sheet and rope which Julie's body had been wrapped in. 'Fibres from the floor are visibly indistinguishable from fibres on the sheet and the rope,' she said. 'No piece of brown carpet was found in the workshop, just these fibres.' This was probably the carpet Julie was sitting on when he killed her.

Sams's answer to this was that Julie's body was never in his workshop. He later changed his story and said the other man could have taken the sheet and the rope from the workshop.

It was clear we were dealing with a complex character, and we would have to adapt our interview techniques as he was in danger of clamming up on us. I decided that, while not accepting the existence of the other man, we would use him as a vehicle to obtain information.

The ploy worked. Sams began to spill the beans, in his own way. He said, 'It was the other man who wanted to kill Stephanie and killed Julie Dart because she did not follow his instructions.' I took him to mean that Julie saw where she was when he said, 'Even if Stephanie had seen where she was, I would have released her unharmed.' He used this to make the distinction between the other man, a murderer, and himself, who had let Stephanie go. In the last interview at Birmingham on Sunday evening, he was told that Susan Oake had identified his handwriting. 'How would she know?' he scoffed, dismissing his ex-wife, whom he now knew was instrumental in his arrest, and what she said as an utter fabrication.

We had learned a lot from the West Midlands interviews with Sams, and even more from those Paul and Tim had conducted. They had interviewed him on six occasions, the first starting on Saturday at 2.31 pm and the last concluding at 7.26 pm on the Sunday.

That evening he was charged with the kidnap of Stephanie Slater, her unlawful imprisonment, and demanding money with menaces. He would appear at court in the morning, and we would ask that he be remanded to Millgarth police station cells in order that we could continue questioning.

I knew we needed to have a robust interview strategy when we got him to Leeds. We also needed to stop the flow of information which had been gushing forth in the newspapers. He was allowed to see these, and all they did was boost an already inflated ego. Sams was arrogant, and we needed to turn that arrogance and use it against him.

I decided he would not be accorded the celebrity prisoner status he'd received in the Midlands. I put out the word that he be treated like any other prisoner who came through Millgarth's doors.

I ordered that no member of staff was to mention the name of Millgarth police station. Millgate instead of Millgarth was the address of our last letter from the killer, and Sams had made the same error in his 'The Facts' letter. Paul and Tim wanted to ask him where he thought he was at the start of his first interview here.

Paul Britton came to watch tapes of the interviews. His view that Sams was a games player was unchanged, and he didn't think he would make admissions in response to direct questions. 'It will have to be like a game of chess,' he said. 'There may have to be twenty questions to move from A to B.'

We also discussed how he had previously been treated and made to feel important. We agreed he would deal only with DI Paul Maxwell and DS Tim Grogan. To deal with me or any other senior officers would flatter him. He knew I was behind the scenes, and had seen me on the various TV appeals, but he would not meet me now. Instead I became the 'dark shadowy figure', lurking behind the scenes, orchestrating his destiny.

On his journey to Leeds, he passed Armley prison. 'I was in there in 1978 when Neilson was there,' he told Tim Grogan, referring to the infamous Black Panther, Donald Neilson. 'He was a Category A and nobody was allowed to speak to him. Everybody used to say, "Look, there's Neilson." That's what people will be saying about me, isn't it?' he boasted. Neilson was jailed for a number of post office robberies and the kidnapping and murder of the heiress Lesley Whittle. I wondered whether Sams had modelled himself on him.

Although I had instructed that he was to be treated as a normal prisoner, it did not stop the station superintendent forming a reception committee in full uniform in the area by the cells to greet Sams.

He had been resolutely arrogant in his Slater interviews, manipulating his questioners to his advantage, revealing very little. I felt this had reassured him that he could succeed in batting out the murder allegation. But would he be bright enough to maintain his lies and not vary his story from what he had said in Birmingham? Now, in Leeds, we had the psychological high ground.

The first interview at Millgarth commenced at 3.57 pm. Tim said to Sams: 'Do you know which police station you are at?' 'Millgate,' he replied cockily. Round one to us. He went on to admit that the rope used to tie Julie's body had been in his workshop for five or six years, but said it must have been taken by the other man.

His word-processor and disks were being examined at the Forensic Science Laboratory at Birmingham. Sams believed he had erased any information that could trap him.

But experts can find these sections of data and piece them back together like a jigsaw. As Sams sat smugly in the interviews thinking he had covered his tracks, chunks of it were being retrieved. Even though he was sure nothing would be found, he kept the door open for himself by declaring: 'The other man had access to my computer when it was in the workshop.'

We learnt he had passed through Leeds on his way to Keighley to visit his mother on the day one of the letters was posted in the city. Teena recalled that they stopped at Leeds railway station and she bought a yucca plant while Sams disappeared towards the platform.

He now accepted that 'The Facts' letter had been addressed to Millgate police station, exactly as the Huddersfield letter dated 16 October 1991 had been by Julie Dart's killer. His explanation was simple – he had accidentally addressed it to Millgate and the other man must have done the same. Millgate is the name of a street in Newark, a short distance from Sams's workshop.

His arrogance shone through as he tried to show his superiority over his interviewers while all the time digging a deeper and deeper hole for himself. Although I knew he was a killer, at times I had to smile at his matter-of-fact manner when correcting his inquisitors.

He was quizzed about the BR extortion and the sandstone block and rope found on the railway line at Millmeece. Even though he denied responsibility, he could not resist airing his knowledge. We believed that the concrete block had been suspended over the track to hit the arm above the train. 'No,' explained Sams, 'you would only need a piece of stone the size of a tennis ball.' This was the size of the sandstone. 'The speed of the train will cause the damage,' he added helpfully.

Sams did not like failure but agreed that the other man had failed twice with the murder of Julie Dart and the botched BR extortion. He said, 'I believe the description the police issued on *Crimewatch* [September 1991] was of an illiterate, uneducated, self-taught person in his fifties. I think that would describe the person who bragged to me that he had done it.'

The description he recalled was of Michael Benniman Sams. But of course Sams was too conceited to see this, as he ascribed it to the other man.

The last interview on Monday evening needed a dramatic note to end on, something to prey on his mind during the long hours of the night. Some data had already been recovered from his computer, including a list of telephone numbers, one of which was the call-box at Glossop railway station. I knew this would shake him.

As usual, he initially denied this could be true. 'I can't explain it, but I find it very hard to believe.' Also found were the numbers of the telephone boxes outside Glossop post office, where Sams had sent Kevin Watts. There was also the phone box at the crossroads at Oxspring, and a further telephone box at Silkstone, where he admitted he had intended sending Kevin.

We knew he could explain these as they all related to the Stephanie Slater money run, but not the telephone numbers of the kiosks on Platform 3 at Crewe railway station, as they related to the British Rail extortion, which he was denying. He fumbled for an explanation and eventually laid the blame on the 'other man', adding: 'If I had recorded them I would have erased them.' I knew, as he was banged up for the night, he'd worry about what else we might find on his disks.

Handwriting samples were requested. I had no great faith in handwriting experts, who in my experience usually came up with bland conclusions such as 'there are some similarities'.

Sams was left handed, and we requested block and cursive writing executed with both his left and right hands to compare with the letters. The text dictated to him had been compiled to include all the wrongly spelt words. When he finished this test, we discovered he was dyslexic, as he managed to misspell sixteen words exactly as they had been written in the killer's letters to the police. The question was, what would the experts say?

A motorcyclist was waiting, ready to take the samples to Paul Rimmer at the Birmingham lab. The results would be faxed to us, written in the expert's own words so we could use the exact phrases and avoid misleading either Sams or his solicitor David Payne on the strength of the evidence.

More information surfaced from his computer disks. Sams might be blaming the other man for what was on there, but one slip-up came back to haunt him. He told Kevin Watts on the night of the ransom run to go to 'Glossop, west of Manchester'. This very phrase had been found on his computer – the significance being that Glossop was not west but east of Manchester. Sams's explanation was as simple as it was unbelievable – the other man had yet again made the same mistake as him.

On Tuesday evening, I ordered the pressure be stepped up. I said to Paul and Tim, 'Start to point the finger at Sams as the killer.' It was put to him, 'It is not as though you're saying, Michael, I don't know the murderer of Julie Dart, you're saying you do. Is that because it's you?' Sams said, 'Until you find proof of another person's involvement, I can't tell you anything.' Fortunately he was unable to sit in silence, even though his solicitor advised him to, and Paul and Tim knew that, so the questioning continued on the basis of what the other man had told him. 'Julie Dart escaped from where she was being held and he chased after her and hit her with a hammer,' he declared.

Sams's demeanour, his evasiveness and the growing list of unbelievable coincidences left me in no doubt that the other man was a figment of his imagination. I had already developed my own theory as to what happened.

Julie was more than likely held in his workshop and murdered as she tried to escape. At the back, where Julie would have been held, was a PIR on the wooden beam. Stephanie had seen it. It was linked to the phone in Sams's workshop, which was programmed with his home number on redial. If the PIR detected body heat, it would activate the phone and ring his home. Stephanie remained in her container and so saved her own life.

The alarm did go off around the time I believed Julie was there. Teena could recall him going to the workshop one night but not the exact date. When he arrived, did Julie rush him as he opened the door and try to

oster with two photos of Julie Dart.
*Police photo*)

# MURDER
## of JULIE ANN DART

**Both photographs are of the victim.**

Julie Dart disappeared from Leeds on Tuesday 9th July 1991 and her body was found 10 days later on Friday 19th July 1991 in a field off the B6403, a short distance from the A1 trunk road just south of Grantham, Lincolnshire.

Julie was 18yrs of age, 5' 9'' tall, slim and had dark auburn, wavy, shoulder length hair, she also had a chipped and discoloured front tooth.

If you have seen Julie since 9th of July 1991 or have any information to offer the enquiry, then telephone the Incident Room at Millgarth Police Station, Leeds (0532) 413022 or speak to any Police Officer.

ANY INFORMATION WILL BE TREATED IN THE STRICTEST CONFIDENCE

PRINTED AT POLICE HEADQUARTERS, WAKEFIELD R

Michael Sams.
*Police photo*)

Back view of Sams's house. (*Police photo*)

Interior of Sams's workshop, showing counter area. (*Police photo*)

escape? Is that why he killed her? Did Julie's fear of confined places over-come her, leading her to force herself out of the box?

Val Tomlinson at forensics was still working on the brown carpet fibres from the sheet and the rope. Further tests showed them to be forensically indistinguishable and from the same manufactured roll of carpet. Sams had no answer to this.

After a debrief with Paul and Tim, we adjourned to the Millgarth bar. We still had a long way to go. The handwriting results were expected in the morning, but I was not anticipating much from them. I knew Sams was feeling the pressure, but he showed no signs of cracking.

It had been a seven-month journey to Michael Sams's door, and we had one more day of interviewing left before his next court appearance. I had enough evidence to charge him, but did I have enough to convict him?

The twelfth interview began at 11.14 am on 26 February. Sams tried to seize the initiative and said it would be the last in which he would answer questions. He was rattled. He'd spent the night weighing up the evidence against him and knew it was piling up.

But his inflated ego and will to compete with my officers would not permit him to remain silent. He was shown the York, Coventry and Huddersfield letters which the killer had sent to the police. Tim and Paul made small talk around the letters for a while before dropping a bombshell on him. Paul Rimmer had faxed the results of his handwriting examina-tion. The York and Coventry letters were written by Sams and we could discount them having been written by anyone else, he said.

Sams was shaken, but he still denied being the author. I knew he revered experts as he considered that he was one himself on many subjects, and he believed experts should not be challenged. He struggled to explain why he had not only written the same as the other man but had also mis-spelt the same sixteen words.

The evidence was building up and we decided to confront him with all of it in one interview to overwhelm him. The computer data, letters, the use of double-sided tape to fix envelopes in phone boxes, stencils, the use of the Dove Valley Trail, the fibres, the paint, and so on. It made no impression on him at all, and he still denied killing Julie.

He happily talked about his financial affairs and his life. He told us how, while in jail for deception, he spent the latter part of his sentence in the prison hospital when it was discovered he had a tumour in his right knee. When the cancer was removed they were unable to save his leg, and it had to be amputated above his knee.

Sams claimed to have substantial assets of £250,000 in November 1987, before his business took a downward turn when Teena's son Paul died suddenly aged twenty-one of a brain tumour. He said the decline was due to Teena's loss of interest, and by 1991 he was £16,000 in debt.

Sams was asked about the incendiary device referred to in the first letter. We knew that at the age of eleven he had made a bomb so powerful that it shook the school building when it was set off. He explained how he had made it from weedkiller and cordite from old bullets. He then denied he had anything to do with the device mentioned in the letter.

The final interview was short and began with Sams being shown parts of a letter retrieved from his hard disk. He had been emphatic that there was nothing on his computer about the Julie Dart case.

The letter was read to him:

nearing the corner again I saw the white girl who was then alone on the corner, I stopped the car and lowered the window, the young girl then called out " Do you want business?" to which I replied Yes she then ran across the road to the passenger side door and opened it,

Girl "It's £15"

Me "Where"

Girl "Over there behind the wall" probably meant the health centre

Me "That's no good, not inside or the car?"

Girl " In the car will be extra"

Me " How much now?"

Girl " £20"

Me "O,K, is it a safe place

Girl " Yes – its money up front please"

I then held out two ten pound notes which she took, it was only then that she got into the car, she immediately told me her name was Julie and directed me down the road, on the way we had a little conversation in which Julie told me she was 24 years old and lived in the Leeds area. Julie directed me to what I think was the Thomas Danby car park, I was a little apprehensive, but she assured me that no other girls would bring anyone up whilst there was a car there,

After a little while we had penetrative sex with a condom provided by Julie. After sex I asked her to lay there a while and talk, and that

I would give her extra, it was at this time that I noticed she had a couple of bruises on her body and numerous on her legs, I challenged her about these to which she explained that she had been beaten up previously and had borrowed money from a friend to get away and recover, that was why she needed extra money to the wages she got from work, this did not seem very plausible as the bruises seemed fresh, she elaborated her statement by adding that she had just got out of the bath and they were therefore looking worse, also that she worked at the L.G.I. and had got something from the sister to put on them at nights,

I asked her if she had a boyfriend and what did he think of her doing this, she replied' Do..... He does not know anything about it, she was going to give his name but stopped, the second letter sounding 'O' in not. Slightly before the car stoped she asked what happened to the extra I had promised her, apologising I gave her a £20 note, saying that she had provided the best sex I had ever had,

she then opened her bag, she was looking for a biro, having found it she wrote her name "Julie D" on one of my business cards that were about, she said "That's me I shall be around here some evenings, I get dropped off about 10,45 and collected at 11,30

It was then that another car drew up behind, and then said "Thanks xxxxx you're a great guy, but I've got to go now" she shut the door and seemed to run towards the car at the rear

On my way home I threw the business card and the used condom out of the window around the Scammondon Dam area.

I did return a few days later to see her again, but have not seen her

The above is a full description as I believe you would want in a statement, only intimate details have been left out as irrelevant

I cannot give my name or any further details due to the fact I am married , I also once heard one of your chief constables saying what police officers thought of men who used prostitutes, he apparently was a happily married man and should consider himself lucky,

The letter is an excellent example of Sams the games player. He knew I would come to three conclusions: the letter was from the murderer; as Scammonden Dam is on the M62 between Leeds and Manchester, he lived west of Leeds; and a search might reveal the condom and a chance of finding samples of his DNA as well as his business card.

There was certainly enough to identify Julie Dart, but why didn't he send the letter? It was certainly an error leaving it on the computer. Was this yet another mistake Sams would lay onto the other man? This was the first evidence from his computer relating to Julie Dart and her encounter with her killer – only the ending was very different for Julie.

After the text was read to him, Sams asked: 'That was on my computer? Well, I don't know what it is.' He agreed it referred to Julie Dart, but when asked who had put it on his computer he said, 'Back to the other chap again.'

The interview returned to the two handwritten letters they'd discussed earlier. Sams was asked if he had any more thoughts on them. 'Well, you're looking for an excuse again. I told a lie, I told my solicitor a lie as well,' he suddenly decided to admit.

He was again asked if he had written the letters. We expected another fob-off but he announced that he had penned all three of them, not just the two we could prove. The tempo of the interview was now increasing. How could he explain writing the letters without implicating himself as the murderer?

Sams simply said he had copied them for the other man. The spelling mistakes? He copied them as well, word for word. The next question should have been obvious to him – he was asked why the other man could not have done this himself. 'He was using me as a pillock,' Sams bluntly concluded.

Paul and Tim had the bit between their teeth now and asked, 'Doesn't it hurt when someone who's cold-bloodedly murdered a girl comes and talks to you?' Sams replied, 'You said he doesn't exist.' 'But doesn't it have some effect on you?' Sams said, 'No, I'd never like to think that I'd killed her in my mind. I would not like to think I killed her, I don't care what the rest of the world thinks.' This was the closest they were to get to a confession. In those few words he had not admitted the murder, but he had not denied it either.

As the interview ended, Sams regained his composure and said the other man was out there and might make further ransom demands while he was in prison. But when again challenged about his existence, Sams casually remarked, 'Yeah, all right, then, if there is somebody out there.'

At 9.20 pm, Michael Benniman Sams was charged with the murder, kidnapping and unlawful imprisonment of Julie Dart. The charges had been typed and ready for two hours. I waited in the incident room for confirmation that Lynn Dart had been told before releasing the news to the press.

Everyone on the team was elated. Many officers had heard on the grapevine that Sams would be charged and were making their way back to Millgarth for a celebratory drink. I was pleased we had reached a point where we could charge him, but we still had a long way to go to a conviction.

I looked out of the window as my team relaxed around me in the bar. It had taken seven months from Julie's disappearance to charging Sams with her murder. Considering no one had ever seen them together, I felt we had done well. The TV lounge was full for *News at Ten* as it showed a shot of Tom Cook, John O'Sullivan and myself walking into the Swan and Salmon Yard on the Friday after Sams's arrest. I walked to the juke-box and punched in the numbers for 'Midnight Cowboy'.

Our enquiries continued after Sams was charged. Hairs found in the workshop from Sams's dog matched those on the sheet and rope that Julie's body was wrapped in.

A multicoloured curtain which had been hung on nails from the wooden beam in the workshop had bloodstains on it. The blood had soaked nine inches up the curtain from the hem. Tests showed it was from the same blood group as Julie Dart's – further evidence to support our case that Julie had died there.

Sams tried to use his album of pictures of trains taken on 10 July 1991 at Toton Goods Yard in Nottingham, saying he would not have gone train-spotting if he had kidnapped someone. He again underestimated us, as we enlarged the photos and checked the train numbers. British Rail confirmed that none of the trains in the pictures was in the yard on the date Sams said he took the pictures.

We were even able to find a wheelie bin that had been stolen from the museum in Millgate close to Sams's workshop at the time he disposed of Julie's body.

Stephanie Slater's employers, Royal Life Estates, had provided the ransom money and most of it was still missing, but West Midlands had not managed to find it. They had their case sewn up with Sams's confession. We'd have to look for it to provide the knockout blow to Sams's defence. He was now charged with the £200,000 extortion demand on British Rail. The only missing piece of the jigsaw in our case was the ransom money. I had to find it.

I believed the key to where it was hidden lay with Sams, and that maybe something in his past would throw up that clue.

Born on 11 August 1941 in Keighley, Sams was raised by his mother Iris and Ernest Sams, who was not his natural father. He was conceived while Iris's husband, Corporal Ernest Walker, was fighting abroad for his country. But when Iris registered the birth she gave his real father, George Benniman's, surname as Michael's middle name. Would this burden of his past alter the course of his life? If it did not affect his, it certainly played a major part in his decision not to kill Stephanie Slater. When Stephanie told him she was adopted, Sams told her: 'That makes you special, you were chosen.' Did he feel he was one of life's mistakes and was neither chosen nor wanted?

Sams completed his education at Hull Nautical College, gaining nine O-levels and A-levels in pure and applied mathematics and geography.

After serving as a merchant seaman, he left the navy and trained as a fitter of passenger lifts and a central heating engineer. He had excellent technical and mechanical skills.

I was convinced that the answer to where the money was lay in the complex facets of Sams's character. I could account for £35,000 of the money. He had dropped £15,000 on the Dove Valley Trail after collecting the ransom and had kept £20,000 in the workshop for day-to-day use.

It was ironic that, on his way home after freeing Stephanie, Sams ran out of petrol. He had just enough money on him to refuel and get home. He did, however, have £175,000 close by, but he dared not use it for fear it could be traced.

Sams had travelled virtually the whole railway network, so he knew many suitable hiding places. And, of course, our old friend – the other man – got a look-in with Sams stating that on the night of the drop his accomplice took all the money. On arrival at Newark police station, he told the gaoler that the money was buried at three locations a hundred miles away. In the many conversations with police officers and prisoners at Winson Green in Birmingham, he said the money was south of Grantham on a railway embankment.

Sams was such a complex person and such a games player it was difficult to distinguish truth from lies, as both were comfortable bedfellows to him.

I gave the task of finding the money to Tim Grogan. A number of codes in Sams's possession when arrested might lead us to it. One particular code was found in his wallet, on his computer and in his car. It read:

| North | * | | | |
|-------|-----|------|------|----------|
| LHS | 9T | 15ft | 90% | 50 |
| MID | 5T | 12ft | 135% | 20 |
| RHS | 3T | 9ft | 45% | 10/20/50 |

The last column referred to the denominations of the notes – £10, £20 and £50. But what did the rest mean? I presumed that from an unknown fixed point, and facing north, there must be three routes, and each line was an instruction leading to part of the money. Although he used the percentage sign I read the numbers in the third column as degrees of the compass. Taking the first line, I assumed it meant take the left-hand path nine trees along, turn ninety degrees and fifteen feet away was the batch of £50 notes. But given we did not know where the fixed point was it was all hopeless.

Teena found a code, 373 282, stuck inside his shoe. It could be a parts number for a tool or a six-figure map reference. Of course, the sceptics from Birmingham thought it might be the other man's phone number. It wasn't.

In Sams's prison notebook, he'd written:

| MAVIS BLAND | 143 Ridge Ave |
|-------------|---------------|
| (Penfriend) | West Fields |

Sams had no pen-friend that we knew of. The number 143 was for the fictitious address he used when he wrote to Shipways. He used 'Mavis' on the indented writing on the Leeds letter. No Mavis Bland at 143 Ridge Avenue existed.

We found twenty-two Ordnance Survey maps and four A–Z directories at his workshop, some of which he had marked. We tried to relate the codes to the maps' markings, but nothing fitted. I thought we needed specialist advice, and spoke to a whole array of experts from nautical and navigation people to airline pilots. No one could make sense of what we had.

We approached GCHQ, the Government Communications Headquarters in Cheltenham, Gloucestershire, and centre of the government's electronic surveillance operations. Established in World War I at Bletchley

Park, Bucks, it was responsible for breaking the German Enigma code in 1940. Surely, if anyone could break the codes of a one-legged tool repairer from Newark, they could.

Professor John Hunter, an expert on forensic archaeology from Bradford University, was consulted. He told us how vegetation, coloration and growth patterns differ in an area where something is buried.

Sams had the money only between 29 January and his arrest on 21 February. I focused on the week of his arrest, when pressure was mounting as more information about him filtered into the media. If we could determine on which day he moved it, we had a chance.

Luck always helps, and as I reviewed the list of sightings of people near where Julie Dart was found, I discovered one of a man with a limp seen six hundred yards from the spot, though weeks earlier. I reckoned this was Sams, and instructed that he be put on an identification parade.

The witness did not pick him out but Sams admitted visiting a secluded railway bridge, Westby viaduct, on the main East Coast railway line near where Julie was found. He claimed it was months later and he was train-spotting. He said he spoke to a farmer, who was shooting pigeons. After interviewing the farmer, we put the date at days before Sams's arrest.

I was certain it was Wednesday, 19 February, the day he rang Jane Cashman from a call-box at Great Gonerby, north of Grantham. The bridge was not far off his route from Newark. I checked the weather with the Met Office, as the farmer said it was raw and drizzly, which that Wednesday was. Hardly a day for train-spotting, but maybe one for reburying the money.

Westby viaduct is more commonly known as Stoke Summit in train-spotting annals. It was here, on 23 July 1938, that the *Mallard* reached a 126 mph world record for a steam train. What better place for Sams to bury his loot than here? It was also only 1.8 miles across the fields from where Julie's body was found.

I contacted a retired SAS colonel who, in the 1970s, had devised a system for finding terrorist arms caches in Northern Ireland.

On Monday, 28 September, I met the colonel and showed him places of interest to the inquiry, starting at the point where Julie's body was found. We went down the various tracks where Sams had been and ended up at Stoke Summit.

The track to the bridge at Stoke Summit is a farm track, three-quarters of a mile long with nothing but fields on either side. The bridge spans the cutting forty feet above the track with a fenced embankment, giving the farmer access to his fields. At the top of the embankment is a twenty-foot-wide flat grassed area within the fencing, shielded from the line by thick bushes.

The colonel stumbled as he tried to climb over the fence. He did not know it but he was feet away from the money. He liked the railway connection but favoured a disused line rather than the embankment. I knew Sams needed a drawn map, a written code or a mind map, which would allow him to find his treasure even in the dark.

News of SAS involvement in the inquiry was soon in the press. Sams's conversations with other prisoners gave me more useful tips. 'If the SAS has been brought in, they'll find the money,' he said, again revealing his reverence for experts. This gave me an idea.

On Tuesday, 27 October 1992, a meeting was held at the West Midlands Training School, where all interested parties were invited to hear the different theories about where the money was.

Our theory that it was at Stoke Summit was generally accepted. The dissenters were West Midlands officers, those who had been sceptical all along that the Dart and Slater cases were connected. One even proffered his theory, apparently without any evidence, that Sams had burnt the money.

It was agreed that West Yorkshire Police would go ahead with the plan to search around the bridge at Stoke Summit. West Midlands was invited along but turned down the offer, which I found remarkable considering the missing money was from their kidnap case.

I needed a device that would find something buried but not in a metal box. Sams's instructions in his first letter to me was that the Dart ransom money be wrapped in polythene 120 microns thick. He would not make the task simple by burying it in a metal box, easily found using a detector. Mick Brown, head of the Technical Support Unit, found out about Ground Probing Radar, which the Atomic Research Establishment at Harlow had pioneered for sweeping the ground for objects below the surface.

It was used extensively in the oil industry, as the sonar waves emitted into the soil detected underground pipes buried up to twelve feet deep. It had also been used for locating crypts under church floors.

A small Aberdeen company, Oceanfix International, had the kit.

Owner Peter Simpkin charged £1,000 a day to hire it out. Before I even attempted to persuade the force to foot the bill, I needed to know how effective it was. Tim and Wayne Greenwood were dispatched. They were told to get it more cheaply and check whether it could do the job.

They achieved both objectives. The price would be £500 per day, and as to performance – yes. Tuesday, 1 December was the day we'd go money-hunting. But as well as sweeping the area with the radar, I had another plan up my sleeve.

I called on the services of Yorkshire Television journalist Andrew Sheldon. I needed to generate publicity about the operation in the hope that Sams would respond in some way by indicating whether we were in the right place.

Day one of the dig was uneventful. I went to the site the next day, arriving at 11 am. Conditions were appalling – it was bitterly cold and intermittent rain had left a large pool of water across the bridge over the railway line. The search around the bridge had unearthed parts of a plough, rabbit holes and stones, but no money.

I wanted the grassed area inside the fence at the top of the embankment done next. The ground was fairly uneven, and there were two furrows per-haps made by a tractor running parallel along it.

The weather and the constant digging up of stones had dulled the enthusiasm of the search team, whose faith in Peter Simpkin's ability to find the money was slowly waning, even assuming it was buried there.

After thawing out over a pub lunch, I returned to the bridge at 1.45 pm. I could see the search teams' yellow waterproofs from half a mile away, and as I got closer I realised something was happening. A group was wading through the water on the bridge with their arms in the air.

'Oh no,' groaned Gary Caine, a freelance cameraman for YTV who'd been filming for two days in the hope of catching the very moment when the money was found. Gary hit the ground running, switching on his camera as he sprinted towards the bridge. As I reached the grassy area where I'd asked them to look, it was apparent that the scanner had picked out a buried object. The team quickly dug down, and there it was – a black plastic box, a seed tray with a copy of the *Newark Trader* on top, wrapped in polythene. The spade had cut through the top as it had been dug up, and £50 notes could be seen through the gash in the newspaper.

Everyone was in a frenzy. I never really expected we would find the money. At the most, I was hoping for some reaction from Sams to guide me to it. I needed photographs of the money *in situ*, and we called on the services of a Lincolnshire scene-of-crime officer. He agreed to make a plan and take photographs but insisted I give him £2.20 for a hand-drawn plan of the area where the money was found. I muttered to myself that it would have cost Lincolnshire a lot more than £2.20 if West Yorkshire had not taken the Dart murder away from them.

The tray was put into a clean plastic dustbin to preserve it for forensic examination, and I brought it back to Millgarth police station. But I immediately hit a problem – the Chief Superintendent doubted whether police insurance covered that amount of money being kept at the station. Until it was sorted, I arranged for the bin to be kept under constant surveillance in the bar at Millgarth. We all stood around it toasting our success. We raised our glasses and I said: 'To the bin: I never thought the contents of a dustbin would make me so happy.' The money did later go into the superintendent's safe.

Next morning the money was taken to Birmingham, and I got a call to say that Sams wanted to see me. I couldn't believe it; he was saying we had found only half the money but he would tell us where the rest was. Wayne Greenwood confirmed that we had only about £60,000. I sent Tim Grogan and Paul Leach with Sams's solicitor, David Payne, to see him.

Sams said the ransom was in two boxes. We had only one. He said that he and the other man had buried the money together. He had picked his pal up on the A1, blindfolded him and driven him to within two hundred yards of the bridge. Sams had removed the blindfold from the other man, who then put it on Sams. The other man then went off and buried the money. The process had then been reversed, and Sams dropped him off back on the A1. A tall story, even by his fairytale standards.

His plan was flawed. If the other man existed, and was the one who killed Julie Dart and wanted to kill Stephanie Slater, he would have had no compunction about returning, collecting the money and spending the lot. He had ample opportunity, as it had been there nine months before we found it. Neither could he have failed to notice it was beside a bridge on a main railway line. It would take him no time to find the bridge. Peter Simpkin was on his way back to Aberdeen, so we would have to find the rest without him.

By 9 am on Friday, 4 December, we were back on-site. I would start from where Peter had finished and work away from the bridge. Despite the cold December air, the task force officers were stripped to the waist as they toiled away, slicing off the top surface. The area was about a hundred square yards, and there was no guarantee the rest of the money was there.

We used probes, sticks with six-inch metal points, to prod the surface. I gave a hand in various tasks but found the prodding the least tiring. By 10.15 am we were in full flow, and I was happily prodding away in front of Jeff Calter, one of my team. Although I did not strike anything, I found the ground exceptionally soft.

'Dig here, Jeff,' I said, pointing to the ground. Jeff had a garden fork and forced it into the grass about a foot away from where I wanted. 'No, Jeff, here,' I said, taking the fork from him and plunging it in the ground. I felt a jolt. The fork had struck something. I bent the fork back and could see that it had pierced a plastic box. I pulled it up and out came a one-gallon plastic ice-cream carton stuffed with £50 notes, a wad of which had been pierced by the fork's tines.

The smell of victory was musty £50 notes in an ice-cream carton. This was my moment. I was elated and ran around the field with the fork thrust in the air, still with the carton of money stuck on the end, shouting, 'Got you, Sams, you bastard.' This, for me, was the finest moment in the whole inquiry, as I knew we had torpedoed Sams's defence. In digging up the carton, I had buried the other man. A jury could hardly believe the other man existed now we had found the rest of the money.

The carton was in a white Black and Decker plastic bag emblazoned with the words 'We know how. Do you know where?' Was this Sams's final joke? I looked at his codes again. None corresponded with where the money was buried, except possibly MAVIS BLAND, 143 Ridge Ave, West Fields. The money was in line with a ridge or furrow on the west side of the track, and walking from the fence it was roughly fourteen paces to the first lot of money and three to the next. But Sams did not need to write that down. It was all part of his game.

With the Sams trial looming and tension mounting, a little light diversion was welcome. It came when I received a phone call from a Yorkshire Television producer asking me whether I would meet the comedy duo Hale and Pace. I was intrigued to discover that they were making a pilot TV series based on Reginald Hill's book *A Pinch of Snuff*. Gareth Hale was to play Andy Dalziel, a detective superintendent in the mythical Mid-Yorkshire Constabulary, and Norman Pace would be his sergeant sidekick, Peter Pascoe.

This was one of a series of whodunnit detective novels centring on Dalziel and Pascoe. To bring realism to the roles, they wanted to explore the relationship between a senior detective and his sergeant. A copy of the novel was posted to me, which I read and enjoyed.

In March 1993, Norman Pace arrived at Millgarth police station. Gareth Hale was unable to come. I brought DS Tim Grogan into the discussion, and we spent a couple of hours talking about how I would run a murder inquiry, what role the sergeant would play in it, and my relationship with Tim. 'Would he call you "Bob" or "sir"?' Norman asked me. 'Oh, definitely "sir". Even though your sergeant may be a friend, it is not professional or good for other officers to hear him shouting "Bob" at the superintendent down the full length of the station corridor or across an incident room.'

Off duty, in our own time, I encouraged officers to call me Bob; I did not want anyone shouting 'Superintendent Taylor' across the bar of a pub. There are senior officers whose egos demand that junior officers grovel and use their title irrespective of where they are. I always suspect these types have their rank insignia stitched on their buttoned-up pyjamas and demand that their wives and children call them 'sir'. And, of course, this type of officer would not be seen dead socialising with junior ranks, whereas I enjoyed the occasional teatime drink and discussion with officers from my inquiries. I found that they would speak more openly in a social forum than in the more formal setting of a briefing.

I told Norman about an inspector who had had a sergeant transferred to another station for overfamiliarity when he had overheard a young PC address him by his first name. Our meeting ended with a couple of drinks in the station bar, and Norman thanked us for the insights. That was the last I heard.

The following year the programme was screened as a three-part series and was pummelled by the critics. In 1996, the BBC screened a new series of *Dalziel and Pascoe* based on the same characters but now with Warren Clarke playing Dalziel and Colin Buchanan as Pascoe. Few people saw anything in common between Gareth Hale and myself, but Warren Clarke transformed Dalziel into a blunt-speaking Yorkshireman who many of my colleagues and friends – and even my wife – remarked has more than a passing resemblance to me. I have never been sure whether to take this as a compliment or not.

# chapter four

# SHE WAS ALWAYS GOING TO DIE

## Wednesday, 9 June 1993

Apart from a fleeting glance when Michael Sams was committed for trial from Birmingham magistrates' court, I had never seen him in the flesh. Nottingham Crown Court was chosen as the venue for his trial. It would be the first time we would face each other and he would see me, the dark shadowy figure, come into the light.

At 10.29 am on 9 June 1993, Michael Benniman Sams was brought into the crowded court. He stood in the dock wearing a smart blue suit, light blue shirt and dark blue tie, looking as defiant as ever and totally unmoved by the crowded courtroom. This was what he wanted, as many people as possible to witness what he considered would be his greatest hour, when he successfully made the final moves in his game by being found not guilty of Julie Dart's murder and the British Rail extortion.

His eyes flickered around as he took in the layout of the room and those in it. I could tell he knew who I was as his gaze lingered momentarily on me before moving on, scanning everyone else in the courtroom. I felt nothing when I saw him.

Set in the prestigious Court One, the trial was due to last six weeks. Our leading counsel would be Richard Wakerley, QC, and the defence was represented by John Milmo, QC. I would have given anything to prosecute this case myself.

But Mr Wakerley was an imposing figure who I sensed would be an intimidating adversary when cross-examining a witness. He had a good knowledge of the case but he did not understand Sams's character as I did, so I needed him to be open to my ideas.

We compiled a report supporting the case that there was no other man, while West Midlands Police produced one to show he did exist. These actually ended up as one report which showed that all references to the other man came from Sams, either in his letters, interviews or comments to Stephanie.

The other man was an illusion created by Sams. It helped deflect blame from him for the crimes, but I also believe he used it so he could convince himself that he performed all the good deeds, such as saving Stephanie, while the Absent Protagonist was the dustbin where he dumped all the bad acts. It was the other man who wanted to kill Stephanie but it was Sams who saved her life, according to his bizarre way of thinking.

As the trial loomed, I was still picking up other jobs. There were always other operations and investigations to run. In January 1993 I had finally captured the serial rapist David Jackson, who'd been terrorising young women in the park next to Leeds University for two years. Like Sams, he had written a letter to me, and that was his downfall.

Later that same month, I was called to the home of pensioner William Collins in East Park Mount, Leeds. The house was a back-to-back terrace which had been set ablaze. By the time I arrived, the fire had been extinguished, but steam was still pouring out of the front door, its only entrance. Mr Collins was dead, lying on the lounge floor, between an armchair and his settee. Whoever had killed this eighty-four-year-old man had left him with extensive head and face injuries.

Alerted by the fire, neighbours in the tight-knit community had fought with a stranger who had appeared from the smoke-filled house. He was now under arrest on suspicion of murder and arson, but he was refusing to speak or name himself.

It became clear as I sifted through the neighbours' statements that the anonymous man sitting in the cells had not been alone, as they gave descriptions of three different people seen at the house. I had one – two others I had to find. Mr Collins's house had been ransacked, and robbery appeared the likely motive.

When I attended the post-mortem I was sickened by the extent of the injuries inflicted on this pensioner. His eyes, cheeks and lips were bruised, swollen and blackened; he had a gash on his chin, another, larger one on the side of his head, and too many others on his scalp to count. His forearms showed defence injuries. They were battered and bruised from trying to fend off some of the blows. He had broken cheekbones, a shattered jawbone and at least three broken ribs.

He had died from shock resulting from his multiple facial injuries caused by an evil cocktail of punches, kicks and stamping – and all for a few pounds, as his meagre lifestyle and modest home did not suggest he possessed any wealth whatsoever.

It was some hours before we identified Freddie Lee as the man in the cells and his accomplices as Mark Shakeshaft and John 'Sonny' Gavin, who were arrested over the following days. All were charged with murder. The case was complex in so far as I would have to show exactly what each person had done in contributing to Mr Collins's death. I had discovered they had visited his home the previous day and had noticed a bank book with about £2,000 savings in it. So they returned. Shakeshaft claimed he had arrived at the house after the other two and on entering found Lee already kicking the old man in the face and demanding to know where his money was. When Gavin joined in the attack, Shakeshaft started several fires in an attempt to distract the other two from the assault. When they appeared in court they all pleaded not guilty to the murder charge. Nevertheless, Lee and Gavin were convicted of murder and Shakeshaft was sentenced to eight years' imprisonment for manslaughter.

On Bank Holiday Monday I was called to the murder of a twenty-two-year-old insurance manageress, Nadine Farrar. Her body was found in a second-floor bedroom at her boyfriend's home in Sandhurst Place, Leeds. She had been strangled. Her twenty-two-year-old boyfriend, Steven Edmund Barnard, a singer, was arrested and admitted strangling her in a fit of rage. Their relationship had been a stormy one and was on the wane. The previous day they had had sex, but afterwards an argument developed. Nadine told Barnard she had another boyfriend (an unfortunate white lie) as a way of ending their relationship and taking a holiday with her girlfriends in Rhodes.

Barnard flew into a fit of rage and strangled Nadine with his bare hands until she slumped to the floor. She was still alive and he ended her life by putting his stockinged foot on her neck and keeping the pressure there until she was dead.

At his trial he asked the court to accept his plea of manslaughter on the grounds of provocation, but the jury rejected this and found him guilty of murder.

Two days later, an hour after I arrived home from work, I was called out at 9.45 pm to the murder of forty-two-year-old mother-of-two Ann Smith. I drove to the scene, a back-to-back terraced house in Cross Flatts Mount, south Leeds, where Mrs Smith lay dead in the first-floor bathroom. Her sons, Richard, aged sixteen, and ten-year-old Adam, were with the neighbour, who rang the police after hearing a disturbance at the house.

The boys had fled their home after Richard had seen his father, Trevor Smith, standing over his mother with a knife in his hand as she lay in the bath. Smith, a forty-two-year-old lift engineer, was nowhere to be seen. It may have seemed an open-and-shut case but procedures had to be followed and everything verified. If, when arrested, the husband maintained his right to silence, I would have to prove his guilt by other means.

Within a couple of hours, Smith was arrested at his brother's house on the other side of Leeds, having rung the police to give himself up.

It was the early hours of the morning before the post-mortem began. Ann Smith had ten wounds inflicted by a long-bladed kitchen knife to her side, back, hip, arms, shoulder, chin and legs. The side wound had punctured her liver and the back wound extended into her spleen.

Their marriage had been in difficulty for a couple of years, and Trevor Smith had begun to suspect that his wife was having a relationship with another man. On the day of the murder he found a letter that led him to believe his wife was leaving him and moving to Filey. He wrote a letter setting out his feelings for her and his hopes for the future, leaving it on her jewellery box.

Trevor arrived home shortly after 8 pm. He was drunk and became argumentative when Ann refused to discuss the letter he had left. Ann went up to take a bath and he took her a cup of tea and attempted again to discuss their future, but his wife was non-committal as to her intentions. He stormed out, returning from the kitchen armed with a knife, and, after forcing open the bathroom door, he stabbed and killed her.

The court accepted that Trevor Smith was suffering from an anxiety neurosis and reactive depression and he was jailed for six years for manslaughter on the grounds of diminished responsibility.

I felt sorry for the two Smith boys. Innocent victims of a domestic incident which went badly wrong, they were now left without mother or father.

But such is the dark side of life which detectives come to treat as almost everyday, as I did. One minute you can be sat having a meal with your family, the next standing in the mortuary clad in a green gown dealing with some poor soul's death.

And so to Sams's trial. In all my years' service I'd never been to crown court without feeling some butterflies, as experience had taught me that as many things could go wrong as right. The case would be heard by Justice Igor Judge, a senior judge with a no-nonsense reputation.

Sams pleaded not guilty to the kidnap and murder of Julie Dart, the subsequent blackmailing of the police, and the extortion demand on British Rail. To the charges of kidnapping Stephanie Slater, demanding the £175,000 ransom and her imprisonment in his workshop, he pleaded guilty. He would be sentenced for these at the end of the trial, whatever the verdict on the crimes he denied.

Witnesses are not normally allowed in court before they give evidence, but the judge said I could be present as I wanted to hear Mr Wakerley's opening speech and see Sams's reaction to the prosecution case. The atmosphere in the courtroom exuded tension. I felt that I could not only hear my own heart thumping but also those of everyone around me. This is what I'd been working towards for twenty-three months. Richard Wakerley's opening speech was delivered with eloquence and precision over the course of two and a half days; never once did he glance at his notes.

I was more than impressed, as were the journalists in the court and those in the press room to which the proceedings were piped, such was the media interest. The unequivocal opinion was that it was one of the finest opening speeches they had heard, if not the finest. It was for me, and I've heard a few in my time.

The witnesses followed. Some statements were read, but for the purpose of having a greater impact on the jury, and to retain interest, tension and drama in the case, we needed some to appear in person. The picture has to be painted for the jury, they must grasp the reality; the cold-blooded and calculated acts this man was accused of had to be felt by them.

They had to experience the emotion of the witnesses. Thus, on Monday, 14 June, as Lynn Dart walked to the witness box, I hoped the jury could see the pain of her loss.

For me, her anger and anguish of the last two years, and her hatred for Sams, were etched across her face. As she reached the box, she turned and locked her eyes onto Sams. He held her gaze for what seemed an age, until finally he looked down. If you could read her face, it said: 'I loathe you, little man.'

I had explained to Lynn that we did not need to call her but the best way to make Julie come alive in the jurors' minds was for them to see and hear her mother speak about her. Lynn was more than happy to give evidence. She had waited a long time to face her daughter's killer, and this was her moment. Dressed in black, she gave evidence with dignity and poise, though this deserted her for a moment as she stood shaking when she recalled: 'Julie was afraid of confined spaces. Even as a child she was terrified to go in a lift.' That is, without doubt, why Julie would have tried to escape from the tomb she was kept in. After Lynn had finished, she walked to the door, but before stepping outside she turned to Sams, pointed her finger at him and in a trembling voice declared: 'He's mine.'

One of the last people to see Julie alive was a prostitute she had stood with on Spencer Place in Leeds. The woman had since left the streets to rebuild her life, and would be referred to only as Mary to protect her identity. After Sams's arrest and the disclosure that he was a one-legged man, she told us of a punter she had picked up three weeks before Julie was abducted.

The man, driving an orange-coloured hatchback, took Mary to the Thomas Danby College carpark. He threatened her with a knife and told her to undress. She tricked him into letting her get out of the car to take her clothes off, and she ran off. Mary performed one final defiant act. 'I was about ten feet away. I picked up a piece of brick and threw it at the car. I remember it hit the windscreen on the driver's side and bounced off.' When Sams's Metro was checked, on the very spot Mary described there was a dent in the front windscreen.

However, Justice Judge ruled that this part of her evidence should be excluded. This was based on its prejudicial value outweighing its probative value, or as Richard Wakerley put it: 'The judge thinks we have enough; we would not want to lose it on appeal over something we can do without.'

When the court broke for lunch it became a familiar sight to see Richard Wakerley fleeing through the doors clasping a lit cigarette in one hand and his wig in the other. He'd seek sanctuary in our room, the only place you could smoke. It meant we were able to discuss the progress of the trial, but there was one point we always disagreed on. Would Sams give evidence? Mr Wakerley, considering it from a lawyer's perspective, was emphatic: 'No, he won't.' I was equally emphatic. 'Yes he will.' 'John Milmo would not advise him to do that,' Mr Wakerley said. 'Might not be able to stop him,' I retorted.

Stephanie Slater's appearance was one of the trial's more dramatic moments. She arrived on day seven, posed for photographs on the court steps but did not speak to reporters.

It was a magical moment as she recounted to the crowded court what had happened to her at the hands of the man in the dock. The tension reached its height when she spoke of her first night encased in the coffin-like structure in Sams's workshop. 'That night, lying in there, you start to think what happened during the day. I was bitterly cold, absolutely frozen. My arms had gone to sleep. I had pins and needles all night. I did not sleep much, if at all. I thought I had died. I saw a picture of Christ in front of me in the blackness.'

Unusually, some of the jurors sobbed, and all in the courtroom were obviously moved as she recalled her ordeal. Also shedding tears was Sams. In fact, he sobbed from the moment he came into court and sniffed away throughout her evidence. Yet he never shed a tear for Julie Dart, as he said he had no more feelings for her death than he did for those who died in the Second World War. But if he had a heart, Stephanie had touched it, and without doubt, I believe, that saved her life.

Kevin Watts described how a sunny afternoon in Glossop turned into a nightmare as he battled against time following Sams's instructions to deliver the money. Kevin's bravery was apparent.

The drama of the case reached another peak when Susan Oake stepped into the witness box on Monday, 21 June. Wearing a purple jacket and white skirt, she was as elegant as she was articulate as she described the events leading up to her ringing Millgarth. She was clearly uncomfortable at having to face as a witness a man who had been her husband and was father to two of her sons.

As with most high drama, there were times of pure comedy, as when Marg Carne and her daughter unexpectedly turned up at court. I had crossed swords months earlier with Marg when she rang in about a man with a signal box in his garden at Penkridge, Staffordshire, fourteen miles from Millmeece, where the block had been found on the line, and even nearer to where Sams had stopped to train-spot after kidnapping Stephanie.

Marg lived at Long Bennington, six miles south of Newark. She put 'Penkridge Man' forward as a suspect at the time we had publicly made the railway connection. Marg was also a medium. I regarded mystic suggestions as highly unreliable and usually filed them under no action, but as she'd made a legitimate factual suggestion it was followed up and the man was eliminated from the inquiry. This was just not good enough for her, and she would constantly ring the incident room.

I had been told of a visit Tim Grogan had made with Paul Leach when Marg's playful puppy Zeus – in reality a full-size Great Dane – was being a constant nuisance in the lounge as they tried to speak to her about Penkridge Man. At one point Paul asked to go to the toilet upstairs but was warned that, as all the wooden doors had been removed for dipping, there was only a curtain to protect his modesty.

As he went upstairs, Marg disappeared into the kitchen to make more coffee. Zeus had only Tim to play with now, and Tim's patience had long since deserted him. In an attempt to ward off the boisterous mutt, he thrust out his arm and caught the hound with his fist in its sizable testicles, causing it to wince in a doggy sort of way.

Having decided that Tim was no longer any fun, Zeus bounded upstairs in search of the unsuspecting Paul. He had only just dropped his trousers and was sitting on the toilet gazing at the curtain when it flew open and Zeus launched his considerable frame at him. To Paul's horror and shock, the dog plonked his enormous front paws on his shoulders and eagerly began licking his balding head.

Tim was just about to sip his freshly made coffee when a blood-curdling scream filled the house. He and Marg rushed to rescue Paul, who attempted to regain his dignity while Zeus was forcibly removed from him.

During a long inquiry a moment of diversion is a relief. It was for this reason that I was happy to call on Marg during a visit to Newark with Tim and Wayne Greenwood. We were ushered into the kitchen, where in the corner was a table with benches on either side. Wayne and Tim immediately sat as close to the wall as possible and I sat at the other end with Marg opposite.

As we made polite talk, she declared: 'I receive messages from a black hole in space at 14.2 MHz and when I do my eyes turn red.' I nodded my head knowingly. 'Funny that, Marg. My eyes turn red as well sometimes, but that's more to do with Tetley's Bitter than any imploded star in space.' I could see she sensed I was a disbeliever. Dead bloody right. We were just discussing her theories relating to Sams being in cahoots with Penkridge Man, when I heard a rumble.

It started like distant thunder. I noticed Wayne and Tim snigger and tense up as through the door came the beast of the bog, Zeus. 'Bloody hell,' I said under my breath, 'it's bigger than a Shetland pony!' I'm not a dog lover so I was not impressed with the manner in which the hound immediately shed several handfuls of hair down my dark blue suit. I was struggling to see the humour, which Wayne and Tim obviously could, when Zeus thrust its paw, as thick as a man's arm, into my jacket pocket. As the 'puppy' then tried to detach it from the rest of my suit with considerable force, it nearly dragged me out of my seat. 'Don't worry, he's just being playful,' reassured Marg. I could imagine those words ringing in my ears as the mutt dragged me out and buried me in the sodding garden.

But now she was at crown court, insisting to the point of making a scene that there was another man and he had been seen in a pub near Newark with Sams and Stephanie when she was supposed to be captive. Marg said that what she was saying was not a theory but fact. I was on my ground now, and there was no Zeus to intimidate me.

I asked her to give up the name of the person who had seen the other man. She refused point blank, saying the person would not agree to that as he did not trust anyone on account of being abused by a priest as a child. I was as baffled as I was bemused by that.

I told her I would pass this on to Sams's solicitor, David Payne, but could do no more. She was not satisfied by this, and began to threaten as to how she would reveal all when Sams was found not guilty. I told David of this latest suggestion, and after he had seen Sams he said: 'Michael says it is complete rubbish.' If it had not been for the suggested presence of Stephanie at the pub, Marg's spoutings could have helped bring the other man to life.

At the end of each day, I met with Richard Wakerley to determine the batting order of witnesses for the next. I asked when one particular witness would be called. 'We will leave the rubbish till last,' he said. The next day he told me I would be the last witness!

The technicalities of the forensic evidence were presented to the jury. While essential, it didn't have the fascination of the witness appearances. Scientist Val Tomlinson provided vital links between Julie and Sams's workshop with the work on the fibres, the dog hairs on the sheet, and the rope that bound Julie's body.

The evidence she gave on the watery blood on the curtain in his workshop was astounding. Its watery consistency had come about as it seeped up the curtain from the workshop floor. I knew the blood was the same group as Julie's. What I did not know was that, during the tests, Val had purposely cut her own finger, let it bleed for several minutes, and used her blood to simulate a similar effect. Her conclusion to the question as to how much blood would have been soaked up to cause this effect was 'about half a test tube'.

Finally, on Wednesday, 30 June, and twenty-one days after the trial began, I stepped into the witness box. I felt confident the case was going well but was ever conscious that the wheel could come off. When it came to officers giving evidence, I always followed the principle of Big Billy-Goat Gruff, from the song. When Little Billy-Goat Gruff crosses the bridge and is confronted by the troll who wants to eat him he tells the troll that his bigger brother is a much tastier morsel and escapes. Medium Billy-Goat Gruff uses the same ploy. When Big Billy-Goat Gruff comes along he is more than up to the task and kills the troll.

I told the team I would deal with questions of policy and the direction of the inquiry.

The very nature of my evidence as the 'sweeper' – the last witness – meant that the defence had to tell me in advance what they were going to ask me, as I pointed out that I would refuse to answer any questions until I had checked the computer. I was not in the box very long but was able to correct a few misunderstandings which had arisen.

And so ended the prosecution case. The big question was would Sams put himself at the jeopardy of a cross-examination by Richard Wakerley by giving evidence. Word quickly spread that Sams would indeed take the stand. The media were surprised, and once again the trial had reached a high point. There were no spare seats in court, as the anticipated exchange between Sams and Wakerley was being billed as a Battle of the Titans.

I sat and watched at 10.30 am on Thursday, 1 July, as Michael Sams dragged his false leg across the court to the witness box. His counsel, John Milmo, QC, led him through the evidence that Sams had offered as his defence. It was his final chance to breathe air into the lungs of the other man. It also gave Richard Wakerley an opportunity to weigh up his foe.

Sams had rehearsed his answers well and, as he was working with his own defence counsel, was under no pressure. I wondered how long all this would go on. It was boring, because he was lying through his teeth. There were times he was virtually smirking as he painted the picture of the other man, obviously thinking it was going down well with the jury and that he was doing a good job.

'Will you name this friend?' asked John Milmo. Sams replied as casually as if he were being asked if he wanted a cup of tea. 'Not at this moment, no.' John Milmo had hardly bent his knees to sit down when Richard Wakerley leapt up, demanding: 'When will you name him?' The delivery of the question was so different in tone from the almost jovial exchange between Sams and Milmo over the last two days that it shocked everyone, Sams included.

Like a confused man who had just walked into a right hook, he spluttered that he had never seen Julie Dart. Richard Wakerley was not really interested in his reply – his verbal blows were designed to soften and confuse. 'Name him now,' he said.

By 1 pm, Richard Wakerley had battered and bruised Sams in a fashion such as I have never seen before or since. His staccato style of questioning ridiculed Sams, accusing him of being the murderer and playing a game, and laid open before the jury the crass stupidity of a man who was effectively saying, 'I will let the court find me innocent before I name the other person.' Had this been a real boxing match I rather think Sams's corner would have thrown in the towel well before now, but he clung on. He had compelling reasons to do so – his liberty and the rest of his life were at stake.

The drama continued through the afternoon. Sams obviously had an uncomfortable lunch-time. He had underestimated his adversary and didn't recover that day. The afternoon tea break couldn't come quickly enough for Sams, who had visibly changed from the relaxed defendant of the morning to this cowering grey man. I met Paul Britton and Richard Wakerley in our room at the break. Paul said: 'He's on the point of cracking. I think he may confess to the murder.' I knew that whatever Sams's agenda was, confession was not part of it.

After a weekend spent licking his wounds in Birmingham's Winson Green prison, Sams was back in the witness box on Monday morning. As I expected, our games player was not the grey, battered figure that had left on Friday. He was fresh and confident. The questioning was along the same lines as Richard Wakerley sought to expose the existence of the other man as a sham. Sams's answers showed more thought and guile as he dodged to avoid the punches and threw a few back himself.

When asked to describe the other man, Sams said, 'He's five foot ten inches tall, dark, bigger than me and just under fifty. He used to work for British Rail.' Wakerley challenged him, 'Why did you tell the police he was still working for British Rail?' Sams replied comfortably, 'Because I did not want the police to find him.'

Later he cockily challenged his accuser: 'How can you stand there and think I could have killed anyone?' He had coped far better in this exchange, and at no time did he show the distress he had on Friday.

It was probable that the trial would finish by the weekend, depending on how long the jury took to reach a verdict. I was confident but in no way certain that Sams would be found guilty. Jurors have an ability to remain completely passive and I had experienced perverse verdicts in the past, though for lesser crimes.

By Wednesday afternoon all was completed. Justice Igor Judge spent the day summing up in a methodical, fair and commonsense manner. He would finish in the morning and then the jury would be sent out.

That night we knew we were on the final straight. If the jury had to stay in a hotel overnight and deliver its verdict on Friday it would be two years to the day since Julie was kidnapped. I knew we had done everything possible. It was now in the hands of the eight women and four men of the jury.

Bright and early on Thursday morning, we breezed into court. It would be a decisive and busy day, with lots of press interviews and the obligatory celebratory drink if everything went our way. But there was activity that caused me concern; barristers and solicitors were rushing to and from the law library. There was clearly a problem and no one was telling us what it was, though it did not take long for me to get the thread. Two members of the jury, it was alleged, were overheard discussing the case on a bus the previous night.

The information had been anonymously rung into both the court and the local paper. This could certainly give Sams grounds for an appeal if the trial proceeded. I felt sick, as did the whole team. This trial had gone well; could I hope for it to go as well a second time? The saviour of the day was the last person I would have imagined, Sams himself. His legal team explained the problem to him in the cells. Sams decided: 'I don't want to go for a retrial. Let's carry on.'

The judge explained the problem to the crowded court. He said he had questioned all the jurors and the matter had been denied, and given the defence position he had concluded that the trial would continue. I for one breathed a sigh of relief.

It then took Justice Judge less than an hour to finish summing up. He concluded: 'The question is, is he hiding someone else or is he hiding himself?'

The jury retired at 11.42 am to consider its verdicts. Just after 3 pm, I was told that they had reached a verdict and were returning to the court. I struggled through the media pack to take a seat next to Tom Cook. It seemed an age for the formalities to be concluded and for the verdicts to be formally announced. Guilty on all counts, the foreman declared. These twelve people I had never met before and would not meet again had vindicated all our efforts.

'Yes, we've done it,' I said to myself. My scalp was tingling, and my heart thumping like a kettledrum. I felt hot, flushed and happy that the job was done. The game of cat-and-mouse had ended with the mouse Sams now firmly ensnared in the trap of justice.

Behind me, a man shouted, 'Yes, you bastard.' Justice Judge quickly restored calm, told Sams to stand and addressed him: 'You are an extremely dangerous and evil man. The jury has convicted you of murder, a murder in cold blood. You deliberately strangled her [Julie] to death while she was unconscious, when your kidnapping went wrong because she saw more than she should. Undeterred by the horror of what you had done, you tried to turn her death to your advantage. The letters you wrote make chilling reading. No qualms, no remorse, heartless at the grief you had caused. It was misplaced pride and callous arrogance.

'Then came the British Rail blackmail, frightening enough and not followed through because you had returned to your idea of kidnapping an estate agent. You planned and executed that quite ruthlessly. When Stephanie Slater was kidnapped I have not the slightest doubt that she was in desperate and mortal danger. If it had seemed necessary to you she, like Julie Dart, would have been murdered in cold blood.

'You are and will remain for the indefinite future a menace to the community. There is an urgent necessity to protect the public from you. Having regard to the wickedness of these crimes and the danger you represent there will be sentences of life imprisonment for the murder, the kidnaps and the unlawful imprisonment, and ten years' imprisonment to run concurrently for the four offences of blackmail.'

I looked at Sams as he glanced around the court, but his gaze did not settle on any one person. His expression was one neither of shock nor surprise. He knew better than I that the jury would find him guilty. He turned and disappeared through the door behind the dock.

Tom Cook said: 'Well done, Bob.' I shook hands with my team and then went to a private room to speak with Lynn Dart and her family. 'I promised you that we would do it, we'd catch the killer, and we did,' I said to Lynn as we shared a hug and a few tears.

I was delighted at the success we had achieved, but realised it was only a consolation prize for Lynn as it would not bring Julie back to her. I left the family to their own emotions.

Outside the court, I was interviewed by the press. The big question they wanted answering was why had we put so much effort into the case. 'We did it for truth. We did it for justice. But most of all we did it for Julie's sake,' I said. Who else but us could find the truth of what happened to a girl of eighteen who was taken from Leeds one night and ended up, naked and trussed, in the corner of a Lincolnshire field. Murdered.

That night I watched Harvey and Margaret Atkin, Julie's grandparents, on TV. The interviewer said, 'There must have been times when you thought the killer would never be caught?' Harvey replied: 'Oh no, never. Mr Taylor vowed he'd catch him and we knew he would.'

I felt proud of their faith in me and was glad it had been justified. I'd met the family many times. It was not about making an inquiry personal but about ensuring that what was done was professional, and remembering that families are victims too.

Success is intoxicating, but that was the nearest I got to a celebratory drink until I had done a host of interviews over the next three hours. Many representatives of the media who we got to know over the four weeks of the trial also joined us for a drink that night.

I hoped I had seen the last of Sams, but the very next day my slumber was broken at 9 am by a phone call from Paul Maxwell. The Home Office Prison Liaison Department had rung him to say that Sams had asked to see me.

After the trial he was immediately packed off from Winson Green prison. He had enjoyed a status there that I considered wrong and was now an embarrassment to prison staff, some of whom amazingly had been convinced of his innocence. The governor once let Sams use his own office with his solicitor to view videotapes connected to the trial. Sams's new home was Full Sutton maximum security prison near York. I told Paul to arrange to see him on Monday. This time he could wait.

On Monday morning, Paul and I drove to the prison. We were shown into the visitors' hall, set out with dozens of tables in rows. I chose a table a third of the way down in the middle, and Paul and I sat down to await Sams's arrival.

Our small talk echoed around the empty hall until he arrived escorted by a prison officer, who sat thirty feet away. Sams and I had made eye contact many times during the trial, but at no time had I ever spoken a single word to him.

He wove his way through the tables, dragging his leg as he did so. His face looked grey and he had the pained appearance of an unhappy man. I sat impassively as he placed himself opposite me. 'Settled in all right?' Paul asked. 'Yeah, no problems at all, television to watch, watching sport all day.' He was trying to play down the reality that he would be in prison for life by passing it off as if it were a stay at a seaside guesthouse.

'You know me. You know Mr Taylor, in charge of everything on our side. It's our understanding that you wish to speak to us,' said Paul. Sams nodded at me in acknowledgment. I did not offer my hand. I don't shake hands with murderers. He said, 'It's only fair you should know. I mean, obviously I did do it, I admitted it when I got back to the hospital,' referring to when he returned to the prison hospital wing after the trial.

I sat impassively as he went on: 'What upset me most was when I saw on TV and the papers that Mrs Dart had put a headstone there and she wasn't able to put the date Julie died. What I tell you is the exact truth. I don't have to tell you any lies or anything like that. It was about six pm on Wednesday, so that'd be the tenth. As long as Mrs Dart knows what day she died.

'Basically put it this way, when I went out to kidnap Julie Dart there was only one intention and that was to kill her. She was never put in a box, never tied up – sorry, she had her hands tied and she had one of her legs tied, but I had no intention of keeping her alive.

'I picked her up off Spencer Place, on Leopold Street, at about half past eleven. I took her round . . . well, she took me round to the carpark and she was bending down to take her shoes off. All I did was grab the back of her neck and then said, "Right, don't scream, all I want to do is tie you to the seat." I put tape across her mouth and took her back to Newark, stopped there all night with her Tuesday and she was blindfolded. When I heard Jane Fowler who had the dress shop over my workshop lock up and go, I hit Julie on the back of the head and strangled her.'

He had just detailed kidnapping and taking a young woman's life in such a casual and matter-of-fact way, he could have been describing a walk in the park. 'What did you hit her with?' I asked. 'Hammer. You didn't find it because I threw it away.' Paul asked him what he strangled her with. 'Just a rope. She was unconscious at the time. She was on the carpet, that's why you found some fibres from the carpet.'

I asked him whether he thought I would actually pay the ransom. 'Yes,' he said, casually. When I asked whether he put Julie in a container, he said, 'No, all she had was her hands tied at the front. That's how she wrote the letter, with both hands tied together, and that rope on her ankle.'

He was asked why he had not gone through with the run on 14 August 1991. He said, 'There was a car parked where I was going to unload the bike. It was in the back of the car.' Sams had intended to use his moped like he did on the Slater ransom run. Parking nearby he would take the moped out of his car, collect the money and return to his car and drive off.

'Let me just clear this up, Michael. Was there anybody else involved?' I asked.

'No, never.'

'Not in any small way at all?'

'Not at all,' he said.

'The "Julie D" letter found on your computer?'

He said: 'I don't know why I didn't send it. No idea. I wrote it for some reason. I imagine I was going to send that so you would think he'd been one of her clients.'

He said he had neither blindfolded nor gagged Julie. She saw his face, but as he had no intention of holding her until the following Monday it did not matter. He had not disguised his car except to put false plates on.

'I have to ask you, why did you decide in 1991 that the kidnap victim would be killed but by January 1992 you say things had changed and you never intended to kill Stephanie?'

He replied, 'Can't answer that one, no idea at all. That's actually true. I've no idea.'

He said Stephanie knew he had a limp and a false leg. 'Why do you think she did not tell us?' I said. ''Cos she promised me she wouldn't tell,' he explained. Stephanie had not at any time mentioned this to the police.

Was this a further example of his arrogance and lying, trying to demonstrate his control over her? Or was this part of the secret she did not reveal until much later, which was that Sams had raped her?

We talked about the phone calls he made on various occasions, and when asked why there was no call on 6 August 1991 he said, 'Teena wouldn't let me go out, so you never received anything that week.'

I asked him about the missing estate agent, Suzy Lamplugh. 'I know nothing about that,' he said.

One thing puzzled me. 'I can't understand how you arrive at a point in life when suddenly you want to kill people.'

Sams replied, 'I've no idea, I can't explain it.'

He returned to the moment he killed Julie. 'About six o'clock that night, she wanted a wash so I let her. I tied her hands behind her back, she was laid on the mattress, then I got down and just hit her about three times to make her unconscious, that's all.'

Paul asked him about the 'Phil and Mavis' indentation on the Leeds letter. Sams said, 'Yes, I put that on. Got the names from *Coronation Street*.'

Paul asked: 'Bob Southwall, the name you used in the Slater kidnap, anything to do with Bob Taylor?'

Sams shook his head. 'No, Bob came from a magistrate friend I have in Birmingham and Southwall came from the town.' I was slightly relieved to know my name was not involved, but I did not fully believe him as he never used the name Bob until the Slater kidnap. I wondered whether it was another twisted element to his game to name himself after me.

He went on to admit the British Rail extortion and the Millmeece device – the concrete block and sandstone left on the railway track.

I asked him whether it was more acceptable to kill for money. Sams said, 'That is what they are telling me down the halls [prison landing], that if you kill for money you're accepted. I'd have said that in court but I thought people wouldn't believe me.'

As the meeting ended I asked: 'Is there anything else you want to say, a message for Lynn Dart perhaps?'

He said, 'I do feel sorry for her but she'll never accept that. Don't ask me why, I've no idea why I did it. Stephanie would never have been killed. She was terrified. It's the first time in my life that anybody's been frightened of me. I always had dominating women in my life, I've always accepted that but didn't like it.'

After two hours, I left the prison. I had mixed feelings about the sincerity of everything he had said, particularly his insistence that he never intended to kill Stephanie and when and how Julie died.

I fully believe Sams intended to kill Stephanie – she was on a journey to death when she left Birmingham, never to return. But what changed his mind?

My view is that Stephanie humanised herself in his eyes to the point where he undoubtedly fell in love with her and so ditched his murderous objective. She did what she was told. She did not fight.

Why, then, doesn't he admit that? Simple. Sams cannot face up to failure. He cannot admit he made a mistake; his arrogance denies him this option.

At one time, Sams was a devoted, hard-working family man. So what turned him into a killer? It seems he had a change of personality when he suffered a meningeal viral infection in the 1970s, becoming violent to his wife and mixing with bad company. Sams yearned for riches he did not feel would be gained from legitimate hard work. The sum he required to start a new life in Thailand was around £140,000 – the ransom. But traces of the old Sams survived. Stephanie delved into the recesses of his character and found that last flickering ember of compassion which saved her life. I doubt it exists now in Sams, after nine years in prison.

Arriving back in Leeds, I went to see Lynn Dart. 'What's he said?' she asked. Although it was two years since Julie's death, Lynn still had moments of deep depression and grief, but she was eager to hear my news. I had nothing to tell her that would cause any more pain than she was already suffering.

'He said Julie died at about six o'clock on Wednesday night, the tenth.'

Lynn then put the question she must have asked herself a thousand times: 'Why?'

'Lynn, I'll tell you what he said but I'm not sure if it's true. He said he always intended to kill her but Julie did not know this. He took her back to the workshop, sat up with her all night and the next day until the woman who worked upstairs left. Then he killed her.'

Lynn gulped. 'Did she suffer, did she feel pain?'

'No. She was looking away when he picked up a hammer and struck her on the head. She would have lapsed into unconsciousness and would not have felt anything else.'

Lynn needed to know. At least now she could put the date of death on her daughter's gravestone.

*

Sams continues to languish in jail along with the country's most evil men. To this day, I am told by various contacts of his how much he respects me, always referring to me as Mr Taylor. As he sees it, unlike the Ripper he was not caught by a trainee officer but by a senior, experienced detective. In fact, he is wrong. The hunt for Sams involved every police force in the country at one point. He was put behind bars by the hard work of dedicated officers, of which I was one.

I have no particular feelings towards Sams. Without doubt he is intelligent, and during my hunt I imagined him to be a master criminal. I was disappointed to discover he was a one-legged train-spotting tool repairer, but later realised that this did not detract from his criminal cunning. Sams is arrogant with a certain amount of cunning and cleverness. He was hoist on the petard of his own arrogance, and eventually his luck ran out.

If I had gone to see Sams the day after the trial ended, he would have confessed to murdering Julie Dart on the second anniversary of her abduction. I don't know whether this was him continuing to play twisted games, but his opportunity was thwarted. Instead, I saw him three days later. He was playing the game by my rules now.

Stephanie Slater now lives on the Isle of Wight under an assumed name. She owes her life to her tenacity and strength of character in the way she dealt with Sams, not knowing he was a killer. The type of kidnap that Stephanie was subjected to is extremely rare, and I cannot recall anyone else being freed alive without police intervention. Her remarkable recall was what made Sams's workshop so instantly recognisable to the detectives who went there, as she had logged in her memory every sound and flickering light while there.

But what took Julie Dart to work in Chapeltown in the first place? It seemed the unemployed teenager had borrowed money from a male acquaintance. He was pressuring her to repay the loan. She was trying to pay him back out of her social security benefit, but it was too little and too slow for him.

The week before she was kidnapped, he drove her to Chapeltown and dropped her off in the red-light area. Working to pay her debt drove her into the killer's arms. I believe the man who took Julie to Chapeltown is as much responsible for her death as Sams. He remains a free man.

Julie, quite simply, was in the wrong place at the wrong time.

When the staff eventually changed the juke-box's contents at the Millgarth bar, I was given the 'Midnight Cowboy' record.

RIGHT Reconstruction of the wheelie bin in which Stephanie Slater was kept.

BELOW Dove Valley trail, which connected the Dart and Slater money drops. (*Police photo*)

Kevin Watts, the manager at Shipways who acted as courier in the kidnap of Stephanie Slater, pictured with her after her release. (*Raymonds Press Agency*)

Commendations by Chief Constable Keith Hellawell presented to some members of the Julie Dart inquiry team and Regional Crime Squad after Sams's conviction. I am the second from the left of those holding their awards. (*Yorkshire Evening Post*)

# chapter five

# A Foot-soldier's Story: The Yorkshire Ripper

When people ask me whether I can spot a killer, I have to say no. They don't have horns on their heads or 'psycho' tattooed on their arms. For most of the time a murderer looks as normal as you and me.

It is the change in their persona and the resulting evil they perpetrate which obviously makes them different. Some of the most callous murderers I have dealt with have turned out to be courteous, unassuming and intelligent people when interviewed.

But that is their outer shell. Murderers are like eggs. You don't know whether they're rotten until the shell cracks. I always find it fascinating to discover what makes them tick, what turns them from suburban Joe Normal into a Michael Sams. Who would have thought a tool repairer – with one leg – was Britain's most wanted man in the 1990s?

Twenty years earlier I had been on the case of the country's then most wanted man – the Yorkshire Ripper.

I was boss in the Sams hunt but on the Ripper inquiry I was a foot-soldier. Though I have to say, the lessons I learnt from that ill-fated case I was to put into practice throughout my career.

Along with the rest of the north of England, my family and I lived through the bleak seven years during which Peter Sutcliffe remained free to slaughter thirteen women and attack numerous more. I was a detective in Chapeltown CID in Leeds, one of the force's most notorious areas owing to its infamous red-light area and sporadic riots. The division covered a neighbourhood stretching from the edge of the city centre to Alwoodley and Shadwell to the north, considered the 'posh end' of town.

Times were rapidly changing as we moved to policing by consent of the community rather than despite the community. There had been riots in 1974 at the bottom end of the division, in an area known as New Leeds. The red-light area was half a mile square and was mainly made up of terraced streets of three- and four-storey Victorian houses with huge gardens, magnificent in their day. Originally occupied by wealthy Jewish families, they had then become populated with immigrants from the Eastern Bloc countries, such as Latvia, Lithuania and Poland.

The area and the houses took a downward turn when many were turned into flats and bed-sits, and the flotsam and jetsam of society drifted in and out among the long-suffering house occupiers. The crime rate was high, measured by the little that was reported. You had to have been at the division a bit longer than I had to progress from working this area, known euphemistically as the 'bottom end', to the 'top end', where 'millionaires' row' was situated.

It was also an area of the city that had two lives, its day- and nightlife being very different. There was little sophistication – no massage parlours – but up to thirty prostitutes could be seen plying their trade on the numerous street corners from lunch-time onwards as the pubs and clubs became the hunting ground of kerb crawlers in search of women to satiate their sexual needs and fantasies. Some did their business in the punters' cars, others in the nearby alleys or the local park, and occasionally in flats.

A stranger to the area had an equal chance of being propositioned or robbed if he walked the streets at night, but the place could turn ugly at any time of the day or night. One night, I was sat outside the flat of a prostitute, known locally as Thunder Thighs, watching a stolen car down the road and waiting for the thief to return. In the space of an hour, four suited and polish-booted men went in and came out, duly satisfied. The myth of dirty men in raincoats being the customers of prostitutes is just that.

We had our fair share of serious assaults, arising either from someone playing the wrong domino in the taproom of the Hayfield or from a drunken brawl in the Gaiety, these being the only two pubs on the patch. The girls on the streets were occasionally assaulted by punters, but rarely reported it. In the main the area just managed to steer clear of murder.

Hence news that a woman's body had been discovered spread rapidly on 30 October 1975. Wilma McCann had been found on the Prince Philip playing fields at the rear of her own home in Scott Hall Avenue. She had been murdered. It was reported in the media that the Murder Squad was dealing with the case, but the so-called Murder Squad was fictional. The investigating officers were an almost random selection of detectives, some from divisions beyond where the murder was committed.

We'd joke that the main requirement for this squad was to be 'grim faced', as every time a murder was reported in the local media they referred to grim-faced detectives questioning neighbours at the scene.

Wilma's body was not found on our patch but across the boundary road from the bottom end of Chapeltown, where I usually worked. During that afternoon, twenty of us were called to Brotherton House, the Leeds Area HQ, for a briefing.

I thought about the last time I was here, for a murder in Blackman Lane near the university. I was on late shift and was sent out to do the pubs, looking for the perpetrator, whose identity we did not know.

I was never quite sure why we did the pubs. I suppose the theory was that after a murder the killer would be stood at the bar, dripping with blood, passing the time of day with another drinker, telling them how murder was thirsty work. But it did serve to get word around until the next edition of the papers came out.

We did not have personal radios then so we had to ring into the incident room every ninety minutes. I recalled we had done our pubs and returned to the incident room to find that the killer had been arrested and interviewed, had confessed to the crime and was about to be charged.

Today the briefing was given by Denis Hoban, Head of CID for Leeds. He reported the sketchy details we had on Wilma McCann. She lived alone with her four children, the eldest, Sonje, being nine, in a council semi on Scott Hall Avenue. She had left the children in Sonje's care while she went out drinking.

We were not sure at this stage whether she was a prostitute, but her usual drinking haunts, the Regent, Scotsman and Royal Oak, were regarded as favourites among call-girls. The local milkman had discovered the twenty-eight-year-old's body at 7.30 am. She was lying on her back, her white flared trousers pulled down to her knees, her pink blouse and bra pulled up above her breasts, while her coat had been laid over her legs. Her boots had been removed and also neatly placed on her legs.

She had been stabbed fourteen times in the chest and abdomen with a knife and had two blows inflicted to her head with a hammer. The skull fractures were of a distinct depressed nature and their shape indicated that the rounded end of a ball-peen hammer was the killer's likely tool.

We saw the first copies of the crime scene photographs, which were the next best thing to seeing the body *in situ*. Wilma's face had already taken on a waxen tone in the short hours since death had gripped her. Her husband had been found and was being interviewed, but we would need to establish in detail her movements from the time she left home the previous night, as well as trace everyone she had met. The killer was in that group.

The pattern of Wilma's life emerged. It appeared her last port of call on her final night alive was the Room at the Top, a club between Chapeltown and the city centre. It was housed above a row of shops once occupied by a tailor and a piano retailer. I remembered as a ten-year-old going there with my parents to buy a piano for my sister Judith for Christmas.

It was now a row of late-night cafés, takeaways, sex shops and taxi firms. Wilma had staggered much the worse for wear out of the club, bought curry and chips, and was last seen at 1 am in Meanwood Road, about a hundred yards from the club, trying to flag down passing cars. If the killer had been in the club with her and had followed her out, we might stand a chance of finding him.

The club was at the very bottom end of my patch, and I had been there a few times when I was on late shifts, checking on who was about, as it had a reputation for drugs and was frequented by local criminals. All visitors were supposed to sign in but few did, and the clientèle could be described on an average night as drunks, prostitutes, pimps, villains and the occasional detective. Given this clientèle, there would be little hope of tracing everyone who'd been there that night, but we had to try.

This was the first long-running murder investigation I was to work on since becoming a detective in 1973. The police service thought staff a cheap commodity and had not considered how to get the best from us. The hunt for Wilma's killer got off to a shambolic start, an omen maybe for what was to come. We needed cars so we could get out to conduct enquiries. We worked in pairs on twelve-hour shifts, but owing to a lack of vehicles one car had to be shared between eight officers.

In the week, we would set off with four detectives in each car, each with our own enquiries to conduct, get back to the incident room four hours later for our meal and hand the car over to another four officers. At best we would not see that car for another four hours, and then we might not get out in it again. It was only on weekends when half the team was off that there was enough transport.

With such a lot of time on their hands, and rather than be seen hanging around the incident room, detectives would do those calls on which they could walk to or get to on the bus; others would kill a few hours at the cinema, or even go to the gym. The notion of having a car for just two officers so they could do a full eight hours' work was many years in coming, and still to this day meets some resistance.

There was also a theory that Wilma's husband, who she was separated from, had killed her because she had gone drinking and left their children home alone. That theory carried little credence as time went on. We were not used to unsolved murders in Leeds and had only a few on the books, but after a few months we were sent back from the 'murder team' to our respective stations and resumed normal duties.

Three months after Wilma's death, on 22 January 1976, I was just about to start my day shift when my boss, John Watkins, asked me to go with him to Enfield Terrace, just off Roundhay Road at the bottom end of our area. John had been my sergeant when I first came into CID and he knew I was reliable.

About fifty yards from the main road was a yard amid a row of semi-derelict properties. It was full of rubbish, and in the middle of it was the body of a woman. Gazing around that yard on a bleak January morning, I said to myself that no one should die in a place like this.

There were some strange wounds to her body from what I could see, but they did not look deep. What was obvious were the head injuries – I could see at least two among the blood and matted hair. She was lying on her back, and her tights and underwear were partly pulled down. She had a brown coat on and her blouse, jumper and bra were pulled up above her breasts.

I nudged John. 'Does this remind you of anything?' He nodded. Wilma McCann. But this woman neither looked nor dressed like the street girls. She appeared middle aged as she stared into space, her eyes cold. I could see a boot print on her left thigh as if from the sole of a wellington boot.

I was made the exhibit officer for the case, a job I had done once before. I had to receive exhibits, whatever they were and from anyone connected with the inquiry, log them in a book and ensure the integrity of each exhibit against contamination or interference. I would also have to make sure all the necessary tests were carried out on them, whether by forensic or fingerprint experts.

By late morning, the body had been removed to the City Mortuary at Mill Hill, near Millgarth police station. It was an inhospitable place – the smell of death permeated the surrounding atmosphere as well as the building. I spent over six hours there taking exhibits as the woman's clothes were removed and bagged up and the post-mortem took place.

Pathologist Professor David Gee looked at the two head injuries. In one, a circular piece of bone had been punched straight through the skull with the flat end of what he thought was a hammer; the other was an angled blow also causing a depressed fracture. When he looked at the multiple stab wounds he was as bemused as the rest of us. Little crosses were all over her breasts, neck and abdomen. I gave up counting them after reaching fifty-one.

Professor Gee believed a Phillips screwdriver had caused the quarter-inch cross-shaped wounds. As some had punctured her sternum, and considering the number, depth and distribution, he concluded considerable force had been used in a frenzied attack. From documents in her possession, we identified the woman as Emily Jackson.

Emily was a forty-two-year-old housewife and mother of three. She lived with her family in Churwell, the other side of Leeds from where she was found. Husband Sydney was a roofer but did not drive, so Emily would take him from job to job. Their life had taken a strange turn when she started working as a part-time prostitute.

Part of my job was to search her home, where I spoke to Sydney. He was a tall, powerful-looking man who was clearly in shock after Emily's death, a state not helped by the exposure of their curious sexual arrangement. The house was clean and tidy and gave no obvious clues as to the double life the Jacksons led. The neighbours were equally shocked as the details of Emily's nocturnal activities became known.

'Emily would stand in the streets next to the Gaiety pub in Chapeltown. She'd drive over and park the Commer van in the pub carpark, leaving me drinking there while she did her business,' explained Sydney. 'We'd meet up at closing time and she'd take us home. That night I waited a while but she didn't come. She had the van's key so I expected she would come home later and I got a taxi home.'

Sure enough, his van was still there in the carpark. His story, bizarre as it was, quickly checked out. I was satisfied that several times a week this man saw his wife go off on the game while he quaffed ale in the pub, where topless waitresses and strip shows were regular features.

An incident room was set up in the newly built Millgarth police station as Chapeltown was too small to house one. The new five-storey building had a purpose-built incident room on the fourth floor – an enormous open-plan room. The only other room on the floor was the senior investigating officer's office, which I was to occupy fifteen years later during the hunt for Sams and other serious criminals.

The similarities between the murders of Wilma and Emily had not escaped anyone's notice. We had two types of injury to each body, hammer blows to the head, stab wounds to the body, and the characteristic of the bra being pulled up. Both victims had the same part-time habit of selling sex, and their bodies were found either side of the Chapeltown area.

The concept of a serial killer had not registered with us at all. I thought the two deaths being the responsibility of the same man would increase our chances of successful detection, as we would surely be able to unearth more information on him. I set up my desk, complete with a sign saying 'Exhibit Officer', in a corner of the incident room. As the inquiry progressed, one fact I was certain of was that every suspect owned a hammer and a pair of wellingtons.

Though I insisted that all exhibits be handed to me in person, it was not uncommon to arrive at work and find ten pairs of boots and ten hammers on my desk. The growing pile of dirty, sweaty boots behind my chair was becoming a health hazard as the weeks turned into months and we still had no clue as to who the killer was.

On 9 May 1976, young West Indian prostitute Marcella Claxton claimed she was attacked in Soldier's Field near West Avenue at Roundhay Park, Leeds. She was working in the red-light area when a bearded man picked her up. Once at the field, he struck her numerous times on the head, leaving her for dead.

The attack happened at 4 am, so a night detective was dispatched to St James's Hospital to see Marcella, who was a well-known figure in Chapeltown. I had met her previously in the line of duty. As a prostitute she was certainly not the prettiest on the streets and was in no way the brightest. She was also difficult to speak to as she would quickly and easily fly off the handle.

There was a strange relationship between the local prostitutes, the CID and the Vice Squad. CID was not interested in prostitution unless it involved some other crime. We would often talk to the girls as they could be a useful source of information. The Vice Squad hunted them, watching from the shadows as they chatted up punters, then pouncing to arrest them. The girls knew all their car registration numbers and could tell CID from Vice.

Marcella had fifty stitches in her scalp, and when we were finally allowed to see her she had to be interviewed in a cleaner's cupboard at the hospital owing to a lack of facilities. No connection was made between her attack and the double killer, owing to irregularities in her story. Apart from the beard, her description turned out to be hopelessly inaccurate. She had survived the attack, but the idea of any of our killer's victims surviving was not taken on board at that time by the police.

Six months after Emily Jackson was killed, the inquiry had been reduced to a team of one – me. While I had been working from Millgarth incident room, Chapeltown CID had been moved into a Portakabin in the station's back yard. I had a desk at the back and dealt with all the outstanding enquiries. Everything was routine; we had no real suspects.

Nine months passed before he struck again. On 6 February 1977, a jogger found a female's body, again on Soldier's Field, near a block of luxury apartments where Sir Jimmy Savile lived. I was called to the scene. The woman was in her late twenties, with long brown hair which partially concealed her head injuries. She was lying on her front as if asleep. A coat covered her body, and her imitation suede boots had been removed and placed carefully side by side on her legs, just as in the photographs of Wilma McCann. The usual team of pathologist, police surgeon and an array of senior detectives arrived.

It was only when the pathologist turned over her body that the full extent of the injuries were evident. She had been stabbed in the neck and throat and there was a slash wound to her abdomen so severe that her intestines were spilling out. Once again, I was the exhibits officer and would be spending the rest of the day at the mortuary while the post-mortem was performed.

In death, this woman did not have those hard-faced features I had seen on many prostitutes. I felt sorry for her. I think the enormity of what I was witnessing came home to me. She was, without doubt in my mind, the third victim of a killer of whose identity we had no idea at all, and who we seemed helpless to stop.

We identified our victim as Irene Richardson, twenty-eight, a single mother of two children who were in foster care. She had spent the weeks before her death trying to find somewhere to live and earn some money to set up home and get her children back. She, like so many before her, had chosen the tax-free employment offered on the streets of Chapeltown. This was how she had met her killer.

The incident room was once again at Millgarth. There were some tyre tracks at this latest scene, but we had no way of knowing whether they belonged to the killer's car and, even if they did, it was not much of a lead.

The killer had by now been branded the Yorkshire Ripper. Three victims and a killer at large constituted a pressure that was becoming noticeably visible on senior detectives' faces. In the history of the force we had never had such a run, which now stretched over a sixteen-month period. I had only been on the inquiry five weeks when I departed for a Criminal Investigation Course, at Hutton Hall, the Lancashire Police Training School at Preston.

The Ripper's activities were the talking point of most detectives on the course, and more so when news that a fourth victim, this time in Bradford, had been added to his tally. Divorcee Patricia Atkinson, thirty-two, was mother to three children who lived with their father. She lived in a bed-sit a short distance from Lumb Lane, the heart of Bradford's red-light district.

She was found lying on her bed covered with a sheet. Her clothes had been pulled up in the telltale fashion and there were hammer injuries to the head and body. She had been killed on Saturday, 23 April, only eleven weeks after Irene Richardson. Tina, as she was known, had been out drinking in the pubs and clubs around Lumb Lane before she met her killer around midnight.

The inquiry now took on a new dimension, as the Bradford detectives would run this case. There was enormous rivalry between Leeds and Bradford detectives, which was worsened by their integration into West Yorkshire Police in 1974. What had been Leeds City Police, Bradford City Police and the larger force that surrounded the two, the West Riding Constabulary, all became one force. The one thing Leeds and Bradford seemed to dislike more than each other was the West Riding lot. For most of us, the rivalries were tongue in cheek. For some it was deadly serious.

The new force policy would see hundreds of Leeds officers working in Bradford and vice versa. They would wave at each other as they travelled to and from work on the Leeds–Bradford road, the main link between the two cities. It was like a Red Arrows display as their cars criss-crossed at the junctions.

Before my course finished I was promoted to sergeant and posted to

Millgarth in uniform, starting in May 1977.

The city centre division could be walked from one end to the other in thirty minutes, and it too had a red-light quarter around the Corn Exchange and the pubs in the immediate vicinity. Some prostitutes, nearing the end of their careers, would provide sex for the small change in the punter's pocket rather than do no business, so they could nip back in the pub to buy another drink afterwards.

I had been at Millgarth just over five weeks when the Ripper struck again on Saturday, 25 June, returning to his original hunting ground in Chapeltown. This time his victim was sixteen-year-old Jayne MacDonald, who was attacked while walking home after a night out in Leeds city centre. She lived in Scott Hall Avenue, a few doors away from Wilma McCann. She was cutting through the red-light area when the killer struck her with a hammer from behind, dragged her into a children's playground and killed her.

There were scrape marks left by her platform shoes as she was dragged across the open ground. She had stab wounds to the back and chest, the latter enlarged by repeated stabbing in the same place. In it was lodged the neck of a broken bottle. She also had injuries to her head consistent with a hammer blow.

Jayne was not a prostitute, and suddenly the public awoke to the reality that they were not as safe as they thought. Times were different then, as it was not only the police who treated prostitutes as second-class citizens. Many sections of the public had little sympathy for the killer's victims, as they considered the prostitutes had put themselves in danger by choice. Now the thought that any woman who was out late at night could be a potential victim made everyone sit up and take notice.

Many more voices had been added to the chorus of criticism of the police and of our failure to catch the killer. From every shop window the angelic face of Jayne MacDonald shone out on appeal posters. When on patrol in Leeds I talked to prostitutes, who were buzzing with stories that the killer had cut off parts of the victims' bodies and taken them away. Even that did not stop them, although they now worked in pairs or threes. Chapeltown was the same – the economics of the sex trade were that men still wanted women and the women who worked the streets still wanted the business. Some had taken to working from flats, using a handful of regulars they trusted, but a few women still walked the streets.

In the seventeen months I worked in Leeds city centre the Ripper attacked six further victims, killing four of them. Prostitute Maureen Long, forty-two, was attacked in Bradford two weeks after Jayne MacDonald. She had gone with the punter for sex in his car on spare land near her home, but as she crouched down to urinate before doing business he struck her on the head, ripped her dress to the waist and repeatedly stabbed her in the chest, stomach and back.

She was left for dead, but although she lived to tell the tale she was no use as a witness as she described her attacker as having wiry blond hair, which turned out to be wrong.

While I was keeping my eye on the Ripper's activities my daily responsibilities were different. My inspector, John Watkins, and I arrested a leading light of the Ku Klux Klan, Bill Williams. He had applied to enter the country to address a meeting of the National Front, but had been refused by the Home Secretary as an undesirable. He then illegally entered the country to address the NF at a secret meeting in a Leeds city centre pub. We had been told to be at Leeds railway station to be on the lookout for him and his bodyguard, a mountain of a man called Rabbit who always wore a Tam o'Shanter.

We were waiting by the ticket barrier, trying to look casual and chatting, when John ordered, 'If they do a runner, you take the big one.' 'Thanks a lot,' I replied, as my eyes locked on a lone figure weaving through the barrier. 'That's him,' said John. We confronted and arrested Williams as he walked onto the station concourse. He immediately admitted who he was, so we took him to the charge office for detention. He showed no animosity towards us and chatted away, confessing that this was the first time he had ever been arrested and asking whether he could have his photograph taken with John and me. We gracefully declined on the basis of not wanting a burning cross in our front gardens.

From his briefcase he gave me a copy of an application form for the KKK, which I still have and which, needless to say, remains blank. He had travelled from America, had slipped into the country and was no doubt only a few hundred yards from his destination when we arrested him. For his sins he was deported.

Twelve weeks after the attack on Maureen Long, Jean Jordan became the Ripper's latest victim. 'Scotch Jean', a twenty-one-year-old prostitute, was killed in Chorlton-cum-Hardy, Manchester. She'd been struck eleven times on the head with a hammer and had numerous stab wounds to her chest. Further injuries inflicted days after her death consisted of a slash wound across her body, and the Ripper had tried to sever her head. She was found nine days after she was killed and in her handbag, found nearby, was a crisp £5 note.

The Ripper returned to Chapeltown for his next victim, another prostitute, Marilyn Moore. The dark-haired and bearded punter who said he was called Dave picked the twenty-five-year-old up from virtually the same spot where he had snared Emily Jackson and Irene Richardson, in the heart of Chapeltown's red-light district. He took her to spare land near by, and as she got out of his car to clamber into the back seat Dave struck her a glancing blow with a hammer. Her screams were heard by people close by and scared him off. As it turned out, Marilyn gave what was to be the most accurate E-fit of the killer, but although her attack was thought to be part of the Ripper series little reliability was accorded to her E-fit, her recall being questioned owing to her head injuries.

I remember seeing the Dave E-fit at the time, along with the many others compiled by various witnesses. It was never singled out for what it was, which was a very good likeness. All the other victims who survived his attacks could not give reliable descriptions, owing to the memory loss from their injuries, but Marilyn did.

Only five weeks passed before he struck again. The body of Yvonne Pearson, twenty-two, from Bradford, was hidden under a settee on wasteland. She was not found until Easter Sunday. Then there was Helen Rytka, eighteen, who he killed in a wood yard in Huddersfield. She was the only victim he had sex with. Fifteen weeks later, he travelled over the Pennines to Manchester to kill Vera Millward, forty-one, in Longsight. All the victims after Jayne MacDonald were prostitutes.

Staff were working all hours, but I tried to be compassionate when a PC told me one of the WPCs on my team had rung in to say her dad had died. We were stretched with people off sick and on courses, but I said I'd square it with the inspector for her to have three days' compassionate leave. When she returned to work I said, 'Sorry to hear about your dad.' Only then did I discover the constable had misheard her. 'It was my dog not my dad that died.' I cringed. At a time when we were short staffed, I had arranged compassionate leave for the death of her dog.

My career as a detective resumed when I was transferred to CID at Holbeck in South Leeds, a part of the city untouched by the killer. It seemed that a period of calm had descended. The longest gap between the murders was fifty-three weeks. We did not reach that milestone again.

Forty-six weeks had passed when he struck again in April 1979 – his victim building society clerk Josephine Whitaker.

He had broken his pattern by killing Josephine at 11.40 pm in Saville Park, Halifax, only 250 yards from her home. This was not a red-light area and Josephine was not a prostitute, and unlike Jayne MacDonald she was not in a vice area.

The public outcry and reverberations in the media put the police under enormous pressure. The Ripper left some clues in Saville Park – his boot prints were discovered, which showed that one boot had considerably more wear than the other. But what did that mean? Were we looking for someone with a limp or was there another reason for it?

It was at this time that I returned to the Ripper team at Millgarth and found that the once spacious open-plan incident room had been turned into a giant filing cabinet. It was taking a piece of information three weeks to go through the system, and meanwhile no one had a clue what was on it. Peter Sutcliffe eventually had four separate cards in the system, so whenever he was looked at officers only ever retrieved one-quarter of the information we had on him.

George Oldfield, West Yorkshire's most senior detective, was in charge of the inquiry. He was a larger-than-life figure with a ruddy face. It was not much of a surprise when the 11 am tea and coffee tray went round and on it was a solitary glass of water for Mr Oldfield to accompany his Scotch. He was not an easy man to approach with his praetorian guard of superintendents surrounding him, certainly not for a humble sergeant. The wounds of rivalry were opened once again with the friction between the old West Yorkshire, which George belonged to, and Leeds senior detectives, creating an air of discomfort.

A colleague was sent to be Mr Oldfield's gofer after just failing to pass his CID exam. Clearly his chances of becoming a detective depended greatly on making a good impression on his new boss. Oldfield had hung a board on the back of his office door with a map showing which inspectors and chief inspectors were at which police station. One day my friend banged the door too zealously and a dozen of the precariously held magnetic name labels crashed to the floor. Looking about to see whether he had been seen, he frantically stuck them back up. In some cases he knew where they came from, in others it was a guess. Some time in the following week, personnel staff popped in to see what changes the boss wanted, saw the map and implemented them. My friend silently looked on as his shuffle-round was suddenly carried out and senior officers found themselves with new postings.

I know now, as they then probably realised, that multiple murder investigations cannot be efficiently supported by a paper-and-card filing system. It was inadequate to deal with the massive amount of information the Ripper inquiry generated. Nor, as they did then, can officers now be expected to eliminate suspects on spurious alibis provided by wives, mothers, girlfriends or workmates on the basis of what people usually did days, months or years in the past.

The alibi system depended on the person providing the alibi being truthful and remembering accurately. Even work records can be falsified. It seemed at times that the pressure was on to find and eliminate the innocent rather than look for the killer. The danger of making elimination criteria too narrow is that you may exclude the killer.

There were more suggestions coming in than could be coped with, and the Ripper letters and 'I'm Jack' tapes diverted the inquiry along another path that, we now know, was to have dire consequences. On most murders at that time, the senior detectives would keep to themselves some information about the killer. It would be held back from the team and the public to weed out the false confessions. This still happens with some senior detectives but most, like me, would tell the team everything, otherwise they might, through ignorance, miss a good suspect.

My fellow foot-soldiers and I believed there must have been something in the letters, or more probably the tape, that had been edited out, because as far as we were concerned there was nothing new in them and nothing that had not been in the public domain. To rule out a suspect if he did not have a Geordie accent allowed thousands of men to be swiftly eliminated from the system. It was a disastrous decision and I still cannot believe it was accepted by the inquiry's police chiefs.

Neither were they too keen for any suggestions from the floor – again with disastrous results. DC John Osborne suggested the uneven wear on the killer's boot prints found at the Josephine Whitaker murder scene was because the killer was an HGV driver. John had been one himself prior to joining the service, and one of his boots always wore out well before the other owing to the pressure of applying the clutch pedal. His suggestion fell on deaf ears.

Another member of my team, DS Tony Ryan, looked at where all the offences had occurred. By this time it was acknowledged that the 1975 attacks on Anna Rogulskyj and Olive Smelt were the Ripper's first two.

Tony's theory was that, like many sex offenders, the Ripper committed his first assaults close to his home and then had to travel farther afield to avoid detection.

Keighley was where he first struck in the early hours of 5 July 1975. Anna Rogulskyj was thirty-four, single and not a prostitute. Arriving home after a night out, she discovered her cat was missing. Thinking her boyfriend had taken it, she set off walking the short distance to his home.

It was around 2 am when a man in North Street propositioned her. She rejected him and walked on. He then struck her on the head from behind three times with a ball-peen hammer and dragged her into an alley, where he pulled up her blouse and made superficial slash marks on her stomach. He was disturbed by a nearby resident calling out at him and ran off. A twelve-hour operation at Leeds General Infirmary saved Anna's life.

Mother-of-three Olive Smelt, forty-six, was his next victim, on 15 August 1975. After a night out in Halifax with a friend, Olive was yards from home at 11.45 pm when a man who had been walking behind her commented about the weather before striking her twice on the back of her head with a hammer and then scoring an X on her lower back with a hacksaw blade. He was disturbed by an approaching vehicle. Olive suffered two skull fractures and needed brain surgery.

Keighley was five miles by road from Bingley, where Peter Sutcliffe lived at that time, and Halifax was around ten miles away. Chapeltown is a little over sixteen miles, driving through Bradford and Leeds centres. There had been attacks in Keighley, Halifax, Bradford, Manchester and Huddersfield. It was nearly two years before he attacked in Bradford, which lay at the centre of all the attacks. Was that because it was on his doorstep and he dared not venture there until he was confident in his killing?

Six weeks after Olive Smelt's attack, the Ripper claimed his first murder victim. Had he refined his skills on Olive and Anna?

In hindsight Tony Ryan's theory was sound, but when it was suggested at the time to the incident room superintendent it was, like John Osborne's theory, ignored.

The £5 note inquiry was based on the belief that Jean Jordan's killer had paid her up front for sex, and when he later returned unsuccessfully to look for the note, he further mutilated her. She had placed it in a secret pocket in her handbag. The note was a recent issue and was traced by the Bank of England to a sub-branch of the Midland Bank at Shipley, where it was received only a couple of days before it found itself in Jean's possession. It was among a batch used for the wages of around thirty firms, which employed in total around eight thousand men. One was T. and W.H. Clark's, who employed Peter Sutcliffe as a driver. Detective Chief Superintendent Jack Ridgeway, in charge of the Jordan murder, believed the £5 note was a vital clue. George Oldfield's scepticism was obvious from comments that filtered down to us.

Bradford University student Barbara Leach was his next victim. On 1 September 1979 she'd been with her pals to the Manville Arms, Great Horton Road, Bradford. At 1 am, the pretty twenty-year-old left them outside and walked down the road to clear her head. The Ripper struck her with a hammer, dragged her into a back yard and stabbed her with a sharpened screwdriver.

There was no pattern now in his behaviour. Barbara was not a prostitute but a lone woman out late at night, which indicated either that he believed she was a woman of the night or that he did not now care who he attacked.

The best part of a year passed without any more attacks until civil servant Marguerite Walls was murdered on 20 August. The forty-seven-year-old was attacked in Farsley, a suburb of Leeds, as she walked home from her Department of Education and Science job. She was in a dimly lit secluded street, just after 10 pm, when he approached from behind and hit her on the head several times with a hammer, dragged her into the gardens of a large private house, and strangled her with a cord. He then stripped her naked, apart from her tights, and left her clothes near by. She was discovered at 9.30 am the next day, and a murder incident room was set up at Pudsey police station.

I had by then moved on to the Eastern Area Robbery Squad, a misnomer in title as we had responsibility for rapes and serious woundings as well as robbery investigations. We were an eight-man squad who were usually a first choice for murder teams. I was once again working from Millgarth, where our office was situated. We had worked on ten murders in the last twelve months.

During the first day's briefing, Jim Hobson, the Chief Superintendent and Head of CID for Leeds, made it quite plain that this murder was not to be treated as connected to the Ripper case and we were not to utter any thoughts that it might be. I turned to my team and said: 'I can't believe this. We are being told that there are now two homicidal maniacs killing women in Leeds. Surely the first and most obvious thought is that it's the same guy.'

It was not long before it began to be accepted that, although he might have changed his style, there really was only one suspect – the Yorkshire Ripper. Maureen Long, who had survived her attack three years previously, was spooked, as she lived within a hundred yards of where Marguerite Walls' body was found and was convinced he had come looking for her, thinking she was one of the few who could identify him.

I could understand her fear, but the truth was that he could have been sat next to Maureen on a bus and she would not have had a clue who he was. A combination of the amount of alcohol she had drunk that night and the severity of her head injuries ensured that any memory she might have had of Britain's most wanted man was expunged for ever. In fact, when he was arrested Sutcliffe said he had seen Maureen from a distance while out Christmas shopping with his wife.

There were no leads at all with Marguerite Walls' murder. A sexual motive was doubtful, even though her clothes had been removed. She was a hard-working, squeaky-clean woman.

Only weeks passed before he attacked again. But yet again, there was no public proclamation of this fact. Uphadya Anadavathy Bandara, a thirty-three-year-old doctor from Singapore, was in Leeds attending a conference. She was attacked on 24 September 1980 as she walked home along Chapel Lane, close to the Yorkshire County Cricket Club ground in Headingley. The stranger came up behind her, looped a rope around her neck, struck her on the head with a hammer and left her for dead.

But Dr Bandara regained consciousness to find a uniformed police officer standing over her. She had been dragged down the street, and her shoes and handbag thrown over a wall. Probably the presence of a police car in the street had prompted her attacker's departure. She could recall that he had a beard. Again, no one was saying if it was our man.

Six weeks later, at 8 pm on Bonfire Night, he struck again back in Huddersfield. Teresa Sykes, sixteen and mother to a three-month-old baby, was walking from her local shop to her home when a man struck her on her head. She fell to the ground, but her boyfriend at their home near by heard her screams. The Ripper was standing over her and about to deliver further hammer blows, but Teresa's boyfriend raced towards them and chased him off.

Teresa was able to tell the police that her attacker had black hair, a beard and moustache. Four of his victims now said their attacker had a beard – Marcella Claxton, who was not believed, Marilyn Moore, who had also made what turned out to be a very good E-fit; Dr Bandara; and now Teresa. Regrettably all this information was not pulled together because of other misconceptions, such as the Geordie accent, leaving senior officers with doubts about which attacks the Ripper was responsible for. Those victims who survived and had spoken to their bearded attacker were adamant that he did not have a Geordie accent.

My team had just been released from the Walls murder, now heading towards the ever growing unsolved murders file, when the Ripper was writing his final chapter of death. On Monday, 17 November, Jacqueline Hill, who was studying English, had left Leeds University later than normal, having attended a seminar. The twenty-year-old caught the 9 pm bus to the Arndale Centre at Headingley, a quarter of a mile from where Dr Bandara was attacked.

She was walking to the halls of residence on Alma Road when the Ripper struck her a blow to the head with a hammer before dragging her thirty yards onto waste ground to kill her, stabbing her with the sharpened screwdriver in the chest and once in her eye.

It was an appalling example of slackness that, after a fellow student found her blood-spotted raffia handbag within thirty minutes of the murder on the pavement where she had been abducted, the police made only a cursory search, finding neither her body, just thirty yards away, nor her glasses or one of her mittens. They simply returned to the station and entered her handbag as found property.

It is hard to believe that after seven years of murders and attacks on women, and with one happening less than two months earlier in their division, the officers acted this way, especially as there was bloodstaining on the bag and Jacqueline's name was inside it.

Jacqueline was found the following morning by a shop manager in the Arndale Centre. The local police should have been out there searching at first light and found her body, but regrettably they did not.

My team and I were drafted onto the Jacqueline Hill murder within hours of her being discovered. As there were neither fingerprint nor forensic links between any of the attacks, it was pure guesswork which were the Ripper's. So as not to put all our eggs in one basket, we would again treat this as a separate enquiry while accepting it was the Ripper's work.

We worked over Christmas, but I could sense an air of despondence. I felt we had lost control of what we were doing. We were hunting Jacqueline Hill's killer while the Ripper Squad were hunting the Ripper and following up suggestions made by the public as to who he was.

Suggestions had descended to the bizarre as it became open season for the disgruntled to put forward ex-husbands, neighbours and workmates.

People rang in to say the Ripper was an alien or wore a diver's wet suit to commit the crimes, and that was why he never left any traces at the scenes. If the Ripper Squad never received another call, they had six months' work to get through. The incident room's floor in Millgarth was fit to collapse with the amount of paperwork it housed.

Friday, 2 January 1981 was the start to yet another year with no light likely to be shed on the identity of the killer – or so we thought. The police had still not put together the dark hair and the beard and, even if we had, Sutcliffe would have been eliminated from the inquiry as the Ripper Squad were working on him being a Geordie. But that night things would change.

Britain's most wanted man arrived in Sheffield's red-light district at 10 am to select his next victim. He was driving a Rover with false number plates he had stolen from a scrapyard in Mirfield, a town between Huddersfield and Leeds. He was putting into practice Tony Ryan's theory about having to travel farther afield to avoid detection. Sheffield was new killing ground for him.

Olivia Reivers, a convicted West Indian prostitute, was on the street for business. She got in his car and directed him on a journey that was intended to take her to her death, to a secluded private driveway half a mile away. He had with him the tools of his murderous job, a hammer and the sharpened screwdriver he had used previously. They'd been talking for twenty minutes when the police arrived.

Sergeant Bob Ring and PC Bob Hydes clearly knew what the couple were up to but went through the process of checking out the man, who gave his name as Peter Williams. It was then they discovered the number plates were for a Skoda. Reivers was put in the back of the squad car while Peter slipped away on the pretext of going for a pee but really to dump his hammer and knife.

He was taken to Hammerton Road police station in Sheffield, where he admitted that his real identity was Peter Sutcliffe and gave his home address in Bradford. He again asked to go to the toilet; this time a ruse to secrete another knife he had in his coat lining into the cistern. As the number plate theft had taken place in Dewsbury division in West Yorkshire, he was transferred there.

At 8 am on Saturday morning Sutcliffe was being booked in at Dewsbury police station by the custody sergeant. Force instructions required the Ripper Room to be notified of anyone arrested in a red-light area; the sergeant was smart enough to pick up on this and ring it in. The records at Millgarth incident room were checked and they revealed the incredible number of times Sutcliffe had come into the inquiry – his car had been sighted in red-light areas on a number of occasions and he had been interviewed during the £5 note inquiry by Manchester Police, though he had already told them all this at Dewsbury.

When Bob Ring came back on duty, hearing the man was a Ripper suspect, he drove to where they had arrested him and found the hammer and knife. A later search found the knife in the cistern at the police station. Sutcliffe remained defiant in his denials of having had anything to do with the murders until Sunday afternoon, when he was being pressed about leaving his car to urinate. It was suggested he had done so for a more sinister purpose.

Sutcliffe: 'I think you have been leading up to it.'

'Leading up to what?'

'The Yorkshire Ripper.'

'What about the Yorkshire Ripper?'

'Well, it's me.'

And so, at 3.30 pm on Sunday, he began his statement, admitting killing seven women and attempting to murder another seven. With short meal breaks and a recess for a few hours' sleep, it took until 1.10 am the next day before his chilling recollections were finished. He would later go on and confess to a further six murders of women.

His wife Sonia was brought to see him at 10 pm on Sunday. The last time she had seen him was on Friday evening, before he left for Sheffield. Sutcliffe asked that he be allowed to tell Sonia that he was the Ripper.

DS Des O'Boyle, who took down a large part of his confession, remained in the room as the dark-haired teacher was brought in and seated next to her husband. As he turned to face her, she demanded: 'Peter, what on earth is going on?'

'You know all those women who were killed by the Yorkshire Ripper? That was me. I killed all those women.' Des silently waited for her reaction, and when it came, he says, it was one of the most bizarre he has ever witnessed.

'Peter, what on earth did you do that for? Even a sparrow has the right to live,' she replied.

Des recalled: 'Here was Britain's public enemy number one, the most wanted man, a self-confessed thirteen-times killer who had spread fear and terror across the north of England for seven years – and Sonia just accepted his confession there and then. There were no tears, recriminations, expressions of shock, physical or loving gestures. That was it, and she was then ushered out of the room.'

Peter William Sutcliffe was thirty-four when he was arrested. His trial was set for 29 April 1981. We had four months, an incredibly short period, to put together a file of considerable complexity. My team was assigned to Chief Inspector David Pickover as part of the clear-up squad assisting in preparing the files for Sutcliffe's attacks on Anna Rogulskyj and Olive Smelt, and the murders of Wilma McCann, Emily Jackson and Irene Richardson. Other teams were doing the rest. Security was so tight that we were allowed access only to the parts of his written confession related to the cases we were involved in.

I also had to find Trevor Birdsall, Sutcliffe's long-time mate who had accompanied him when they cruised the red-light districts. He had been out with Sutcliffe on the night he attacked Olive Smelt. Birdsall was now in the hands of a national newspaper, and I was dispatched to Bradford's Norfolk Gardens Hotel, from where I expected I'd simply bring him back to Millgarth to obtain a statement, as we could not be sure whether he was implicated in any of the crimes. His value to the press as the Yorkshire Ripper's best mate was immeasurable. Every detail about the killer and his life would be read and reread by millions of readers.

I walked into the hotel, and it was like a journalists' convention. I met the newspaper's editor, who initially refused to produce Birdsall or even tell me where he was. Eventually he said he was a hundred miles away in Blackpool.

I finally managed to arrange to meet some of his staff the next day, when we would be told Birdsall's location. We met him at the Castle Hotel, where he was immediately arrested, put into our CID car and driven at speed to Millgarth. The speed of our actions wrong-footed the hacks. I think they believed we were going to sit down and speak to him in their presence. No chance.

The newsmen sensed that treachery was in the air. They had been footing the hotel bill for Birdsall and his wife for several days. They chased our car every inch of the way back to Millgarth and then camped outside.

Threats never work with me. I would have been reasonable and tipped them off when he was leaving so he did not fall into the arms of a rival paper, but on the first night he stayed with us they tracked me down to my local pub and threatened me. A hapless hack said: 'My editor knows your chief and if you don't tell us when Trevor is leaving Millgarth, one phone call and your career is over.'

My reaction was equally acerbic: 'If your editor knows my chief that well, then get him to ring him and he can tell you when Birdsall is leaving, because I won't be now.' They got their man in the end and we got our statement, but they had to camp outside the police station in round-the-clock shifts.

The trial began before Mr Justice Boreham in the Old Bailey's famed No. 1 Court on 5 May 1981. Sutcliffe was charged with thirteen murders and seven attempted murders. The jury did not believe Sutcliffe's defence that voices were telling him to clean the streets of prostitutes and on a 10–2 majority he was found guilty. The judge recommended that he serve at least thirty years.

Afterwards, West Yorkshire took a drubbing which neither the force nor those involved in the case could ever forget or allow to happen again. They made computerisation a priority, and have been served well since by its highly professional Holmes incident staff, who set up, administer and maintain the computerised system which ensures that everything about any name in an investigation can be flashed on-screen in seconds at the touch of a button.

I personally learned many lessons from the Ripper case which shaped me for the future. I have always preached that promotion and rank do not give you exclusive access to the best ideas – witness John Osborne's HGV driver theory. They may well come from the most inexperienced member of your team. As a senior investigating officer you have the responsibility to accept or reject ideas, but not necessarily to come up with them yourself. This is not to say that you do not need to know anything at all, as you do require the experience to recognise a good idea when one is put forward.

It is the training and experience of today's senior investigators which cause me concern, as other cases have highlighted since. Chief constables still sanction transfers and promotions of staff with inadequate skills for the posts in question. I know of cases where officers are fast-tracked to senior detective roles without ever working on a single murder inquiry. The passage to the senior ranks is still not truly about what you know. Who you know still carries much weight, and examples of this can be seen in every force in the country, where inadequately trained police officers are still placed in crucial posts.

Good communication and listening to your team are key factors in a successful investigation, and this is where the Ripper inquiry went wrong. The foot-soldiers who challenged the system or made suggestions were often told dismissively to get on with their work. Suggestions were unacceptable, as the whole inquiry was drowning in paperwork. Many forces that have never been involved in such major investigations have even today not taken on board some of the issues that were raised. Should a Ripper stalk their area, they will fall into the same traps that were there twenty years ago.

Despite the changes, could this country see another Ripper? I believe that today there are a number of serial killers roaming free. By picking the right place to commit the crime, the right target, being cautious in the manner in which they kill as well as varying their methods, they may have committed dozens of murders across the country. They could well eventually be arrested for other murders, but without forensic links, fingerprints or similarities in their methods there may be no clues to the true extent of their activities.

The Crime Faculty at the Police College at Bramshill looks at murders for links with other crimes, but they have to be fairly obvious. In most cases, if a killer like Sutcliffe changed his modus operandi, or his geographical pitch by moving away from red-light areas, as Sutcliffe did when he strangled Marguerite Walls, linking would be more difficult but not impossible.

A research unit is an essential element in an investigation; untainted by the pressures of the investigation, it can give an objective assessment of proposed lines of enquiry and the likelihood of other crimes being connected. If this is not part of the set-up, and staff are not allowed to voice their views, you run the risk of adopting a dictatorial approach and will end up not carrying your team with you. Officers will lose confidence in their leader; then you have the lions-led-by-donkeys syndrome, and in time the lions will lose their appetite and it is the public which suffers. This was one failure of the Ripper inquiry.

However, the twenty-first-century rank-and-file detective challenges senior officers more than his predecessors, although there are still some who expect blind obedience and do not like their views being questioned by their juniors.

Prostitute murders rank as some of the most difficult to investigate and solve due to the nature of the victims' work, punters' reluctance to become witnesses, and a lack of interest in their activities on the part of those who live in or pass through the streets where they ply their trade. Their bodies are often found in lay-bys with no clue as to where they came from or who dumped them there.

Although the day she was kidnapped was probably the first time Julie Dart went onto the streets of Chapeltown, it took two months and a BBC *Crimewatch* appeal to bring forward a prostitute she had talked to on the night she had the misfortune to meet Sams.

Most members of the public show little sympathy for these girls, taking the moral high ground regarding their demise, though falling short of saying they deserved what they got. This makes public appeals generally fruitless in terms of obtaining useful information. These women take to the streets for a variety of reasons – being desperate for money, having run away with their children from a violent partner, being forced onto the streets by a pimp or a drug habit, or as housewives needing the money to keep their family together, make ends meet and pay the mortgage when their husbands are out of work. Needs must when the devil drives. None deserves to die. They are people, and in parts of Chapeltown are as much a part of its life as night and day.

Plenty of effort went into investigating the Ripper murders but it was channelled in the wrong direction. It was a groundbreaking case that grew and grew, and as it did so it became too big for the minds of men to comprehend the whole picture without the aid of a computer.

Investigating a crime using an unreliable description of the suspect is fatal. I had no description of Julie Dart's killer, and until we linked the case with the kidnapping of Stephanie Slater no description of Sams existed, but even then I had to keep an open mind in case it was not the same person. I follow the rule that you deal with the probable before contemplating the unlikely.

Some of Sutcliffe's victims survived and described their attacker as having a beard, but not a single one stated he was a Geordie. In fact, Olive Smelt repeatedly told the police that he had a soft Yorkshire accent, but she was never listened to. Today Olive would be seen by specially trained officers and her evidence given greater credence.

The public interest in the Ripper case ensured a constant flow of information from the public and other police forces. The rate of information coming into the incident room exceeded the investigation team's ability to process it. When this happens, you are on a one-way road to nowhere.

Chapeltown today continues to house the city's red-light area. There are fewer prostitutes on the streets but they remain easy targets. There has been no real change in police attitudes to prostitutes, as the move towards political correctness and tolerance in the service has not extended to the women who pursue the world's oldest profession. There are still those who focus on the victim and not the crime, and have difficulty raising the same level of enthusiasm in catching a prostitute's killer as they would the killer of an office worker.

More prostitutes work from flats, seeing regular customers. But those who still do the streets take few precautions beyond working in pairs or threes so that there is always someone to note a punter's car registration. But both Sams and the Ripper were cautious enough to change the number plates on their cars.

Over the years, I revisited Chapeltown numerous times to deal with a variety of incidents, including two murders. One victim, Damien Sutton, died three days after being shot in the head in the Hayfield pub carpark on 8 October 1995. The twenty-year-old was shot no more than a hundred yards from where Jayne MacDonald was murdered by Peter Sutcliffe. His shooting was witnessed by dozens of people who were leaving the pub, as well as by a number of Damien's friends.

I was called out at 8 am the next day when the doctors gave up hope of any recovery. Damien was in a coma and on a life support machine. The crime scene had been obliterated when I arrived – not even the telltale blue-and-white-striped police tape cordoning it off remained. This was a hostile area for the police, especially at night, and all I saw when I visited it early in the morning were drugs dealers plying their trade on the streets where hours before a young man, a member of their community, had been shot.

There was no doubt that the pub's customers would have heard the shot being fired and seen Damien's attacker fleeing the scene in a car. The first police officers to attend had noted the names of witnesses and to that list had added those they knew in the crowd who were refusing to give their names. It was like pulling teeth to find out which of Damien's friends were with him when he was attacked, and when we did they had little to say.

I set my team the task of interviewing the witnesses. The handful of names we had, represented only a small number of the people who were there. Unfortunately this part of Chapeltown followed the premise of 'See no evil, hear no evil and tell the Babylon nuthin'' (Babylon is Jamaican patois for the police).

Damien's life support machine was turned off three days later; his death was inevitable. I attended the post-mortem. I had guessed that a .22 bullet had caused the small entry wound, but now discovered it had entered his skull just behind his right ear and passed through his head. Externally there was little to see but a black mark where the congealed blood had sealed the wound.

Even Damien's death did not crack the wall of silence I faced. I had done several TV appeals for information without any success, until I got a telephone call asking me to personally and confidentially visit a local man who had something to say and would speak only to me. He lived locally and when I arrived at his door, I was ushered into the lounge where I sat down. Out of habit I would always quickly take in a room, discreetly glancing round. I was taken aback to see a motorised golf trolley standing in the corner of the room behind the settee. It would have been out of place in any lounge but we were on the twelfth floor of a block of flats! I chuckled at the thought of an unsuspecting visitor at the lift doors, leaping for safety as he came hurtling out of the lift on it. The man gave me what I wanted – a name and a reason. It seemed Damien's death was a matter of a lack of respect on the part of the younger West Indians towards the elders in the community; drugs were not involved.

Once I had a name and a motive, many others told us the same story or something similar, but written statements were hard to come by. A rogue news story that Damien had been shot with his own gun was both unhelpful and, I believed, untrue. Negative news like that turns the public off – they are less likely to want to get involved if they think the dead person contributed to his own demise.

Damien was not known to have been in possession of a .22 pistol that night, but the gun had disappeared before the police arrived, taken by either his killer or a bystander. It would never be found.

My suspect, Alan George Black, a disc jockey and tailor, had fled the area, but the discovery of a box of .22 cartridges in the flat he was staying in was a helpful start. There were rumours that he had gone to the West Indies but these proved untrue as he came out of hiding a month later and gave himself up in Bradford. The thirty-three-year-old was charged with murder, subsequently convicted of manslaughter and jailed for four years.

Another Chapeltown murder victim was twenty-nine-year-old labourer Steven Seddon, who was killed on 5 September 1992 at his home in Scott Hall Grove, near to where Wilma McCann and Jayne MacDonald lived.

It was 3.30 am when I was called out. I drove to the modest rented semi on the suburb's fringe to look at the scene.

Steven had been out for a Friday night drink but was now dead. He had suffered a brutal beating – his face was a mass of swelling and bruises, his nose had been broken with such force that the skin had split on the bridge, and his body was covered with abrasions.

Professor Michael Green performed the post-mortem and concluded that death was due to the inhalation of blood from his facial injuries. Steven had lain on his back in a helpless state behind the lounge door and died choking on his own blood. His two young children were upstairs but could not open the lounge door. Unbeknown to them their father's body lay behind it. Had there been anyone to give him first aid or simply turn him on his side he could easily have lived.

A neighbour heard screaming at 1.30 am, but had only gone to the house an hour later because of the loud music coming from it. It was then he discovered Steven's body. From the concentration of blood spattering, I knew that this was where the attack had taken place, while a trail of blood to the open back door showed me the way the killer had gone as he left. It could have been a burglary gone wrong but became a routine murder inquiry when we began retracing Steven's movements the night before.

Steven Seddon, a single man, had been out drinking with Mary Frances Coleman, a twenty-year-old, who lived in the same street as him. While out, they were seen by Coleman's former partner, thirty-six-year-old Stephen Paul Brown. He was so enraged that he waited until the couple returned to Seddon's home and broke into the house through the lounge window. Although he was told that the relationship was platonic, his anger was not assuaged, and he violently attacked Seddon, punching and kicking him before turning on Mary Coleman and inflicting severe facial injuries on her.

Brown left the house with Mary Coleman, and it was the sound of music booming through the open front window which alerted neighbours. Brown was traced to a nearby address and arrested. He was charged with the murder of Steven Seddon and assaulting Mary Coleman. Although the jury cleared him of murder, he was convicted of manslaughter and sentenced to seven years' imprisonment and a further two years for the assault on Miss Coleman.

Criticism of how West Yorkshire Police handled the Ripper case was unavoidable. Then Home Secretary William Whitelaw requested that Sir Lawrence Byford, one of HM Inspectors of Constabulary, conduct a review.

He presented his findings to the House of Commons on 19 January 1982, stating: 'There were major errors of judgment by the police and some inefficiencies in the conduct of the operation at various levels. In particular, excessive credence was given to the letters and a tape from a man claiming responsibility for the series of murders and signing himself "Jack the Ripper".

'Another serious handicap to the investigation was the ineffectiveness of the Major Incident Room which became overloaded with unprocessed information. With hindsight, it is now clear that if these errors and inefficiencies had not occurred Sutcliffe would have been identified as a prime suspect sooner than he was.' Indeed, the report did not tell any of us junior officers what we did not already know. Lessons were learnt – but in the most tragic of ways. Even Sutcliffe realised that for years he was literally getting away with murder. 'It got to the stage where I thought I was invisible because I never got caught,' he said.

So why did Peter Sutcliffe commit the terrible crimes he did? Was he mad or bad? Or was it a case of murder by proxy?

He revered and adored his mother, Kathleen Sutcliffe. The shy and quiet Peter much preferred to stay indoors with her rather than join in the rough-and-tumble games his younger brothers and sisters enjoyed. And he seemed to have little in common with his chauvinistic, cricket-mad father, John. But Roman Catholic Kathleen was a saint in his eyes, and few women if any could be her equal. It was even reported in August 2001 that he had officially changed his surname by deed poll to his mother's maiden name of Coonan. She died three years before he was arrested.

If you dismiss the voices from God and the headaches, blackouts and depression resulting from a 1966 motorcycle accident as part of a contrived attempt by Sutcliffe to get the murder charges reduced to manslaughter through diminished responsibility, then what motivated him to murder and maim so many women?

When being interviewed after his arrest, he freely admitted: 'Of course, it all began in 1974 when I was done out of a tenner by a prostitute in Manningham, Bradford. It poisoned my mind against them.' He also spoke of exacting sexual revenge on them and of a compulsion to kill.

But was this really what kicked him off or was it his feeling of betrayal when he discovered that Sonia, his first serious girlfriend who became his wife, was seeing another man? When he learnt he was being two-timed, he went off to Manningham, picked up a prostitute and took her to her flat, but bottled out of having sex as she undressed. He had given her £10 up front for her £5 services and said he'd get the change back at her place. But she refused to give him the money, and did so again a few weeks later when he bumped into her in a pub. In his eyes, this prostitute had humiliated him in much the same way he felt Sonia had.

He and Sonia wed, but how did she fit in with his now warped view of women? Sutcliffe's father, John, described his eldest son: 'He was a mummy's boy and she was proud he had got on in life, buying a detached house and the like. He was very quiet and shy until he was seventeen and he began to get more confident. He was meticulous about his clothes, always looked smart, though he wasn't one for the girls. In fact he only ever brought one home.'

This was, of course, Sonia Szurma, the arty, teetotal, dour trainee teacher who became his wife.

'The first thing about her you noticed was she was so domineeringly quiet,' said Sutcliffe senior. 'She gave you the feeling without saying a word that she was disappointed in everything and everyone she came across in Pete's family. She thought she was a cut above us.

'Pete and her would occasionally hold hands. Wherever he sat, she'd always be right next to him on the chair arm. She stuck close to him so he couldn't get away from her. He was henpecked. She was the gaffer in that relationship.'

There is no doubt he had a compulsive streak in his character, but I doubt it amounted to a personality disorder. He came into the police inquiry that many times someone would surely have spotted him as a nutcase, but they did not.

I always believed Sonia did not know of Sutcliffe's murderous activities. I felt she was the last person he would have wanted to know. But when he killed, was it murder by proxy, killing the same person over and over again? Was there a sense of power, a thrill when he did it, which drove the emasculated Peter on to do it again? His compulsive personality became focused on women, but why? Was he killing Sonia over and over again?

# chapter six

# ANGEL FROM HELL

## July 1981

A dead body is the usual and most obvious starting point for a murder investigation. One of my most satisfying cases was a hunt for a triple killer – without even one, never mind three, corpses.

Unusually, in this case we had a pretty good idea who the murderer was. That's normally the hardest problem to solve. But for us the most difficult thing was finding the victims – three dead men.

Almost immediately after I had finished with the Ripper investigation, the Eastern Area Head of CID, DCS John Conboy, rang me and, without telling me what it was about, asked me to choose two other detectives from the Robbery Squad and come to a meeting at Brotherton House, Leeds.

I chose Tony Ryan and Ronnie Burks, and off we went to the meeting on the hallowed first floor where, in the Leeds City Police days, the Chief Constable and his senior officers had their offices. I met the other detectives we'd be working with – DCs Geoff Darley, Steve Bottom and Derek Lincoln from Garforth Divisional CID (Garforth is a suburb to the east of the city). It was only two months since Peter Sutcliffe had been jailed, but the sense that the force had bungled the case still lingered heavily. The failure of senior officers on the Ripper case to listen to their juniors' views ensured that Geoff would now get a chance to air his thoughts and satisfy my curiosity as to why we were here.

At that time Garforth had a population of 16,000 people. Its main industry was light engineering, and houses in the area were sought after owing to its closeness to the city. It was typical suburbia.

Geoff Darley told us he had suspected for some time that a local Hell's Angel, Paul Anthony Hobson, known as Tony, was involved in the disappearance of two local men, Christopher Robin Cooper, who was last seen alive on Saturday, 26 July 1975, in Garforth, and, two years later, Philip Clapham, just seventeen, who was last seen alive on Friday, 29 July 1977, drunk outside a pub in the town.

Both men knew Hobson, the president of the local chapter of the Hell's Angels, very well. He was twenty-six, a colourful and charismatic character, admired by some of the local youths and feared by others. He was a powerfully built man who always wore his colours, the traditional Hell's Angel cut-off denim jacket and dirty jeans. His hair and beard were unkempt, adding to his stereotypical image as a Hell's Angel.

Although Geoff had been making noises for some time that he believed Hobson to be implicated in the men's disappearance, he got no more than local support for his theory until a third person was added to the list. Geoff saw an article in a local paper in 1981 about David George Hirst, a twenty-year-old married man who had also gone missing. David worked at White Sea and Baltic, a chemical firm in Garforth, and was last seen on 22 December 1977, as he left work with Hobson, who also worked there as a charge-hand.

This couldn't just be a coincidence. Three people missing from a small, quiet town over a two-year period, and the common denominator was Garforth's own resident Hell's Angel, Tony Hobson.

David's wife, strangely enough, did not report him missing to the police until Christmas Day, as she thought he'd had enough of her and the children and gone off to start a new life. They lived in a different area of Leeds, covered by Gipton Division, where a missing-person record was opened, so he was not reported missing in Garforth after leaving work. It was pure chance that Geoff saw the article appealing for information to end the mystery of the two-year disappearance.

John Conboy told us: 'I want the inquiry to be run in secret. We have a suspect, Hobson, who is thought to be the last person to see these men, but no bodies. The question is, is it a coincidence these men have disappeared?

Are they living somewhere else? If so, find them. Otherwise Hobson, on his own or with others, murdered them and disposed of their bodies.'

As sergeant, I was in charge of the five other officers, all detective constables. We set up an incident room on the first floor at Brotherton House in an office next to Detective Superintendent Gordon Harveys, who would oversee the inquiry. We decided to approach the managing director of White Sea and Baltic and discreetly ask him to pick off staff around Hobson we could speak to, trusting them not to tell him of our inquiry.

We got together the three missing-person files and reinvestigated the disappearances. We worked in pairs, each looking at one case. I worked with Geoff Darley on the Christopher Robin Cooper case, Derek Lincoln and Ronnie Burks on David George Hirst, while Tony Ryan and Steve Bottom worked on Philip Andrew Clapham.

Christopher Robin Cooper, thirty-seven, worked at the Leeds Rates Office. Married to Valerie, he lived in Cyprus Terrace, just down from Garforth Main Street, in a terraced house not too far from Hobson's parents. He was an amateur photographer, a shortwave radio enthusiast and a member of a local gun club.

He was regarded as immature for his age, and suffered from hearing and sight difficulties and a nervous stomach; he had been prescribed Valium for anxiety. It seemed out of character for him, a gentle giant, to mix with the younger people he did and to be interested in the Hell's Angels cult. Chris, as he was known, welcomed Hobson and his Angel cronies into his home, and was regularly seen in their company.

On Saturday, 26 July 1975, his wife Valerie left home at 7.50 am to go to work. They arranged to meet at 4 pm to go shopping, but she never saw her husband again. Shortly after Valerie left, Chris's father Edgar arrived at 8.30 am and took him to Wakefield and Leeds while he made some business calls.

Chris was dropped off at the end of his street at 12.40 pm by Edgar. He told his father he was going home to decorate the bathroom. Edgar never saw his son again. At 1 pm, Chris was seen riding pillion on Hobson's motorbike in Wakefield Road, Garforth, by one of Hobson's friends, David Eastwood, but he could not say who he was actually riding the bike with. That was the last sighting of Christopher Cooper.

When Valerie returned home at 10.30 pm, she saw that his camera equipment was missing and assumed he had gone off to do some photographic work. Expecting him to come in later, she went to bed. She told

Geoff and me of a strange incident that took place while she was in bed.

'I heard someone downstairs in the night. I thought it was Chris so I went down but no one was there. I could smell gas. The fire in the lounge was turned on but the gas wasn't lit. I walked into the kitchen and all the rings on the electric cooker were on. I searched round but there was no one in the house. I looked out of the window and saw Tony Hobson walking up the street. I turned everything off and thought no more about it.'

I visited Chris Cooper's parents, who lived in a smart bunglow in Garforth. They were an elderly couple, and certainly Mrs Cooper was a broken woman after the disappearance of her only child. She pointed to the clock on the fireplace: 'It stopped the day Christopher Robin went missing and I have never wound it up since. The day I wind it up again will be when he walks back through the door.' I knew it was unlikely that the clock, stopped at one, would ever be wound up again.

There was not much we could say, but it was good for them to talk about their son again. They were solid, decent people, and their son was much loved and missed. Geoff was a local detective and knew the family, having met them many times before. I listened as Mrs Cooper said, 'There was a time I thought he was the Yorkshire Ripper and that was why he never contacted us. I could have even lived with thinking he was a murderer because it meant he was still alive.'

The Coopers must have been the only people in the country who were disappointed when Peter Sutcliffe was arrested, as it dashed their hopes that their son was alive.

We went over old ground. Their son always sent birthday, Christmas and anniversary cards to his parents, but none since he went missing. It was clear to me he had not run off and started a new life. He was dead. The Coopers understandably did not want to believe that. Failing discovery of his body, there was always hope, however slight, that he would one day walk back into their lives.

Philip Clapham, seventeen, was born to a single mother and adopted at six months by Thomas and Mary Clapham. As a child he developed asthma, which he suffered from until he was twelve when he was diagnosed as having diabetes, requiring him to have regular insulin injections.

By the time he was fourteen he had become so aggressive to his parents and elder adopted brother that he was taken into care, spending a number of years in community homes. He returned home when he was sixteen and worked as an apprentice baker in Garforth.

This period of stability was short lived as he was caught stealing money from the till at work and was sent to a detention centre for three months. On his release, on 3 March 1977, he went to live in a caravan on a site at Garforth Cliffe with Hobson and his friend, Andrew Mark Watson, who was then just fifteen.

A short time later Philip moved into local lodgings, and in May he got a job as a labourer at White Sea and Baltic, Hobson's workplace. Watson was also soon to join the firm as a labourer. Involved in petty crime, Philip was arrested for stealing milk and started living rough, sleeping in a Portakabin that was used as a canteen at White Sea and Baltic.

Although Philip kept in touch with his adopted parents, his lifestyle was on a downward curve. Heavy drinking combined with his insulin injections turned him once again into an aggressive young man.

He saw his doctor on 15 May 1977 and was given a repeat prescription of insulin, which he'd been taking since 1968. Failure to take it would cause him to fall into a coma and die. He could not obtain insulin elsewhere without reference back to his GP, we were told.

Philip's adopted brother, Stephen, last saw him when he dropped him off at 7.30 pm at the Newmarket pub in Garforth Main Street.

Philip's girlfriend, Angela Whitford, met him at 8 pm in the nearby Gascoigne pub, and they were joined by Tony Hobson and Andrew Watson. By closing time, Philip was so drunk he could not stand without help. Hobson and Angela took him outside and laid him on a nearby bench. Hobson then walked Whitford to the bus stop and she went home. This was the last time she saw Philip. He was reported missing on Thursday, 4 August by his mother.

The mystery of Philip Clapham's disappearance deepened in October of that year when a burglary was discovered by James Hudson at his parents' home in Airedale Drive, Garforth.

An empty five-litre bottle of brandy containing around £30 in small change and an antique handgun were stolen. On the living-room floor by the window, Mr Hudson found two medallions, one inscribed with Philip Clapham's name and address and details of his sugar intake requirement for his diabetes.

Philip had a record as a petty thief, so the police circulated his details in connection with the burglary, clearly believing he was still around Garforth. To add a further twist to Philip's disappearance, Geoff Darley had seen Hobson at teatime on 7 November of that year, and Hobson told him he had seen Clapham in Garforth earlier that day, and that he had with him an antique gun stolen from the house in Airedale Drive.

David Hirst was described as slow witted and childlike, but he had passed his eleven-plus exam. A keen train-spotter, he had various jobs after leaving school before joining White Sea and Baltic as a labourer in August 1977.

He married Zena Podsiadly in 1976. They lived in Seacroft, Leeds, and had two children aged three and five. Zena waved goodbye to her husband as he left home for work at 7.15 am on Thursday, 22 December 1977, his last working day before Christmas. She never saw him again. Maurice Leathley, works clerk at White Sea and Baltic, paid him one week's wages and one week's holiday money totalling £79.58 that morning. At lunchtime, he was seen having a Christmas drink in the Gascoigne pub with Hobson, Andrew Watson and other workmates.

They returned to work at 3.30 pm but continued drinking. David was seen leaving and walking in the direction of Main Street with Hobson and Watson. They were all drunk. Witnesses recalled that Hobson and Watson were arguing with David, who was seen crying at one stage. When he had not arrived home by Christmas Day, Zena Hirst reported him missing to the local police. It had been three days since he was last seen alive.

David Hirst did not return to work after the Christmas break, though his employers were not suspicious as shortly afterwards a letter from him arrived at the firm requesting that his employment papers be sent to his home. The company took the letter as terminating his employment with them and posted his P60 to Zena.

Our first task was to speak to the managing director at White Sea and Baltic. Our enquiries would need to be discreet. If, as we suspected, all three men had been murdered, then the letter signed 'D. Hirst' purporting to be from David must be a forgery. But did the firm still have the letter five years on?

Luckily they did. White Sea and Baltic were able to produce the original handwritten letter, which was checked against a recent sample of Hobson's handwriting which we had arranged through his work. Hobson was left handed. Handwriting experts described the signature as a traced forgery and stated that some features of the suspect handwriting suggested that Hobson was the author.

Enquiries into Hobson's background showed that he was employed as a haulage hand for the National Coal Board at the time of Chris Cooper's disappearance. He had been off work sick from Saturday, 26 July, the date Chris was last seen, until 8 September.

Hobson's work records stated that he had been treated for a hand injury at Leeds General Infirmary. Hospital records showed that Hobson attended the hospital at 2.15 pm that Saturday for a fracture to his left index finger, a deep cut to the left middle finger, and an injury to the outside of his right elbow. As to how they occurred, the records stated he claimed he had fallen on his outstretched hands and injured himself.

But if he was at the hospital, who was riding the motorcycle that Chris Cooper was seen on the back of? Something must have happened in a short space of time. Hobson had been at the hospital at 2.15 pm and Chris was seen earlier at 1 pm in Wakefield Road, Garforth. A journey to Leeds at that time on a Saturday would take around thirty minutes. We had to presume that Hobson's injury happened in whatever circumstances led to Cooper's death, and he had then gone to hospital. Chris must have died between 1 and 2 pm.

A lot of Hobson's friends seemed to work with him, so discreet enquiries would be difficult. We knew we had to speak to someone who was close to him who could be trusted, and was in touch with him on a daily basis at work. The managing director singled out maintenance fitter Stewart Jackson as that person. This was a gamble, as he could blow the whole investigation wide open if our trust in him was misplaced.

Geoff and I went to see Stewart one evening at his home. Like Hobson, he was older than the yard lads. He lived in a tidy terraced house with his wife and family. We talked around the real purpose of our visit as we made the decision to confide in him. I felt that not only could we trust him, but the burden of collapsing a triple murder investigation would be sufficient pressure for him to keep the whole thing secret until we told him otherwise.

'I was in the Gascoigne pub that Christmas with Hobson, Watson, Hirst and others on David's last working day. As I left the works that afternoon, I saw him with Hobson and Watson and another mate of theirs, Nigel Holmes,' he recalled.

What he told us next I found extremely interesting. 'I returned to the firm one summer's evening, though I can't be exactly sure of the year. It was around the time of David's disappearance. I noticed that a large area in the field at the back of the works had been dug over. It was next to the concrete roadway that ran along the back of the premises. It was unusual as the field was wasteland and not used for anything.' Could he show us where it was? I asked. 'Should be able to tell you roughly where, give or take a few feet.'

Stewart said he had asked other yard employees about this patch and Hobson had remarked, 'I buried a stolen motorcycle there.' Knowing Hobson's enthusiasm for bikes, he accepted this and dismissed it from his mind.

He also told us he had seen Hobson with several firearms and that he kept one in his locker. One was a .22 bolt-action rifle with the barrel and the stock cut down. He had seen Hobson firing it in the field.

We had now identified those we considered the key players. Tony Hobson and Andrew Watson were central to it all, as was Hobson's girl-friend, Karen Robinson, who lived with him, and then there were Nigel Holmes and David Eastwood. But what hard evidence did we have? A short time after Chris Cooper was last seen on his motorcycle, Hobson was being treated for injuries to his hand.

Along with Watson, he was with Philip Clapham outside the Gascoigne pub when he was last seen. If Hobson had killed Clapham he must have taken his medallions off his body, burgled Airedale Drive and left them there ten weeks after his death. Then, keeping up the charade when he saw Geoff Darley in November, he said he had seen Clapham earlier that day with the antique gun.

They were also drinking with David Hirst on the afternoon of his last working day before Christmas. There was also the evidence, although not irrefutable, that Hobson had forged the letter sent to White Sea and Baltic after David's disappearance.

But one essential ingredient was missing – a motive. We knew there had been an argument with Hirst, though we did not know what it was about. It took no great leap of faith for our team to conclude that Hobson had killed these three men. But could we prove it? It would have helped if we had had at least one body.

We talked about what Stewart Jackson had said. Had Hobson buried a stolen motorbike in the field behind his works premises, or a body? If it was a corpse, it would have to be Philip Clapham. Hobson did not work at White Sea and Baltic when Chris Cooper went missing, and Jackson had said it was a summer evening. David went missing in December. Or was it really a stolen motorcycle under the soil?

Hobson was the Master of Arms in the West Riding Hell's Angels chapter and would accompany members to fights with rival gangs with an array of weapons. He then became vice-president and in due course president of this small band of Hell's Angels though, ironically, for most of the time they did not have motorbikes. Instead of roaring through the town on two wheels, colours blowing in the wind, they would get about on less glamorous forms of transport – the local bus. Or two legs, as they strutted around Garforth in their colours, getting drunk in the pubs at night and working in the day.

Hobson was the centrepiece of the chapter, some years older than the rest. He was six foot tall, stockily built and intimidating in appearance, with long dark brown hair, beard and moustache. He had a Charles Manson appearance, and it was this aura which allowed him to carry off their cultist behaviour without too many problems with the young men of Garforth and other Hell's Angels chapters.

The plan we devised was simple. We would arrange for Stewart Jackson to stack pallets on the area of ground where we wanted to dig. We would go there early on a Sunday morning, remove the pallets and dig down to find either a body or a bike. If it was a stolen motorcycle, we'd rebury it, put the pallets back, and hopefully Hobson and his mates would be none the wiser about our visit.

At 6.30 am on Sunday, 16 August 1981, nine of us met Stewart at the rear of the works premises. There was no one else about except us. Although it was summer it was cold when we started, which would make the job even more difficult. There was plenty of banter, and an air of expectation that we would be unearthing Philip Clapham's body at any moment. We had an array of garden equipment – forks, spades, a pick and shovels. I took a spade and thrust it into the ground with my foot expecting it to penetrate to the depth of the blade. Not so. A jarring shudder ran through my body as I hit bricks and stones beneath the surface.

'Bloody hell,' I cursed. 'The ground is solid.' 'I'll have a go,' said Ron Burks, who met the same resistance.

Successively Geoff, Derek, Steve, Ron, Tony and I had a go. We all took it in turns, expecting only to take a couple of hours to dig down about five feet. The little progress we had made exposed another problem. The soil was not only mixed with half-bricks and stones, it was saturated and smelled like a toxic soup.

Stewart Jackson explained: 'Oh, there was a large leak of raw turpentine into the ground here. That's what you can smell.' I looked at Derek

Lincoln, who, waiting his turn, was puffing away on a cigarette. I was digging, and watched the ash from my own cigarette fall slowly into the shallow trench. As if walking on broken glass, I gently put the spade down, tiptoed out of the hole and quickly stubbed my cigarette out.

After digging for two and a half hours, we had made less impression on the ground than the turpentine fumes had on the backs of our throats. It seemed a hopeless task. We were enveloped in turpentine and, with the morning sun getting hotter, the fumes got worse and my eyes wouldn't stop watering.

A mid-morning break for bacon sandwiches was welcomed. We knew it could take days to find the grave, if it was indeed there, and days we did not have. Before we finished, everything had to be left as if we had never been there. After forging on for another hour and a half, we had still dug down only two and a half feet.

I think what did it for me was the radio, which had been quietly playing while we dug. Suddenly it seemed the volume increased as out burst Bernard Cribbins singing, 'There was I, digging this hole, hole in the ground ...' Someone quipped, 'I hope it isn't a request for us from Tony Hobson.' We all fell about laughing. It's a serious business, digging for someone's loved one, but we were only human and humour broke the tension and made bearable the fact that at any moment we might unearth a body. The more we dug, the greater the smell of fumes. We were barking like dogs, our eyes stinging and streaming from the fumes, when we gave up the task at lunch-time.

We would need a mechanical digger to get any depth in the soil this side of Christmas. We abandoned the task, put the pallets back and finally removed our tracks by brushing around the pallets with branches, an old Indian trick I picked up from watching too many westerns on television, only they tied brushwood to the tails of their ponies to cover their tracks.

By 12.30 pm, having hopefully removed all trace of our presence, we left to buy Stewart Jackson a drink in one of the local pubs Hobson didn't use. While chatting over a pint, Stewart said, 'I've been thinking, I remember why the digging was so noticeable. It was because the rest of the ground was covered in snow.' I knew instantly that the body we were digging for could not be Philip Clapham.

Stewart went on: 'I think I was off but came into work. A tanker of chemicals from Germany was due on the last working day before Christmas but was delayed and was arriving the next day. Me and some of the yard lads volunteered to come in to sort the delivery out. That's when I saw the patch of dug ground.'

He also said that Hobson and maybe Watson had come in that day, and that was also when he had had the conversation with Hobson. We checked the records, and sure enough a tanker was due the day David Hirst went missing which in fact came the next day. We could not verify that it was snowing, but concluded that it must be David in the ground and it must have been Christmas 1977.

We had gone as far as we could. If we spoke to any other people closer to Hobson we were likely to tip him off. Gordon Harvey sanctioned the use of a mechanical excavator. The arrest of those we suspected of being involved in the triple murders was set for Tuesday, 25 August 1981. Geoff and I would arrest Hobson, and other members of the team would get Watson, Holmes, Eastwood and Karen Robinson, Hobson's girlfriend.

Watson was Hobson's closest friend; Holmes had been in their company when Hirst went missing; Eastwood had seen Cooper on the back of Hobson's bike, but amazingly had not said who was riding it. Hobson had a limited wardrobe – he was always in jeans and his denim jacket, and his long unkempt hair and beard would have made him recognisable even if he was wearing a helmet. How could you recognise a motorbike and not the rider? Karen Robinson, being Hobson's lover, could also have been involved.

The mechanical digger was moved near the works premises the night before so it could arrive at 7 am – the same time we moved in to arrest Hobson and Watson at work. If a body was buried at the premises, we might gain some psychological advantage when they saw the digger and us arrive and realise we meant business.

But all good plans can go wrong. We discovered shortly before we arrived at White Sea and Baltic that Hobson had decided to take the day off. All was not lost, but we needed to get to his house before he got any phone calls from his mates at work or the others on our hit list.

Four of us arrived at Hobson's home – Geoff, Inspector Gordon Garfit, Constable Dawn Cranidge and myself. Gordon and Dawn waited by the gate while Geoff and I walked to the door. There was little conversation between us; we knew what we had to do.

I knocked on the door but got no immediate answer. I was well aware that Hobson had access to weapons and ammunition, as he had been seen firing them at work. I stood to one side of the door just in case he put a shot through it. I was horrified to see Geoff kneel down and shout through the letterbox, 'Tony, open the door.' 'Bloody hell, that's a bit risky,' I said. We had no firearms but if Hobson 'kicked off' and started to fight I had decided to dive on him. I could not hear any noise inside but traffic from the main road yards away would have blotted it out.

The door opened and there was Hobson, half dressed and half asleep. He showed no emotion. 'Come in, lads,' he said, as if welcoming us to a party. When inside I said, 'I am Detective Sergeant Taylor. You know Geoff Darley. I am arresting you for the murder of David Hirst.' 'Come on, lads, give over. You're not serious,' he replied.

A search team was left at the house while Hobson was driven the ten miles to Wetherby police station. We had no real conversation in the car. He was sizing us up, as I certainly was him. After he was booked in, Geoff and I took him straight to the CID office to formally interview him, starting at 8 am.

It was not Geoff's first time interviewing Hobson but it was mine. I needed to get the measure of this man, who had contemptuously used Geoff and Garforth CID to falsely keep Philip Clapham alive.

It was clear from the first he was not going to roll over easily, and we would have to prove the allegations. I started the interview by saying, 'Right, Tony, let's talk about David. When did you last see him?'

'We all went for the Christmas drink.'

I then said, 'You went back to the firm after you had a drink. What was the last time you saw him?'

'Albert, the foreman, let us go early. We'd been sat in the Portakabin after the pub. It would be about four, he went for the train. Come on, lads, murder – that's not me,' he said, as if I had known him all my life and was well aware it was out of character.

'People don't disappear from the face of the earth like David Hirst did. Do you know he had an eye disorder?'

Hobson did.

I then said, 'He would be blind now. He had some special glasses made. They're still at the optician awaiting collection, so don't tell us "murder, that's not me", because we know it is.'

Hobson said, 'Come on, I didn't kill Dave. He went for the train.'

Geoff asked him about a fight they had had in Main Street when Hirst was said to have ended up crying. 'No, there wasn't 'owt happening in street. Where did you get that from?' he blustered.

He was asked about the patch of disturbed earth but dismissed this, saying he did not know anything about it. Then Geoff, without telling him what it was, showed him the letter that had been sent to the firm purporting to be from Hirst. 'Is this your writing, Tony?'

'Yes, it looks like it. What is it?' Hobson stunned both of us by admitting it was in his writing, although he added, 'Well, it's my writing, but I can't remember writing it.'

When it was put to him that Hirst was dead and he had sent the letter to cover up the fact that he had killed him, he retracted his admission that it was his writing until he was shown a copy of a 'Security and Safety' report we had arranged with his company for him to write in order to obtain a hand-writing sample. Geoff said, 'Look at this, it's the same writing.'

Hobson said, 'So that's why I did that report. It took me two bloody weeks.'

We did not progress the interview any further, and I told him we would be finding out what his friends had to say. With hardly a flicker of concern he said, 'Are they here as well?'

As our next interview began, I settled in my chair for the battle of wits I expected. Before I had a chance to open my mouth, Hobson declared: 'All right, it's not just David Hirst. You want three names – Chris Cooper, Phil Clapham and Dave Hirst. I killed all three. Where do you want me to start?' These were the words we badly wanted to hear, but hearing them was still a shock. Geoff and I glanced at each other, not daring to show our feelings. This was vindication for Geoff of the battle he had waged from the start just to get the possibility that Hobson might have murdered these people recognised. I was pleased for him.

'Start at the beginning,' ordered Geoff.

'Well, that Chris Cooper started messing with my bird. That's a capital offence in the Hell's Angels so I took him to Parlington Woods. I was going to beat him to death with my hands, he was absorbing all the punches, he was slow. I hit him wrong, you know, and bust my hand; I finished him off with a spade. I hit him over the head with it. Bloody hell, there was blood all over. I buried him. I went to the hospital with my hand – check their files – about an hour and a half later.'

The girlfriend he mentioned, Elaine Thompson, had died in a road accident months before his arrest and, showing his first sign of remorse, he said, 'She's dead now, killed in a road accident. Glad, really, for the shame I've brought.' I asked how he managed to bury the body so quickly. 'I dug the hole earlier that week. It was planned, you know, a capital offence. You should be able to find him. His helmet is with him, I threw it in the hole.'

He coolly went on to his next victim: 'Phil Clapham was prospecting [an initiation process to become a full Hell's Angel] to get in the Angels. He was causing a lot of bother for us. He was always pissed and getting Angels involved in fights. He'd caused some bother that night with the Mickie lads [Mickefield is a nearby village] and they were coming back. He was dossing in the Portakabin at work. I went to sort him out and he told me to bollocks. I walloped him with a hammer at the side of his head. It caved half his head in and I threw up straight away.

'It's an office now, the Portakabin. I buried him over the back of the concrete. I asked Andy [Watson] to help me bury him. Told Andy I'd got a job to do, got two spades, put Phil in his doss bag and buried him in the field on the Saturday. We were there while half past six. Thought I was all right till I found out about this bleeding cable [the firm was due to lay an electric cable where the body was and might find it] about a year later. We had to move him. He's now about a yard from the concrete.'

I butted in: 'So this is the hole that you spoke of burying a motorbike in?'

'I knew they'd buy that story, but it was Phil. There's no bike.'

In a matter of minutes, this man had casually admitted killing two people as if having a chat with friends. 'Go on to the next,' I urged.

'Dave Hirst never fitted in. While we talked about motorbikes, he'd be telling us the fucking wheel size of the bleeding *Flying Scotsman*. He had to go. I made a mistake with him. I promised to get him some cannabis but realised he couldn't keep his mouth shut.

'I stalled but he kept hassling me over the drugs so I decided to nobble him. I had my .22 sawn-off in my locker so I took him for a walk. He thought he was getting drugs but I took him to this hole over to Fairclough's. The gun was in a Tesco bag, I think, and I could feel the trigger through the bag. I shot him in the back of the head, shoved him in the hole and buried him.' I asked whether he still had the gun. 'Yes, it's at home upstairs somewhere. It's sawn off, you'll know it. Look, lads, I can show you where I buried all three, if that helps.'

'OK, just one question first. Who was with you when you murdered these people?'

Hobson looked me directly in the eye. 'There's only me. Andy just helped me move Phil and bury him.'

We ended the interview and took him in handcuffs to show us where the men were buried. He was driven from Wetherby to the back of White Sea and Baltic where the excavation was in progress. Hobson pointed to a spot opposite a chemical tank. 'That's where Phil should be.'

We then traced the route he had taken with David Hirst as he unwittingly walked to his death. We walked out of the work's entrance, past half a dozen of his colleagues who stood looking on in dazed amazement, but not a word was spoken as Hobson nodded to them.

We turned right towards the premises of Fairclough's builders, three hundred yards away, and walked onto the large carpark at the back of the building. Hobson pointed to a spot. 'I reckon Hirst's about here.' I marked the ground with a cross.

Our next trip was down the lane to Barwick-in-Elmet. I wondered, as we drove the mile and a half to Parlington Woods, whether Hobson realised that this was probably the last time he would see the countryside where he had spent his youth. I wondered what was going through his mind. His life as he knew it had just ended. He would be spending the rest of his days in prison, no doubt.

A large insurance company owned Parlington Woods. As we passed a lay-by by the bridge, Hobson said, 'I parked the bike there.' He guided us forty feet into the wood, but had difficulty orientating himself. 'They've done a bit of tree felling since I was here. I remember he was near a tree that had been struck by lightning. I reckon his head is only eighteen inches down, he's in a sitting position 'cos the hole was too small.'

The area was marked with tape tied to the trees, and we returned Hobson to his cell. We needed to find out what the others were saying and ensure he was telling us the truth.

David Eastwood added nothing to what he had previously said in relation to Chris Cooper's disappearance apart from admitting that it was Hobson riding the motorcycle when he saw Cooper on the back, but Hobson had warned him to say that he had not seen him that day.

That left Andrew Mark Watson. He was arrested at 7.20 am and also brought to Wetherby police station. Watson, twenty at the time of his arrest, had been married a year, and his wife was expecting their first child. He had no previous convictions and had known Hobson at least since he was fourteen.

Tony Ryan and Steve Bottom interviewed Watson initially about David Hirst and Philip Clapham. He denied any involvement in their disappearance, but the enormity of the situation became too much for him. Consumed with thoughts of not seeing his wife again or his unborn child as a free man, he broke down several times in waves of self-pity. He was brought to the station while Geoff and I were first speaking to Hobson. We all heard a banshee-like wailing coming from outside. I looked out to see Tony and Steve supporting Watson as they took him to the desk to book him in. His legs were like rubber and he was sobbing as he passed me.

He may have appeared to be rubber man but it took several interviews before he admitted acting as a lookout when Hobson shot David Hirst, and being in the Portakabin when Hobson killed Philip Clapham, as well as helping to bury and rebury his body.

At 2.40 pm the following day, the first body was unearthed exactly where Hobson had pointed out. Philip Clapham was clothed and inside a sleeping bag. The turpentine in the soil had preserved his body to some extent, but it was still a ghastly sight. As the body was brought out of its grave, it gave off a terrible stench.

I had no doubt that Hobson was telling the truth, but we needed a body to back up the confessions. I knew now we had Hobson potted. I looked down at Philip's grave. His body had been buried six feet down. Considering our feeble six-man efforts at digging, these two must have been at it all weekend.

His head injuries were massive. We were now confident enough to charge these two crackpot Hell's Angels. They had not only used the disappearance of three people to create a fearsome reputation, they were killers. I knew that anyway.

It was not until 11 am on Friday that Chris Cooper's body was found in Parlington Woods. The ground was very dry, and it was difficult for the excavator driver to manoeuvre between the trees, but in a shallow grave at the foot of one tree Chris's skeletal remains were found. He was on his back in a semi-sitting position, and his clothes now hung baggily on his once well-built frame. He had lain in this quiet and peaceful spot for six years, just below the surface of the soil.

The pathologist carefully uncovered Chris's skull to reveal a massive gaping facture which could be seen running down the centre of his head. The excavator now moved to Fairclough's yard to complete its final task, the uncovering of the last body, that of David Hirst. He could be at any depth, depending on how deep the pit was when he was unceremoniously cast into this rude grave.

At 11.15 am on Saturday, the carpark of Fairclough's builders gave up the secret it too had kept for four years. David's body was uncovered in an old rubbish pit which had been filled in and bulldozed over. He showed no obvious signs of violent death, but when his body was transferred to the mortuary an X-ray of his skull showed the .22 bullet which had entered his brain through his ear was still lodged inside his skull.

The causes of death were all consistent with the explanations given, and the victims were all identified from dental records. But why had they been killed? The main interview with Hobson was to last for eight hours. His confession was made in remarkable detail, and such clarity that no one could suppose this man was insane.

The search teams found the .22 gun under the bed at his terraced home. It was a 'rat gun' used on ships with small gunshot cartridges for killing rats. It had been sawn down, and he had filed down the .22 bullet rounds to fit it. An empty cartridge case was also found in the bedroom. Hobson confirmed this was the gun and the cartridge case from the bullet used to kill Hirst.

In his interview he described how he lured Chris Cooper to Parlington Woods on the pretext of showing him some guns, but he had been there a week earlier and dug a grave which he had covered with branches and leaves and which contained the spade that he would use to fill it in after killing Cooper.

Chris had started messing with his girlfriend, Elaine Thompson. Hobson said, 'That was it in my mind. Any damage or theft of your motorcycle, any taking of your colours like your jackets with the emblems, any messing with your woman, and that person was dead.' He said it was a capital offence under Hell's Angels law, as laid down in 1949 in California.

He described how he had fought with Chris, who was stronger than he had thought. 'My chest was on fire. I wondered if he was going to end up burying me.' But he reached for the spade in the nearby grave and struck Chris a fatal blow down the middle of his head.

After covering Chris's body with soil, he sat totally exhausted beside the grave and had a cigarette, then took Chris's keys, went to his home and stole his camera equipment. However, he did not admit returning later that night, entering the house and turning the gas fire on.

Philip Clapham was living rough, drinking excessively, and that night at the pub had caused trouble. Hobson said, 'Clapham was drunk on the seat, Andy was there as well. I told Clapham, "Come on, let's get you out of the way before all hell's let loose. You're going to get us all massacred or us colours nicked."

'Me and Andy took him back to the Portakabin. I confronted him but he didn't care. I don't know if Andy said 'owt. I wanted his jacket, he threw it at me, mouthing at me all the time. I lost me bottle and we started fighting. He wouldn't keep his mouth shut. I grabbed the hammer and swung it at his mouth. I missed first time.

'Andy was kicking him. I shouted to Andy to kill him. He hit him on the head with something, I don't know what. I then hit him about twice.' I asked how many times Watson had hit him. He said, 'I don't fucking know, I wasn't counting, twice maybe. There was blood and bone all over. We took half his head off.' He later said he had used a hammer and Watson a bar.

'I shouted, "Shut up, stop, listen." He wasn't breathing, he was dead. I felt as though half of Garforth were watching through the window. I grabbed his cut-off [jacket] and we went.' Hobson said Philip's medallions had come off in the fight so he put them in his pocket and they spent most of that weekend burying his body. He went on to admit to burgling Airedale Drive in an attempt to convince the police that Philip was still alive.

He then detailed how he dug a grave fifteen feet from where the new cable would be laid, keeping the topsoil and clay separate to ensure that no ground disturbance would be noticed when the cable hole was dug. Watson was physically sick as they tied a rope to the sleeping bag that Philip's body was in and dragged it as fast as they could into the new seven-foot-deep grave. Hobson then packed the layers of clay and soil around the body.

He went on: 'A lad called David Hirst was set on. From the word go, he was hopeless.' Hobson had told Hirst he could get him some cannabis, which resulted in David pestering him. This had been no idle promise as there were over twenty decent-sized plants growing in Hobson's loft.

David's persistence reached a point where he could not tolerate it. He, like Clapham, had failed to show respect to Hobson and had called him 'a wanker'. 'He was a nuisance. I decided a week before he'd have to go, thought I'd get him the sack. I told Andy in the pub that day that we had another job to do. I told Andy I was going to get Hirsty, properly finish him off.'

After leaving the pub they returned to White Sea and Baltic and continued drinking. He told David he would take him to meet a drugs pusher who'd supply him with cannabis, but the journey was always going to end in Fairclough's yard.

They walked side by side through the yard. Hobson had his finger on the trigger of the gun through the plastic of the bag. As they passed the scaffolding erected as a barrier around the rubbish pit, he raised the gun to the side of David's head and pulled the trigger. 'He just stopped walking and still looking ahead he just said, "Bastard!" I'll never forget it. Then he just fell over as if his legs had locked.' David's body was pushed into the pit and buried beneath the rubbish already in there.

Hobson took the £80 holiday pay from David's pocket and used it to buy cocaine later that day. 'Watson knew what he had to do; he was to yodel or whistle if anyone came, he was close enough to see what happened.'

As the interview ended, I asked, 'Did you think you'd get away with it?'

'I thought they might turn up in about eighty years when building a motorway or summat, but I would be dead and gone by then. Can I ask if you were armed that morning you came for me?'

'Why?' asked Geoff.

'Because I saw the woman [plainclothes officer]. I thought she'd come about the damp course. I thought I'd politely tell her to fuck off. If I'd known it was you lads I'd have come down with the gun and given you a barrel as I opened the door. Just one, only one works. You'd have got me, then it would be all over, none of this.'

I realised he had looked out of the window and had not seen Geoff or me at the door but had spotted PC Dawn Cranidge. He obviously didn't hear Geoff shout through the letterbox, otherwise one of us might have been shot. It hadn't happened so his words didn't shock me or give me the feeling of having had a narrow escape, but then he did not know that we were unarmed.

I put it to him, 'Is it right you have a death list?'

'Yes, but only for those who cross me. Who gets the credit for nailing me?'

I could see some concern on Geoff's face at this question, and he said, 'Why, will they go on the list?'

Hobson said, 'No, nowt like that. It's a kind of grudging respect.' Geoff did not declare his role in Hobson's downfall, so neither did I.

It was not until forty-eight hours after his arrest that Watson admitted striking Philip on the head with a hammer as he fought with Hobson. He was brought into the room where I was sitting with Geoff and Hobson. Watson told Hobson that he had admitted striking Philip and being the lookout when he shot David.

Hobson was charged with the three murders and also with preventing the lawful and decent burial of the corpses. Watson was charged with the murders of Philip Clapham and David Hirst and similarly with preventing the burial of their bodies.

Watson was again interviewed at Wetherby police station on 17 September while there for a remand hearing at the town's magistrates' court. He admitted being with Hobson when Chris Cooper was murdered and helping Hobson dig the grave the week before. He said he struck Chris about the head with a piece of wood. Watson was later charged with his murder and preventing his burial.

On their next court appearance the following Thursday, Hobson had more to say. He was feeling betrayed, after hearing in prison that Watson had said he was afraid of him and had acted under duress. This got Watson into the hospital wing, segregated from Hobson.

Geoff and I went to see Hobson in the cells. 'Now then, lads, I've a bit to tell you about Watson. He was there when Chris was killed. I was on top of Chris, had him by the throat. I shouted to Andy, "Hit him there," and put my hand on Chris's head, but the silly bastard hit my hand and bust me fingers, you can check that. I got up and my hand was pissing blood and I saw Andy hit him on the head with the spade. He buried him. I could do fuck all with me hand, I just kicked muck in with me feet.' The spade was thrown away in the wood, possibly in the lake.

This completed the last few pieces of the jigsaw. Watson had admitted being there when Chris was killed in an interview the previous week, but neither of them had accounted for the massive fracture Chris had down the centre of his skull, and the injury to Hobson's hand.

Hobson finally admitted: 'I am not a nutter. It was not done for money. It is just hard for anybody to understand. Some people have God; I have only had the Hell's Angels. It is the nearest thing to religion. If my time came round again I'd do it again to anyone else who crossed me. These are the rules laid down by the Hell's Angels in California in 1949 when they were formed.' This was the last paragraph of Hobson's written statement to Geoff and me. The words he carefully chose would ensure he spent the rest of his life in prison.

At Durham Crown Court in April 1982, Hobson pleaded guilty to all charges, but Watson, who was fourteen at the time of the Cooper killing, denied them. Watson's counsel was Harry Ognall, QC, who, twelve months previously, had prosecuted the Yorkshire Ripper at the Old Bailey.

On 13 May 1982, after four hours' deliberation, the jury found Watson guilty on all the three charges of murder. On charges of preventing the lawful and decent burial of the corpses, the jury found him guilty on two counts. They could not agree on the Hirst case, where he acted as a lookout and did not physically assist in the burial. In the light of the other findings, the charge was not pursued.

Watson had to be supported by two prison officers as he stood in the dock to hear sentence being passed by Justice Kenneth Jones, who told him he would be detained at Her Majesty's pleasure. The judge then turned to sentence Hobson. 'These were horrifying murders – horrifying for their brutality and horrifying for the deliberation which you brought to the killings of at least two of those young men. You say you have made a religion of evil. Many misguided young people also belong to this abominably evil cult of the Hell's Angels.

'But you are to be marked off because you have shown yourself to have the capacity to kill not one but three human beings in cold blood. I have no doubt that you are a ruthless killer. These do exist. You are one of them.' He then sentenced Paul Anthony Hobson to life imprisonment with a recommendation that he serve at least thirty years.

Hobson was taken to Winson Green prison in Birmingham to begin his sentence; but there was one outstanding issue I wanted to sort out with him – the suspicious death of James Woodhead. He was the grandfather of Elaine Thompson, Hobson's dead girlfriend.

Mr Woodhead was seventy-four and lived with his invalid wife in a semi-detached house in Seacroft, Leeds. A relative found him dead in the bath. He was clothed only in his vest but had abrasions to his wrists and knee and, bizarrely, one of his big toenails was missing. The gas and the electricity had been turned off. A carpet was missing from the kitchen while a biker's black scarf was found there and no one knew who it belonged to. To add to the mystery, the house was locked and no key could be found.

A post-mortem was held. Owing to Mr Woodhead's age, there could obviously have been a number of different clinical reasons for his death. There were certainly no obvious violent injuries. The police told the pathologist they had not uncovered anything suspicious. A slight under-statement, I thought. Mr Woodhead was in the habit of turning off the gas and electricity before going to bed, but he surely would not bathe in his vest and with the lights off, unless he was suffering from dementia, and there was no suggestion he was.

We had previously asked Hobson about Mr Woodhead's death but he had denied any involvement. I knew that when he was visiting his daugh-ter, Shirley Thompson, in Garforth, Mr Woodhead's building society book went missing. The thief had tried to draw money from the account and the pensioner suspected and constantly accused Tony Hobson of it.

I went to see Hobson in jail. He was pleasant but there was no way he was going to budge on this one. 'The assistant governor has seen me and told me I could be out in fifteen years. So I reckon if I admit anything else, I'll never get out.' Not to be outdone, I was determined that if he would not admit it then whenever he came up for parole the authorities would have a comprehensive report on the crimes he had committed and on the death of James Woodhead, which I suspected him of causing.

I obtained permission from the Home Office Prisons Department to send these to the prison and a comprehensive report and a complete set of photographs showing the extent of his crimes were sent to Winson Green prison. I was not too surprised when Tony Hobson asked to see me. Now ashen faced, as prison pallor had set in, he said: 'You've done for me.'

Feigning surprise, I said, 'What do you mean, Tony?'

'That bloody report you sent down. I was talking with one of the assis-tant governors and he's told me I'll never get out if the police suspect me of other crimes.'

Tongue in cheek, and well aware we had him cornered, I said: 'Well, Tony, perhaps the best thing you can do is to tell us the truth of what hap-pened that night.'

Hobson drew a deep breath. He knew he had no alternative – the only hope he had in life was to get out of prison before the turn of the century.

'Elaine's grandfather was causing a lot of trouble between us. He kept accusing me of stealing his building society book and taking money out.'

'Did you?'

He said, 'Well, yes, but he did not know that for sure. I thought I would go to his house and sort it out with him. So I rode over on me bike and he let us in. It was late at night. We were in the kitchen. I was trying to convince him he was wrong. He was a stubborn old man and started shouting and carrying on, telling me he knew I'd stolen it and to get out of his house.

'Suddenly, we was fighting. I never hit him but he fell to the floor and was dead. I carried him upstairs and put him in the bath with a few inches of water in, rolled the kitchen mat up 'cos there was blood on it, turned lights and electric off and locked the house.

'I rode back to Garforth on bike with rug under me arm. I dumped it in a derelict house off Main Street.'

'The black scarf found in the kitchen was yours?'

'Yeah, that's right.'

'Did you go with the intention of killing him?'

'No, I thought I could reason with him, convince him it wasn't me, but I didn't. He must have had a heart attack.'

I knew he would not be going back to court, as with the absence of pre-meditation it could only amount to a manslaughter charge at best. James Woodhead's death might be regarded as a loose end by some, but to me it was finishing the job. It was right that his family should know the truth. They had suspected for some time that all was not right with the circum-stances of his death, and no doubt suspected Hobson of being involved.

The question has to be asked: did Tony Hobson commit any other murders? He could easily have done so. After murdering Chris Cooper, Hobson went not once but twice to his home that night, the first time to steal the cameras, the second to lay a false trail. Just as he had with the forged David Hirst letter and the staged burglary, he wanted to deflect attention. He coolly let himself into the house while Val Cooper slept, turned on the gas fire without lighting it, and also the cooker rings. The effect of this would have been a massive explosion when the red-hot rings finally ignited the gas-filled house.

The consequence would have been Val Cooper's death. Who would be suspected? Her absent husband, of course, who appeared to have made off after the dastardly deed. Val Cooper had not previously realised the bene-fits of being a light sleeper.

Hobson was an extraordinary character. He was likable, evident from his wide circle of male and female friends, but he was a killer. He was also charismatic, Garforth's very own Hell's Angel. The problem was he had a darker side to his nature. He lived by a different set of rules to the rest of us.

He reminded me of the story of the scorpion and the frog. The scorpion wanted to cross the river. He asked the frog to carry him over on his back. 'No,' said the frog, 'you will sting me and I will die.' 'I promise you I won't,' said the scorpion. 'OK,' said the frog, and he let the scorpion jump onto his back. In the middle of the river, where it was deepest and fastest flowing, the scorpion stung the frog. As the frog rolled over dying, he looked up at the scorpion and said, 'Why did you do that? We will both die now.' The scorpion said: 'I'm sorry but I couldn't help myself. It's in my nature, you see.'

Paul Anthony Hobson died in Hull prison of cancer before he saw in the millennium. The prison staff regarded him as a model prisoner.

# chapter seven

# THE NEWLY-WED RAPIST

## 26 October 1992

It had been a great evening. The pub was a laugh and she'd enjoyed a few dances with her two girlfriends at the nightclub.

It was after 1 am and she was ready for bed, but she would have to walk home alone after one of the girls had fallen ill and the other had taken her home. It'd be OK, there were plenty of people about, even at 1.50 am. That was one of the advantages of living near the university.

She was just ten yards from a parade of shops at the busy junction when she left the main path at the side of the park to go up a track cutting across the corner behind the shops.

Suddenly, a hooded man pounced from behind and pushed her so violently in her back that she fell to the ground. One hand gripped her throat, the other covered her mouth to stifle the scream welling up inside her.

'He flipped me over onto my back and covered my eyes. As he lay on top of me, I could hear his heart beating,' said the student. Struggling for all her worth, she tried to punch him until he leant over and whispered in her ear: 'Carry on doing that or make a sound and I'll kill you.'

He dragged her in a headlock to an area of four-foot-high bushes, laid her on her back and knelt astride her legs, using his body weight to pin her down.

As she lay in the cold and darkness wondering about her fate, he began quizzing her. 'How old are you?' 'Eighteen,' she said. 'Have you done it before?' 'Yes,' she said, understanding exactly what he was getting at.

He ordered her to sit up, put her left hand on the ground behind her and the other around his waist. He pulled his trousers down to his knees and forced his penis into her mouth, moving it in and out until it became fully erect. He took it out and pulled her jeans down to her ankles.

'I'll kill you if you do not do what I want,' he said as he pulled up her T-shirt and exposed her breasts. He put his hand between her legs and started rubbing her vagina with his fingers, before forcing his fingers inside her.

It was a chilly night. She told him she was cold, so he pulled her T-shirt down, after he had fondled her breasts.

Then he forced himself inside her but withdrew almost immediately without ejaculating and told her to sit up. He again put his penis in her mouth and moved it backward and forwards as he also touched her between her legs.

After a short while he ejaculated into her mouth, causing her immediately to swallow. He coolly got up, pulled up his trousers and walked off, leaving his victim spitting out what was left in her mouth and rubbing her lips on her sleeve.

He started running until he reached the edge of the park. As he stopped to catch his breath before crossing the road to his car, he thought he'd better get back home to his wife. After all, they'd only been married a month.

When I took up my superintendent's post at Millgarth four months earlier, I was told of three sex attacks in an area on the edge of the city centre known as Woodhouse Moor, just next to Leeds University.

Woodhouse Lane passes the university and cuts through Woodhouse Moor. On one side of the road is barren wasteland used for carparking and staging fairground events; on the other is Hyde Park, with tennis courts, a bowling green and large expanses of grass, trees and shrubbery, about a half-mile square. The road is busy twenty-four hours a day and the area is densely populated with students.

The university had suffered badly through the Yorkshire Ripper's seven-year reign of terror, as many female students understandably did not want to come to Leeds. Ten years on and it looked as if another serial sex attacker was on the prowl. There had been three attacks, the first in October 1990 and the next two just twenty-three hours apart on the same day, Saturday, 29 June, nine days before I arrived at my new posting.

The common factors in all the attacks were that they had happened at night and in a particular part of Hyde Park. The attacker was usually hooded and he swooped on his unsuspecting quarry from the darkness of the park, literally plucking them from the safety of the footpath before dragging them like the prey of a hunting animal into the centre of the park to sexually feast on the victim.

A twenty-two-year-old student was the first victim, in October 1990. She began her Wednesday night out by attending a twenty-first birthday party held near the university, and then went to the university bar.

Her evening ended as she left News Night club in Leeds City Square at 12.15 am and decided to walk to her home near the university. She had no reason to be worried as her route was along a well-lit main road with plenty of passing traffic.

It was a cold, rainy night, so she decided to take a short cut through the park. Leaving the footpath, she could still see the main road but was now in the eerie blackness of the park. Suddenly there was someone behind her who pushed her onto the grass. Her attacker, a man, pinned her to the ground by lying over her and placing his hand across her mouth. As she desperately fought, kicking out and screaming, he told her to shut up.

As her energy drained away and her efforts to struggle free failed, he undid her jeans and pulled them down with her knickers to her knees. He forced his fingers into her vagina, undid his trousers, pulled out his penis and commanded: 'Suck it.'

Desperate to get him to stop, she moved her head from side to side to stop him forcing his penis in her mouth. As her strength returned, she began twisting and turning her body and trying to cross her legs.

Her spirited fight was causing him problems, so he gave up on his assault and ran off into the darkness. The shocked and dishevelled student ran to her home. She had put up such a struggle that she was bruised all over her body. She had also lost her earrings.

She reported the attack to the police and described the attacker as white, around five foot nine inches, of medium build and aged twenty to thirty. He had short, straight dark brown hair and was clean shaven. He spoke with a local accent and wore dark casual clothing. She was not sure whether he wore a mask, a scarf or a hood.

The investigation into this attack did not produce any suspects and was recorded as indecent assault and assault occasioning actual bodily harm. I wondered why, given the clear nature of the man's intentions, it wasn't recorded as an attempted rape.

The next attack was eight months later on 28 June, the last day of the summer term. A twenty-three-year-old psychology student had been to a party to celebrate the end of her finals, then to the university bar before going to a disco in the refectory next door.

Around half past midnight she set off to walk home. She lived near the first victim, just off Hyde Park Road, and her route home was the same.

As she walked along Woodhouse Lane, she decided to walk on the grass, a few feet from the footpath.

As she reached the end of the park, she decided, like the first victim, to take a similar short cut between the tennis courts and the back of the shops at the junction, opting for the quicker rather than the safer route.

She had gone only a short distance when she was suddenly and violently grabbed from behind and a hand in a woollen glove was placed over her mouth as she was pulled backwards, causing her to fall on the stony ground. In an instant her attacker was kneeling on her knees with so much force she could not move.

Through the murky darkness, she could see he had a Balaclava over his face, but could make out he was dark skinned. In a voice with a foreign lilt to it, he said: 'You do what I want – or I kill you.' Over and over again, he told her: 'I won't hurt you if you do what I want.'

Frightened, pinned down and struggling to breathe, she wondered what was to befall her. 'I'll do whatever you want me to do as long as you let me breathe,' she gasped. The struggle went on for an age, but she could not break free as he was too strong for her. Suddenly he had a knife in his hand, a small one with a two- to three-inch blade. In a threatening but strange fashion, he ran the tip of the knife gently up her left arm, across her neck and down the front of her blouse.

'I put my hands on his thighs saying I wanted what he wanted, trying to calm him. I was terrified I was going to be killed or raped. He did not speak as he unzipped his trousers and pulled out his erect penis. He was still kneeling on my legs as he put it in my mouth and moved it backward and forward, though he did not ejaculate.'

Then the mood changed as he made her stand up and led her into the depths of the park to a more secluded part. But she bravely sensed this was her opportunity to escape. She slipped out of her coat and ran for her life towards her home, which was seconds away. She reached her street and banged desperately at the door of a friend's house, but there was no answer.

As she turned to run to another house, she came face to face with her attacker, who was waiting for her. It must be every woman's nightmare. She thought she had escaped him but there he was at the gate, still clad in his Balaclava and gloves. He rushed at her, grabbed her again and threw her on the grass, where he knelt astride her.

With strength coming from panic and fright, she managed to get him off her and escape, running through the gardens in the street, screaming for help, cutting and bruising herself on bushes as she fled. She hammered on windows with her fists as she fled, climbed over a high wall and sprained an ankle, but still no one came to her help. In a final act of desperation, she picked up a brick and threw it through a window to get someone's attention. At this, her attacker fled into the night.

The police were informed but a search of the park and surrounding area revealed only her discarded coat. She described her attacker as of average build and speaking in stilted English, making her believe he was possibly of Asian descent.

The location and similarities with the previous attacks led the police to believe they were by the same man, but for one major difference. In the first case the victim had thought her attacker was white.

The ink was hardly dry on the second victim's statement when he struck again.

A waitress from a pub in the Leeds suburbs had travelled into the city centre for a meal with her boyfriend but, as they had argued, she decided to walk home alone. Her journey took her past the university and onto the path in the park which ran ten yards from and parallel to the one along Woodhouse Lane.

It was 11.45 pm on Saturday, 29 June 1991, and just twenty-three hours after the last attack, which the twenty-year-old waitress was oblivious to. The road was quiet, but she had the comfort of the constant flow of passing traffic.

She suddenly noticed a man running parallel with her in the same direction, just behind her but deeper in the park. Then, like a swooping peregrine falcon, he homed in on his prey. He changed his course so that he was now running directly at her. She barely had time to think before he grabbed her from behind.

As with the others, he put one arm round her neck and his other hand over her mouth to silence her screaming, and dragged her into the darkness. She could feel the texture of the knitted glove across her mouth and tried to bite it to force him to free his grip, but this had no effect.

As she struggled, he punched her in the eye. She screamed as two passing walkers came close by. This was enough to spook her attacker and, as she wriggled free of his grasp, he ran away.

The waitress was left badly shaken, her face and hands covered in blood and her eye swollen and bruised. She also described her attacker as of Asian origin and stocky build, wearing a Balaclava.

There was one feature she remembered that stood out about him. 'His eyes. They were wide, dark and very frightening,' she said.

As I studied the cases, I considered that his technique was like that of a beast lurking in the darkness of the park, waiting for a victim. How many more women had he eyed up who had been saved by passing traffic?

The three attacks displayed a pattern. He had not raped any of his victims but only because they had put up such spirited fights and he was disturbed. It was not difficult to guess that his endgame was rape.

He must be regarded as dangerous. There was no pattern in the times or days on which the attacks happened. The park was the only linking factor, but we could not guard it for 365 days a year.

Nine months passed before he struck again, at 9.20 pm on 19 March 1992. A nineteen-year-old student left the university halls of residence to go for a walk. She went along Woodhouse Lane in full view of the busy main road. Halfway down the road, she glanced over her shoulder and saw a man running towards her from the middle of the park. Before she realised what was happening, he grabbed her clothing and pushed her to the ground.

He had stalked his prey, waiting for an opportunity to strike just as he had with the last victim. When his chance came, he ran at her very fast and pounced on her before she had a chance to recognise the danger and take evasive action.

He knelt over her, pinned her to the ground and put his gloved hand over her mouth. She struggled with all her might but he was too strong as he turned her onto her stomach and punched her twice on the head in an attempt to subdue her.

She could not breathe and thought she was going to die, only stopping struggling when he shouted: 'Stop it or I'll suffocate you to death.' She was then turned over onto her back and dragged farther into the park.

Her attacker then pulled up her T-shirt and undid her dungarees, but couldn't get them off.

'Be quiet. If you don't struggle, I won't hurt you,' he said, as he pushed his hand inside her knickers and forced his fingers into her vagina. He pushed up her bra and sucked each of her nipples in turn while still keeping his hand over her mouth.

He unzipped his trousers, took out his erect penis and put it in her mouth. 'Suck it, lick it,' he ordered. She did as he said. She was too scared not to, and was thinking that whatever else he had planned he would surely kill her. After about ten minutes he ejaculated and she instinctively spat out the contents, wiping her mouth on her sleeve. He stood up, fastened his trousers and briskly walked out of the park.

She had endured a vile and degrading attack but she was alive. One of her eyes was swollen and bloodshot where he had punched her. Her keyring was missing, and she believed she had lost it in the struggle.

The attacker was said to be of mixed race, muscular build and in his twenties. Dressed all in black, he wore a scarf across his face with a woollen hat or Balaclava. He spoke good English but with a foreign accent.

I was running the investigation from Millgarth CID office. We had no suspects and no connections between the women, apart from the fact that two had been to the university bar just before being attacked and all three had walked past the university.

Did the attacker live locally? Was the victims' route overlooked from his home or a coffee bar he used? I thought it more likely that he travelled into the area from near by, having chosen it because it had two essential ingredients – the park with its trees and bushes providing cover for his stalking, and the number of lone women who would be passing by within easy attacking distance.

I got my first breakthrough when a forensic examination of the last victim's clothes revealed a DNA profile. It had been obtained from saliva mixed with semen from a stain on her sweatshirt sleeve where she had wiped her mouth after the assault. With it came the downside – we had no major suspects to test the DNA profile on and we were struggling with only half-decent descriptions of the attacker.

The ferocity of the assaults seemed to be escalating, as with each he appeared to refine his method of attack. This in itself suggested these attacks were his first. Had he committed previous attacks he would not be on a learning curve, refining his style, as he was now.

Just over two months later, on 26 May 1992, he attacked for the fifth time, though it was not reported for several months. The victim was another student. The twenty-six-year-old had met friends for a drink at a pub in the Merrion Centre.

She walked part of the way back home with friends but left them at 11.40 pm by the Fenton pub just below the university on Woodhouse Lane.

It was only a ten-minute walk home past the park. She did not feel threatened as she could be seen for several hundred yards from both directions.

Having walked about one-third of the distance down the side of the park, she saw a man running towards her. She could only just make out the black-garbed figure when he pounced. A hood and scarf covered his face, leaving only his eyes visible. He grabbed her from behind, locked an arm around her throat and dragged her into the park.

She struggled so violently that she broke free from his grasp, but as she sat up her attacker, kneeling behind on the grass, tried to grab her throat and put his hand over her mouth.

She had initially thought he was a handbag thief but the reality was dawning that this was not so. She was turned and laid face down on the grass while he sat on her back, pinning her down.

Attacks like this, so frightening and savage, can easily leave a victim frozen with terror as it dawns on them what is happening. Not so with this young woman. It was her attacker who was about to freeze. She grabbed his testicles, digging her fingernails in with strength reinforced by rage, and screamed out to two men who were walking a dog near by.

The attack ended as suddenly as it started. As the men walked over, the attacker ran off into the night. Despite what she'd been through, the victim shrugged off what had happened and did not report it to the police until she saw the publicity relating to the next attack, just a month after the perpetrator's marriage. The nineteen-year-old student who in October 1992 became the newly-wed's sixth victim described him as being of mixed race and wearing a black coat with a hood over his head and a black scarf across the lower part of his face.

Her watch was missing, and she presumed it had come off in the struggle. It was found near the scene of her attack when the park was searched.

Detectives from Millgarth CID had been making enquiries and keeping watch on the park after the last attack in March 1992, but were not there that night owing to the seven-month gap since the last incident.

Forensic examination of the sixth victim's clothing revealed a DNA profile of her attacker again obtained from a stain on the victim's sleeve where she had wiped her mouth after the attack. It was the same profile as the one obtained after the March attack.

The university and Students Union were obviously concerned by the attacks and the risks to female students, as the shadow of the Ripper's reign once again shrouded the area. This latest attack was the most violent of all and had, as I feared, progressed to rape.

An incident room was set up at Millgarth and the inquiry was put on the Holmes computer system. The Task Force, a specially trained unit of uniformed officers, was called in to undertake house-to-house enquiries. Its job was to log occupants of the houses around the park so we could check whether any met the suspect criteria and decide whether to take a sample from them for a DNA profile.

The difficulty was that the suspect criteria I had were vague, as I had so little to work on. I set them as non-white male, eighteen to thirty, taller than five foot four. Many of my colleagues thought he might live within walking distance of the park, and that was why the attacks took place there.

He might do, but equally I thought he could be attracted to the spot because of the abundance of young women who walked about the area alone late at night. But common sense dictated that I needed to ensure that the suspect was neither a local resident nor another student before looking farther afield.

The late-night timings of most of the attacks ruled out the use of public transport for the rapist to get home, so he either walked or had transport, a car or a motorcycle, though none was seen.

Only the first woman had described her attacker as white. Was she mistaken, or was this attack not part of the series?

His tally of victims was growing. His motive was clearly sexual and his method rarely differed, though one unusual feature was how he knelt on the women's legs to immobilise them. All the women had been walking down the same stretch of road and there were similarities in their profiles.

Three victims were students and one an ex-student. Was the attacker a student himself? This could be the reason for the Balaclava, as he might be recognised on campus, or was it just a precautionary measure?

I spoke to the Students Union and senior members of faculty about what could be done to reduce the risks to female students. Women-only buses were arranged, and personal attack alarms were given to female students.

They were also given advice on what they could do to minimise risk. The difficulty I faced was that, because we were trying to catch the attacker rather than scare him off, our activities were not visible, and so students were left with the feeling that we were not doing anything. The attacker could be at the university, so we had to be careful how much we told the students, as it could be counterproductive if it got back to him.

Observations of the park area involved officers on the roofs of university buildings, and we deployed policewomen as decoys to try to flush the attacker out. It was a large area to cover, and unless my officers held hands and physically ringed the park I could not guarantee that he could not slip in or out without being seen, so we concentrated on observing the roadside footpath from where he grabbed most of his victims.

House-to-house enquiries were problematic as many of the addresses around the park were bed-sits. Given also the existence of a sizable multi-racial community in the area, and little to eliminate suspects by way of description, it looked as if this was going to be long slog. Sex attackers of this type rarely go away. They go on and on until they are caught, but we could not wait years with his list of victims growing.

My next major step was a blooding, where we would try to get DNA samples from all male residents in the immediate area who fitted the suspect profile and who could not be satisfactorily eliminated by other means. Before we did that, we needed to know who exactly lived in the area, so we would be aware if our suspect had left before we got to him. In an area with such a large transient population this would be a difficult task.

Although the inquiry team had been expanded to include officers from other divisions in Leeds, little positive progress was being made. The extensive media coverage had brought an offer of help from Professor David Cantor, an expert in offender profiling. He theorised that the attacker was either a 'marauder rapist', attacking women near his home, or a 'commuter rapist' who might live miles away and was travelling to the area to carry out his attacks. An interesting theory, I thought. It's a bit like a race with only two horses – putting £10 on each, you can't lose. I think I left it on the basis of don't call us, we'll call you.

I had already considered both possibilities and did not discount either, as each had plus points. The possibility of the attacker travelling some distance was the more daunting prospect, as it was the difference between our suspect being a fish in a small local pond and him being in the North Sea. The former could be managed; the latter was a major problem.

If he did not live in the immediate area, our best chance to catch him was when he returned to commit a further offence. Officers were watching the park with night-sights, spending hours in subzero temperatures, but our man did not reappear. The massive media coverage may have put him off. The question was, would he return at some later stage, as he had done before, or find another place to pursue his sick criminal venture?

Christmas loomed, and the majority of students went home for the festive break. In their absence, the threat level was assessed as much lower, so the inquiry was scaled down until the new term started.

So when I returned to work on 4 January I was devastated to be told that there had been another attack. The victim this time was a girl of sixteen. The attack had taken place at 9.30 pm on Saturday, 2 January, but owing to her distress she did not report it for two days.

She lived in a community home on the outskirts of Leeds, and said she had been shopping in the city that Saturday. She went to the Merrion Centre, where two of the previous victims had been, and spent the day meeting friends and 'dossing around'.

After going to a bowling alley, she set off home towards Hyde Park at 8.45 pm. Her route was not that taken by the other victims. She went through Leeds General Infirmary and out the other side onto Clarendon Road, which leads to the other side of Hyde Park from where the previous victims were assaulted.

On arriving at the park, she decided to walk diagonally through the murky depths of its centre. As she was explaining to us how she neared the bowling green in the park, she suddenly ended the police interview, saying she was too exhausted to go on.

She continued her statement at 10 am the next day. While we were conscious of the trauma she had suffered, we were badly in need of information. We had the basic facts, but that was not even enough for us to confidently go to the press with a description.

Her statement picked up from where she had left off. It was 9.35 pm, and as she neared the bowling green she heard a rustling sound behind her. As she was about to turn around, a hand came from behind and covered her mouth. She was too frightened to scream or react in any way.

RIGHT Peter Sutcliffe, the Yorkshire Ripper (now Peter Coonan). (*Yorkshire Evening Post*)

BELOW Hell's Angel murder inquiry team. Back row, left to right: Chris the JCB driver, Geoff Darley and me. (*Ron Burks*)

ABOVE Tony Hobson, Hell's Angel triple killer (far left) and Andrew Mark Watson (third from left) at Watson's wedding. (picture research by *Phil Callaghan*)

LEFT David Jackson, the Woodhouse rapist. (*Yorkshire Evening Post*)

Her attacker dragged her to a grassy area, pushed her onto the ground and sat astride her as she lay on her back with his knees trapping her upper forearms to her sides.

The manner in which he pinned her down was particularly significant. It was exactly how he had used his body weight to pin his previous victim down.

She screamed hysterically and lashed out with her legs, but his weight and superior strength overpowered her, she said. The graphic detail of the attack unfolded in her statement, and I shuddered at the horror of the girl's ordeal, which culminated in her attacker raping her before coolly walking off, leaving her lying on the ground.

Shaking and crying from what she had endured, she decided not to report it to the police then and there but to return to the community home. By the time she boarded the bus, she said she had stopped crying but was still very distressed. After arriving home, she took a bath.

Although she had ample opportunity to report the attack to the home's staff or her friends, she did neither, and it was only because of her bizarre behaviour the next morning that matters came to a head.

During the course of that Sunday, she kicked her key worker when he told her off for scratching a table. She then took a razor blade from her room and repeatedly slashed her left forearm, explaining her actions in her later statement as a means of dealing with her anger owing to her inability to verbally express her feelings.

At midnight on Sunday she asked another girl, 'What happens when you tell someone you've been raped?' Her comments were passed on to her key worker, and the next morning specially trained officers from the Child Abuse Unit arrived. Although she was medically examined there was little hope that any forensic evidence would be found owing to the thirty-six-hour delay in reporting the attack.

She described her attacker as Asian, aged twenty to twenty-five, taller than her (she was five foot four), slim with short hair and a wispy moustache. While vague, it was similar to the other victims' descriptions, but in this case the attacker had not covered his face. There was a chance this girl could provide a good E-fit picture of our man.

It took an inordinately long time to complete the victim's statement. As I studied it, I picked out the points that indicated to me it was probably the same attacker. The place was right, in that it had happened in the park, albeit on the opposite side from the others.

But I had mixed feelings when I finished reading her statement. There were sufficient similarities with previous attacks to fully exploit the media publicity, both to find the attacker and to warn women in the area. The attack had raised the stakes at the university, which was voicing its concern at our inability to catch the attacker.

But experience taught me to treat her statement with caution. It is difficult as an investigator to equate what rape victims do and what we feel they should have done. The shock and trauma of an attack can have strange and varied effects on people, but I felt that somehow this was different. She reported the rape late, causing the loss of both medical and forensic evidence. She did not describe any conversation on the part of the attacker, yet in all the other incidents he had talked, albeit aggressively.

It was not just a case of trauma freezing her memory, as she recalled in great detail all the physical aspects of the rape. The attacker had spoken to the other six victims, as no doubt it excited him to converse with them during his assault. To my mind, it was an essential, integral part of the whole attack for him to talk to them, either to express his control and accentuate his feeling of power, or to try to humanise the whole thing in his mind, as if it were a kiss and a cuddle with a girlfriend.

A different type of attacker might use silence in a threatening manner and gain pleasure and a sense of power from terrifying his victim in this way.

The girl told how cold and frosty the night was and how hard the ground was, yet for all the writhing and struggling in the ten-minute encounter, this slightly built teenager had just one bruise above her right knee and another on her inner left thigh. The absence of injuries would not in itself have been a problem if she had said she simply succumbed to his superior strength and gave in to his wishes, but she said she fought like a tiger.

While I was sceptical about her statement I had no choice but to run with this as a genuine attack and accept the probability that it was the same man, now branded the Woodhouse Rapist by the media.

The attacks had generated such media interest that at six o'clock on the Tuesday night I was interviewed live by *Calendar News* for Yorkshire TV. I tried to put across the many similarities in the attacks, stressing that the police were doing everything they could, and warned women not only around the park but in the whole of Leeds not to go out alone in the hours of darkness.

I expected that the attacker, more than likely a Leeds man, would be watching the news, taking in what I was saying about him and what was happening with regard to police activity in the area. In these cases the balance always needs to be struck between keeping what we are doing a secret and setting a trap for the attacker, and being open and letting the public know what is happening, so women can take the necessary precautions to avoid becoming victims.

Whether or not the latest attack was connected was significant, but only to the extent that we might be looking for two men. I had nothing but the sixteen-year-old's word that she was attacked, no corroboration such as supporting forensic or medical evidence. Whether I believed her or not was immaterial; we would need to verify her every move that day, especially during the hours before and after the attack. I needed to know her story was watertight, so would have to sensitively test her statement. Might the bus driver remember her, a slightly built young girl getting on the bus dishevelled and distressed?

The inquiry into the latest attack went into its second week with little progress, but events were about to take a different course when I walked into my office on 14 January and my secretary handed me a pile of mail. Flicking through, I noticed one letter addressed to Det. Supt B. Taylor, Millgarth Police Station, Leeds LS2. It had arrived the previous day, which I had taken off.

My secretary, Sally Hughes, routinely opened my mail unless it was marked 'private and confidential', which this was not. Reading the letter, she realised its importance to our rape inquiry. Sally had the foresight to take it to the incident room, where a senior member of the team read it. He did not regard it as significant and gave it back to Sally to put in my pile of mail.

I had only thirty minutes before I was due to do a TV interview in the incident room, so I quickly scanned the letter. My first instinct was that it was probably a sick joke because it was signed 'Jack the Stripper'. It was not uncommon to get letters from cranks, most of which were filed without any action. But as I sat and read it through a second time, I began to get a feeling that this was no hoax.

DET SUPT TAYLOR
I'M THE ONE YOU'RE LOOKING FOR REGARDING MOST OF THE INCIDENTS ON WOODHOUSE MOOR. IF YOU DON'T BELIEVE ME CHECK THESE FACTS. THE GIRL I GOT IN MARCH '92 HAD SHOULDER LENGTH BLONDE HAIR

AND WAS WEARING A DARK DUNGAREE STYLE OUTFIT UNDER HER COAT. I TOOK HER KEYS OF HER. THE GIRL I GOT IN OCTOBER '92 HAD BROWN PERMED HAIR BEYOND HER SHOULDERS SHE WORE A WOOLEN CARDIGAN AND CASUAL TROUSERS. I MADE BOTH OF THEM DO ORAL. THE OCTOBER GIRL WAS LYING WHEN SHE SAID THAT I RAPED HER. AS YET I HAVE NOT RAPED ANYBODY, WHICH BRINGS ME TO MY NEXT POINT. THE JOKER WHO RAPED THE GIRL ON JANUARY 2ND '93 WAS NOT ME HE WAS JUMPING ON THE BAND WAGON. HE WAS A FOOL, HE SHOWED HIS FACE.

YOURS SINCERELY
JACK THE STRIPPER

I knew full well that I had not released any information about the victims' appearance or clothes. The letter referred to the two attacks linked by DNA. Although I had been pressed in media interviews, there was one important feature of the attacks I had never revealed – all the victims had long hair, just as the writer had described. How could he know?

I considered that long hair was one of the criteria he used to select his victims. It ensured he did not snare his prey only to find he was grappling with a male, who might bring his reign of terror to an abrupt end with a well-placed punch.

I checked my notes. The March victim did have blond hair and dungarees and, more importantly, she did lose her keys in the struggle. The letter-writer said he had taken them. Most of the description of the October victim's clothing was also right, except she wore a jacket, which he no doubt mistook for a cardigan.

What was the point of the letter? Was he mocking us or was it indignation at being accused of the attack on the sixteen-year-old, which he was not responsible for? I was not happy with his phrase '. . . as yet I have not raped anybody'. I took it as a warning that he had no intention of stopping his attacks. He might not think what he had done was rape but it certainly was in the eyes of the law, which deems rape to be penetration to the slightest degree of the female vagina by a male's penis. Ejaculation is not necessary.

To write personally to me suggested he was pretty confident of not being caught. He'd obviously not heard about Michael Sams. When word got round my team that a suspect had again written to me, one of them, DS John Church, announced to the incident room: 'Lucky Bob strikes again.' The nickname has stuck with me ever since.

I was excited by the letter, which was a major breakthrough. On the face of it, it told me nothing about him; however, it might enable us to connect him to the letter later if I could get a fingerprint or DNA, and now we also had a sample of his handwriting.

I put the letter into a plastic bag, sealed and signed it RET 1 as an exhibit, and then went swiftly to the incident room. This little gem would not be mentioned in my TV interview, which was now only five minutes off.

As I walked into the room, BBC North were setting up their camera. I exchanged pleasantries and moved over to my deputy, DCI Gordon Garfit, and told him about the letter. Roger Pearson, a sergeant who had a pivotal role on the inquiry, reading statements and actioning enquiries, took the letter to arrange for the necessary tests. The first would be ESDA, a method used to reveal impressions on paper, which might reveal indentations, as it had on one of Sams's letters, highlighting the 'Phil and Mavis' message.

The TV interview went ahead but at times my mind was on the letter. I was asked a question which referred to the two universities in Leeds, and I simply could not remember the name of the other establishment, which adjoins Leeds University, even though I had studied there for a law degree only a few years before. Once I had focused my mind on the fact that it was Leeds and Leeds Metropolitan Universities, I started the interview again.

Everything in an inquiry is deemed urgent, so when you get something that genuinely is urgent it is often dealt with routinely. The letter went for ESDA testing, and when there was no immediate response I assumed there was nothing of interest on it and put it to the back of my mind.

But on Monday, 18 January, my week got off to a good start when news came through that we might have something. The sheet of paper Jack the Stripper had used to write his missive on came from a pad and bore indentations of another letter, probably the one written before ours.

Roger Pearson was excited, to say the least. He patiently separated the two to try to find any details of an address from the indented letter.

He also found an indented but unreadable signature, preceded with the initials D M, but was particularly thrilled at being able to decipher part of a name and address. The words 'Mr Jack ...', part of a two-figure number beginning with a 2, and the first part of a street name, Neville, were high-lighted.

I knew Leeds well and was aware of a number of streets named Neville, but with the part of the postcode we had Roger pinned it down further and worked out that it all fitted a man called David Martin Jackson, of Neville View in East Leeds. The Department of Social Security confirmed Jackson's signature from documents they held, and checks showed that it matched the indentation with the DM initials.

Jackson was of mixed race, and this was consistent with most of the vic-tims' descriptions. He fitted the general description but this was vague, and we were struggling to get background information about him. We could find no record of past criminal conduct; it appeared he was just a very ordinary person.

He had married in September 1992. If he was our man, he had com-mitted the October attack within days of returning from his honeymoon. He was also a member of the New Testament Church of God in Leeds, near where his new in-laws, who were decent people and central figures in the church, lived.

It all seemed wrong. Surely this young newly-wed was not our man, a rapist? The house was at the end of a cul-de-sac and in an area where we could not guarantee confidentiality, so we would not make any covert enquiries with neighbours. I spoke to the community constable to see whether there was anyone he knew who could be approached, but there wasn't.

The only neighbours who can be trusted are those who are introduced to us through a mutual contact, or someone who does not like the person we are asking about. But without an introduction you will not find that out until you knock on their door and expose your hand. Even if you do it in the guise of being from, say, the Department of Social Security, the neighbours will invariably tell the subject, especially when he is as clean cut and respectable as Jackson seemed to be.

After gathering as much information as we could on him without knocking on his door, I sat and read about my latest pen-pal. We had a letter containing information about two of the victims, which could only be known to a police officer or the attacker. I was reasonably happy the letter was not from a hoaxer or a police officer being vindictive or out for a laugh.

The letter connected the attacker in some way to Jackson, who had without doubt written the penultimate letter on the writing pad. There was the additional pressure that to delay taking action might put other women at risk.

Jackson would have to be seen. He was either our attacker or had a strong link to him. We had little prospect of any of the victims identifying this man if it was him. I decided our line of questioning must be to see whether he had an alibi for any of the attack dates. Did his handwriting match the letter and was his DNA a match?

The description of the attacker's clothes was not good but I needed to know whether he had worn, or his friends or relatives had seen him in, similar clothing. I would get family photos at the house checked as they might also give useful evidence. Any clothing could reveal hair or fibres linking the victims to him.

Thursday, 21 January 1993 was the day set for the arrest. I still did not know as much about Jackson as I would have liked, but I could not afford nor wished to delay any further. We'd be at the house at 6.30 am to ensure we did not miss our quarry.

I knew we could talk to him until we were blue in the face, but if his blood didn't match, and he could explain the indentation of his address and signature on the letter, he was the wrong man, and we would need his co-operation to find the person linked to him who was the real attacker.

At 6.35 am, David Martin Jackson was arrested at his home in Neville View, which he shared with his wife of four months, Jennifer. During a search of the two-bedroom semi, a Leeds street map was found with a card marking the page featuring Hyde Park and the adjoining Woodhouse Moor, as well as a notepad of the type on which the letter to me had been written.

Derby-born Jackson and Jennifer, a twenty-eight-year-old nurse, appeared shocked at the allegations. He was taken to Millgarth. John Church had been involved in the case from the very start, so I decided that he and DC Joanne Regan would interview Jackson.

Joanne was a natural choice. She was an excellent detective, and her presence during the interview of a man I believed to be a rapist, who took pleasure in the control and sexual dominance of women, would unsettle him. It was a tactical, psychological move. It could backfire as he might be too embarrassed to talk about such matters to a woman, but I was prepared to give it a go.

The interviews began, and he soon confessed to the 1992 March and October attacks when confronted with the likelihood of his DNA matching the attacker's and the letter linking him to the crimes. 'Yeah, I did attack them two. I did make them give me oral sex, but I didn't rape the second one,' he said.

He admitted what he thought we could prove, though his denial of rape was probably due to his ignorance of the law. He also emphatically denied attacking the sixteen-year-old and all the others.

He was asked about the letter. 'I wrote it. It was stupid. I wanted you to know that I didn't do the one in January and there was a real rapist out there.' How considerate and helpful of Jackson, a serial sex attacker, to let me know there was another about, I mused.

We did not need to wait for the DNA result to charge him. He had admitted two attacks and to writing the letter and had no alibis for the dates of any of the assaults except the one in January 1993, when he claimed to be at Long Eaton in Derbyshire with his family. I was not surprised at this, as I was already having serious doubts about the last incident.

Jackson was charged with all the assaults except that on the sixteen-year-old and was remanded in custody. Sure enough, a couple of weeks later DNA analysis of his blood matched the DNA found on the victims' clothes.

I felt that the two attacks for which we had DNA evidence would provide the cornerstone of our prosecution case, and we would use the legal precedent of 'similar facts evidence' to show that there were indisputable similarities with the others.

The cracks began to appear in the sixteen-year-old's story. When her three friends were seen, they agreed with everything she said apart from her walking home alone. One said she went home with her and they caught a bus forty-five minutes before she claimed she was attacked.

The bus she said she caught after she was attacked actually passed by some fifteen minutes earlier, which would have been before her alleged rape. There was now sufficient doubt to challenge her version of events. She was brought to the police station and interviewed, but even in the face of strong evidence to contradict her rape claim, she stuck to her story and was reported for wasting police time, as we were more than satisfied that she had made up the whole story to fit with what she had read in the papers.

But ironically she had been the unwitting catalyst that prompted Jackson to write to me, and so led me to his door. I did not have much time to dwell on the success of Jackson's arrest as the following day I was called to the scene of the murder of eighty-four-year-old William Collins.

It never surprises me that anyone expecting a lengthy jail sentence pleads not guilty, especially for sexual offences. Jackson would lose everything if proven to be a rapist, his wife included, I didn't doubt. She could hardly be impressed to find that within one week of returning from honeymoon her new husband was masked in a Balaclava and scarf and preparing to rape a young woman.

The jury system in my mind has little to offer twenty-first-century justice. Juries are outdated and ineffectual to the point that at times their decisions are outrageous. The concept of the accused being tried by his village peers has long since lost its relevance. Most barristers I know prefer a jury, as it always offers a chance of an acquittal against the odds and makes advocacy more exciting.

The judge, whatever his view, does not even come into play unless the jury announce a guilty verdict. It matters not how he directs the jury on the evidence and law if they choose to ignore him and go down the route of 'a nice lad like that couldn't have committed these crimes' – all the hard work of the investigators and the prosecutor is for nought.

Hence, when I was told that Jackson would deny all charges, I just got on with the job in hand. The question was, what would be the basis of his defence? After all, he had admitted two offences.

Jackson had chosen one of the leading QCs on the northern circuit, Robert Smith, to defend him. Paul Worsley, QC, equally admired as an advocate, would prosecute.

The trial, due to last three weeks, was to be at Leeds Crown Court.

I knew that Jackson had provided alibi evidence for the March and May 1992 attacks, and was also claiming that, when two women were assaulted on one day in June 1991, he was at a Brighton religious convention. He had hidden behind a mask to commit his crimes; now he would use everything, even religion, to try to wriggle free.

His alibis were contrived. He was cunning – he knew he only had to sway the jury into believing one alibi for a DNA-linked attack and they would have to reject the other. His ploy was clever, as he could argue that, if he had fabricated his alibis, why hadn't he done the same for both DNA-linked attacks? So while I was initially surprised that he had not offered an alibi for the October 1992 DNA-linked attack, I knew exactly where he was coming from. Also, if he was providing an alibi for an attack for which we had DNA evidence, then he must be planning to challenge the DNA evidence by saying it was not a match with his.

Jackson would manipulate and use his wife Jennifer and his in-laws, Clotelle and Clarence Jones, to support his alibis. Ultimately it would be a matter for the jury to decide whether the evidence linking him to the crimes was convincing or whether Jackson was an innocent man. But if the jurors got it wrong a rapist would walk free.

If he had convinced family and friends that he was the victim of unscrupulous police officers hell-bent on ruining his marriage, career and life, then he was halfway home. Now he only had to convince a jury of this, and persuade them that he was a most unlikely candidate for a rapist. As a solid churchgoer and recently married with an attractive wife, why would he need to stalk young women?

I knew his problem was that he was unable to confront in his own mind what he had done. I had seen it before. It was easier for him to create a lie and believe it than confront the truth. He now actually believed he was innocent, which meant he could be convincing. The problem with living a lie was that he was bound to be found out. I was banking on him betraying to the jury the true inner man in some way.

Minutes before the trial commenced on 24 February 1994, I met Paul Worsley for our final conference. 'What do you think his defence will be?' he said. I had already thought long and hard about this. I knew his defence would be audacious, as the more outrageous it was the more believable it would be in his mind.

'His only defence,' I said, 'would be to suggest that a police officer has contaminated the March victim's clothes with his own sperm, sent them to forensics, where a DNA profile was obtained, then done the same with the October victim. He then sends a letter which links Jackson and, when he is arrested, the officer switches Jackson's blood sample for his own and sends it off to the lab. Bingo, they all match.'

Paul Worsley's response was predictable. 'That is too preposterous to consider.' I went on, 'There's more. The test forensics used to obtain Jackson's DNA does not work on semen from a man who's had a vasectomy. Apart from the forensic scientist, all the other men who could have swapped samples have had the snip.' I could see from Paul Worsley's face that he was not happy to follow this line.

The ambush defence, as the police call it, is when the accused pulls out his defence like a magician producing a rabbit from his hat late in the trial, usually building it around perceived weaknesses in the prosecution case.

Unfortunately we don't usually find out what it is until the defence puts its case towards the end of the trial, after the prosecution has concluded and therefore at a time when we are unable to rebut it. As it happens on the hoof, it does not permit prosecuting counsel time to prepare to cross-examine the accused and expose the flaws in his case. This would be one such case, I guessed.

And so the trial began, and Paul Worsley outlined the prosecution case. We had not included the very first attack in October 1990 as the victim had said her attacker was white, although later she said she was unsure. It was felt that its inclusion would undermine the prosecution case of 'similar fact' evidence. I do believe she was the first, but a combination of drink and the darkness probably blurred her vision of the attacker.

The first witness called was the victim from the first of the two attacks in June 1991. The court was packed as she made her way to the witness box, which faced the jury. The judge was to her left, Jackson to her right. As she read the oath, she burst into tears.

Although the prosecution took her through her evidence first, in a kind gesture designed to make her ordeal less arduous Robert Smith assured her that her account would not be disputed. Regrettably, it is usually essential to the prosecution case that the jury see the victims in order to personalise the facts and hear a first-hand account of the suffering, distress and horror the attacker subjected them to.

Paul Worsley could easily have read her statement to the jury, but this would have been unlikely to create the same impact as seeing the victim. In any event, if we had not called the victims, the defence, suspecting some ulterior motive, would not have accepted their written statements as evidence, and so would have forced them to be called anyway.

I was first called as a witness to prove the receipt of the letter and to explain why the investigation originally involved seven attacks, though Jackson was charged only with five. The defence was clearly seeking to suggest to the jury that there was another attacker operating in the same park.

Handwriting expert Anthony Stockton, from Wetherby forensic lab, was next. Referring to the Jack the Stripper letter, he was emphatic: 'It is my opinion that Mr Jackson was the author.' Robert Smith asked him whether he could exclude with certainty the possibility that some-one other than Jackson was the author. Mr Stockton replied, 'No, since I haven't sampled everyone's handwriting in the whole world and elim-inated them, that would be an impossible task to do.' He was adamant that the likelihood of anyone else being the author was so remote it could be ignored.

Scientist Mike Barber, who had performed the DNA analysis, gave evi-dence that the DNA from the clothes of the victims of the March and October 1992 attacks matched Jackson's DNA profile, which he had obtained from his blood sample, saying it was a one in 100 million chance of it being anyone else's.

I was by now feeling quietly confident, though I was uncertain what red herrings the defence would throw in. I was called back to the witness stand to be questioned over why I decided to execute the warrant at 6.30 am, and was accused of doing this to cause maximum distress to Jackson rather than it being a sensible move to be sure of finding him at home, which was our real aim.

I was unaware that the day we arrested Jackson was also his wife's birth-day, but when this was thrown in I could see where the defence was going. It was about to be suggested that the police had 'fitted up' Jackson. Even so, I had no worries; I had fitted up neither Jackson nor anyone else in my police career. I do not have a single worry that I will be wheeled out in a Bath chair to the Appeal Courts to be accused of some miscarriage of jus-tice in any of my cases. I believe competent investigations and prosecu-tions founded on fact are the best way to get the right verdict. It's what I've practised and preached throughout my entire career.

My original supposition that the defence would suggest that the police had tampered with Jackson's blood sample seemed to be taking shape when police surgeon Dr Judith Evans, who had taken his blood sample, was questioned in depth about the syringe she used to take his blood, which, after the needle and plunger handle were removed, had become the sample container. She was asked whether it could be tampered with. It could, she said.

Jackson's defence was becoming clearer.

DS John Church was to be cast in the villain's role by Jackson. Through his counsel, he alleged that John had been into his cell on an unauthorised visit to 'soften him up', though there was no other evidence to support this.

When the prosecution had finished, I had been called to the witness box on four occasions to give evidence and to clear up various points. I was content that we had made out a good case. It was now time for the defence to fire its Exocet missiles at us.

On the trial's seventh day, Jackson was escorted from the dock to the witness box. He had been remanded in prison custody from the day of his arrest, and this was the nearest he had been to freedom since then. His face displayed signs of the deep intensity of his character, and the searing gaze of his eyes betrayed the complexities of the inner man.

The witness box was at one end of the judge's bench and faced the two rows of jurors. A middle-aged man was in the direct sightline of Jackson's eyes, and bore the intimidating intensity of his stare to such an extent that only minutes after Jackson began his evidence he collapsed in his seat, ashen faced.

At first I thought he had suffered a heart attack, as another juror who said she was a nurse laid him out on the floor. An emergency ambulance crew took him, pale and breathing with the assistance of oxygen, to hospital in a wheelchair. I later discovered he had probably suffered a stress attack. He did not return and the jury was reduced to eleven.

Jackson began giving evidence. Portraying himself as a happily married man, he showed the jury photos of himself and Jennifer on their wedding day and on their Florida honeymoon. He said he'd courted his new wife for five years after meeting her at a church convention, regularly visited his in-laws and was a committed Christian.

But then the tempo increased as he declared: 'That is not my DNA. It is not my blood. An analysis of a fresh blood sample will clear me.' He was invoking the very suggestion I had put to Paul Worsley, which he had rejected as unthinkable.

British justice is insufficiently flexible for the judge to have taken the obvious course, which was to adjourn the trial and order a retest. If it had been, Jackson would not have used this defence. To add insult to injury, he also said: 'I have been begging my barrister to have my blood tested. I know the profile will be different to the profile they have got there. I know I am innocent.'

The jurors were given the unenviable task of deciding whether he had been falsely accused as a result of a dishonest police officer switching blood samples or whether these were the bare-faced lies of a sex attacker who would do anything but confront his guilt.

With a week left to run, and DNA testing then taking up to three weeks, a retest could not be conducted before the end of the trial. There were two options open to the judge – abandon the trial for another blood test or continue. He never gave it another thought, and the case proceeded. The defence was ridiculously simple. It had been shown that the sample could be tampered with as the ends of the syringe could be removed, but not that it actually had been. Jackson directed the blame onto a police officer switching samples.

Even when asked how he knew the contents of the Jack the Stripper letter, details of which he had described to the interviewing officers, he said: 'I was able to read it because one of the officers put it on the table in front of me.'

He dismissed the indentation on his notepad. 'I used the pad when working in Leeds Library. The real author must have written the letter using my pad.' His knowledge of the attacks came, he said, 'Because I followed the news coverage at the time.'

Cross-examining, Paul Worsley asked Jackson how, in interview, he had been able to correctly describe the March and October victims as slim women. Jackson's riposte was amazing: 'Well, you wouldn't rape a fat girl, would you?'

This was an incredibly insensitive and unpleasant comment; only his arrogance blinded him to that. I could see that he had offended the women jurors, particularly the plumpish forewoman. The thunder was plain to see in her face. Jackson's naivety had shown through once more. His indiscretion was not likely to endear him to a jury he was asking to believe that his confession was due to intimidation.

The defence case concluded with his wife Jennifer and her parents giving evidence. They related what they honestly believed when they said he could not be the attacker. Covering alibi times, he told them that he was either picking up Jennifer from her nursing shifts at the city's Seacroft Hospital or was at a religious convention in Brighton. I found out after the trial from someone who worked with Jennifer that Jackson never collected her from work. Her parents did, or she'd catch the bus.

Throughout the trial there was noticeable tension in the court gallery, which had been packed every day. The jury complained at one stage that Jackson's supporters, not family members, were giving them intimidating looks. These were also directed at myself and my colleagues, but we had experienced this many times before and ignored it, though I did sense that it could develop into a race issue of white police officers fabricating evidence against an innocent black man.

It has never failed to amaze me how an accused can so easily persuade their family and friends to rally round with dubious alibis when confronted with the assertion that the police have fitted them up, bullied or threatened them into a confession. The travesty was that I knew this was Jackson's DNA. His saying that his legal advisers had told him there would be no legal aid money for another test was just a smokescreen. I waited for the judge to intercede and ask Jackson whether he had considered paying for the test himself and to tell the jury the cost so they could put it all into perspective, but he didn't. I was amazed at this.

It cost only a few hundred pounds to have a DNA test done privately. Jackson had been in custody for fifteen months for crimes he claimed he did not commit. Even if it cost a few thousand pounds, if he was certain of his innocence he would have borrowed it, as he would know his DNA would not match. These matters were not explained to the jury but were left for them to work out.

It was simple. Either he had committed the crimes, some or all of them, and the alibis were mistaken or false, or this was not his DNA profile and the police had switched his blood sample.

The final speeches saw both barristers drive home the main points of their conflicting arguments. 'Someone has a guilty secret,' hinted Paul Worsley, while Robert Smith said the police involved in the case ranged from 'the efficient and patently honest ... Detective Superintendent Taylor heading the investigation to ... Detective Sergeant Church whose actions in this case leave much to be desired'.

This was a clever ploy – bull up the boss and take one of his junior officers off at the knees. John Church was a decent officer and felt unimaginably insulted that these allegations should be laid at his door. Would he be vindicated?

On 14 March 1994, the jury of six men and five women retired to consider their verdicts. After six hours deliberating, they returned guilty verdicts in relation to the indecent assault on the March 1993 victim and the rape and indecent assault of the October 1993 victim. These were linked by DNA.

There were still six charges for the jury to consider, and they were put in a hotel overnight to resume their deliberations the next day. This was a great result so far. The jury had clearly rejected the suggestion that

Jackson's blood sample was switched and the police were corrupt. They only had to consider now whether there were sufficient similarities to link these two attacks with the others.

The following day, just after 2.30 pm, the jury filed back into court and the forewoman stood up to deliver the remaining verdicts. The silence in the court was overpowering, the atmosphere laced with tension and hostility as we all waited.

Three of the victims were sitting in court to hear the spokeswoman declare that Jackson was guilty on all six outstanding charges. I looked at Jackson, who stood dispassionately as his fate was sealed.

Mr Justice Harrison then turned and spoke to him. 'You carried out a campaign of sex attacks that left young women afraid to go out at night. You came from a Christian family who you have let down.'

He was jailed for twelve years.

As I left the court, I saw a woman who had been in the public gallery every day giving a TV interview. I did not recognise her as part of his legal team, but she described herself as Grace Higgins, a member of the Society of Black Lawyers and the family solicitor.

She declared: 'We shall be pursuing an appeal at the earliest opportunity and we shall also be launching a nationwide campaign to free David Jackson. As far as we are concerned David is innocent of all charges brought against him.' Later Jackson's wife and family disassociated themselves from her comments.

There was talk of this being the biggest miscarriage of justice since the Tottenham Two. As all the attacks had taken place in the park adjacent to Woodhouse Moor, I wondered whether David Jackson was now the 'Woodhouse One'.

Why would a man embark on such a criminal course? He had a home, a loving family and a new wife, but he was prepared to gamble all this for sexual thrills. Whatever Jackson's sexual needs were, his relationship with his wife did not satisfy them. His actions were planned, as he chose a park on the other side of the city from where he lived but close enough to the main roads to escape before his victims could report what had occurred.

David Jackson is a Walter Mitty character. He described himself as a publisher specialising in computer textbooks, but this had little substance and in fact he was unemployed at the time of his arrest. While his wife worked late shifts at the hospital, Jackson pulled on his Balaclava and slipped into his fantasy world to carry out horrific crimes.

A glimpse of the real Jackson can be found in his early youth. At thirteen, he was seen by a neighbour staring into a young girl's bedroom from his Long Eaton home. 'He used to stand at the end of the garden and look into the bedroom of a house across the way,' the neighbour recalled. It was at this time he was given a police caution for indecent exposure when he flashed at passing schoolgirls from his bedroom window. Was this the germination of a slow-growing seed?

Jackson's appeals against conviction were rejected. He never showed a morsel of remorse, and no doubt still believes he was the victim of a police set-up. I do not know why he wrote the letter to me. Maybe it was ego, but his foolish boasts and arrogance gave me the positive lead I wanted. He served his sentence and was released in 2001, still claiming his innocence but without ever having his blood retested.

At the end of a major trial such as this, a minor celebration is usual. The three victims who were in court that final day came with me and my team to begin the cathartic process of putting this all into the past with a drink and a chat at the Town Hall Tavern, a pub that has seen plenty of tears and laughter after many a trial.

As I stood with these young women, their relief that the trial was over was plain to see; their gratitude to all my team was immeasurable. I was delighted for them. They were beginning the first day of the rest of their lives. Meanwhile, ten miles away in Wakefield, the life of Wendy Speakes was quietly ebbing away.

# chapter eight

# SOMEONE WAS GOING TO GET IT

During my thirty-one years' service I have witnessed some really shocking sights, along with the raw pain of human tragedy, but some things you are never equipped to totally understand, as I found when the murder of an attractive office worker took me into the uncharted waters of the sexual deviant killer. Stranger killings, where there is no known link between victim and killer, are rare. Most detectives will never deal with one. I was to deal with two – Julie Dart, and now a woman who led, like most of us, a very ordinary life. If only the same could be said about her murderer.

It was the day after the end of the Woodhouse Rapist trial, and I was enjoying my first day off for some time. My peace was broken at 2 pm when Control rang. A woman's body had been found in her house at Balne Lane, Wakefield. I jotted down a few basic details about what time she was discovered and by whom so I could start building a picture of the scene in my mind.

Without being rash, I liked to hit the ground running at a murder scene to quickly ascertain that basic procedures were carried out, such as ensuring that the scene was properly preserved and not contaminated. My theory was simple. You get one chance at the scene while you have it under sterile control – the value of something found after the examinations are concluded could easily be questioned in court.

I worked occasionally in Wakefield and knew some of the CID staff at

Wood Street, the city's police station, which also had the dubious pleasure of being only a hundred yards from the force's headquarters.

The rain was torrential as I pulled up before the end house in a terraced row of ten. Blue-and-white police tape already stretched from number 10, the murder scene, to the pub next door, the Cliffe Tree. I was logged in at the scene at 3.17 pm by the police officer guarding the house.

As I stepped from my car, Detective Chief Inspector Gerry Dickinson, the local CID head, greeted me. I had met Gerry many years before when we both worked on the Regional Crime Squad. He had an infectious sense of humour, a great sense of duty, and bore a striking resemblance to TV detective Jack Frost, played by David Jason.

Gerry took me into the conservatory at the back of the house, where the scene-of-crime staff already had their kits laid out. I was instantly annoyed. 'What the hell are they doing? They should be examining the bloody room, not using it as a base.' Gerry said, 'Yes, I know, it's a bit late now.' 'They should have shut the pub down for a couple of hours until the mobile police station got here,' I said. Gerry nodded.

This was not a good start. The one clue to solving this crime could have been in this room and might now have been obliterated, or they could have walked out with it on their shoes. We simply did not know and might never know now exactly where in the house the killer had been.

I got Gerry to talk me through what had been done. Aware of my views on the conservatory, he said, 'I'd better tell you before you see it on the log of visitors to the scene, the uniform super has been down for a look.' 'Did he have a protective suit on?' 'Afraid not,' said Gerry. I was fuming. I'd expect this from a probationer constable, not a superintendent.

The practice of non-essential people attending murder scenes for a look was something that made my blood boil, and my mood did not improve when I looked up the stairs, which were steep – any visitor placing a hand on the banister rail could obliterate the killer's handprint, if he had left one. The divisional superintendent's visit had not added anything to the investigation, but he could have destroyed vital evidence.

Gerry briefed me on the dead woman, Wendy Speakes. A fifty-one-year-old receptionist, she worked at Albatross Marketing in Ossett, just outside Wakefield. She lived alone, having been divorced for ten years, and had two daughters – Tracey, who was married and lived in Essex, and Leah, who lived in Altofts near Wakefield. Wendy also had a part-time job as a barmaid at the Forresters pub in south Wakefield.

Wendy's boss from Albatross, Deborah Crossley, had become increasingly concerned after she failed to arrive for work and had not answered phone calls. Deborah called Wendy's daughters to ask whether she was ill. As no one knew any reason for Wendy not to attend work, Deborah agreed to visit her home with her father, Robert Crossley.

When they arrived at Wendy's house at 12.45 pm, they found the front door unlocked. As they tentatively stepped inside, they called out Wendy's name but got no response. After a quick search downstairs, Mr Crossley went upstairs and saw Wendy's body sprawled across a double bed in the first bedroom on the right. She was obviously dead.

'Do we have any suspects?' I asked Gerry. 'None, but it looks like someone slept on the settee in the lounge.' I began my tour of the neat terraced home that I would come to know over the years almost as well as my own. The lounge was small and comfortable, but the two-seater settee had a duvet on it. Strange considering there were three bedrooms upstairs. 'Why should anyone sleep on the sofa? Did Wendy have someone staying with her?' 'Don't know. We're looking into that,' said Gerry.

Alone, I walked around the house. It was important to absorb as much of the murder scene as I could. Photos and videos freeze everything in time, but they do not give the same feeling as walking in the murderer's footsteps, which is the first step, so to speak, towards getting inside his mind. It is a strange feeling knowing you are in a room which hours before was the backdrop to fear, terror, hate and indescribable savagery.

A strange atmosphere of peace now shrouded the house as I carefully walked around, looking for anything which might offer a clue as to what had happened, why it had happened and who the killer was.

The room was clean. It had a single person's look to it. Around the breakfast bar were high-backed stools, and on the seat of one was a woman's black bag. At its base was a pair of black court shoes. I could picture this woman slipping off her bag and shoes after her day's work, thankfully unaware of what was to befall her. A wall unit's bottom cupboard door was open, and shoes were strewn across the floor between the cupboard and the stairs. The sink unit and work surface were clean except for a used dinner plate.

I climbed up the steep stairs, glanced into the first bedroom on my right and saw Wendy's lifeless body. The double bed seemed to fill the room. On top of the nearby dressing table was a pair of women's black shoes placed prominently and neatly together. A pair of women's black slippers was on the floor near Wendy.

The double bed was covered in a white duvet, its surface smooth but for a few ruffles where Wendy's left arm lay across it and where I supposed she had been attacked. A torn piece of candlewick bedspread lay near her hand. It was maybe twenty-four by nine inches and looked like an old rag.

Next to and slightly under her left arm was a pair of black stockings with loops tied at their ankles. Bizarrely, they were twisted together. The foot of one stocking was near by, having apparently been ripped off. Discarded near her body were the stockings' empty packet and its thin cardboard insert.

The room lacked the usual trinkets and make-up of a woman's bedroom in everyday use.

Wendy was slumped on the floor. Her face was resting on her right hand. She was sitting on her feet and part of her right thigh was bare and smeared with blood. I could see her right side from her naked thigh to her shoe. Her black tights had been pulled down and she had on a pair of powder-blue mules. She wore a black skirt and top. Her body between her shoulder blades was heavily bloodstained. It was as though she had collapsed to the floor from a kneeling position.

At 1.39 pm, a police surgeon certified Wendy's death. The question was in what circumstances? I had little doubt from what I'd seen so far that Wendy had been murdered. From the day you join the police service you are introduced to death. I've seen hundreds of dead people in my time, most killed in tragic circumstances. It is never an easy sight to deal with, but as I gazed down on this poor woman, killed in her own home, I knew as always that emotion had to be divorced from the job of finding her killer.

I didn't go into the bedroom as I wished to leave it for the forensic scientists and pathologist. I turned and walked down the landing to the end, where a window looked into the Cliffe Tree. To my right was the bathroom. To the left was a spare bedroom, which appeared undisturbed. The largest bedroom was at the top of the stairs, opposite where Wendy had met her death.

And so, on Wednesday, 16 March 1994, I walked into Wendy Speakes's bedroom – and her life. I gazed around and began to get to know her – what sort of woman she was, how she dressed, her reading habits (her daily newspaper had been left on her bed). Her double bed was unmade with her pyjamas at its foot. The full-length pink curtains were closed. Pairs of tights and a white blouse were on the floor in front of the wardrobe. The room had a lived-in rather than a ransacked appearance.

I glanced out of the window, which overlooked Balne Lane. Opposite was a printing company, Green Print, whose four-storey premises dominated the outlook. To their left was a railway embankment and a path that headed towards the top-security Wakefield prison. Was Wendy's killer a one-time neighbour of hers from the jail? To Green's right were further smaller industrial units.

As I gathered my thoughts, Hilary Parkinson and Kathy Turner, scientists from the Wetherby Forensic Science Laboratory, arrived. We briefed them as to what we knew at this stage so they could determine the best place to start. With Professor Mike Green, the Home Office pathologist, the scientists began their first task, which was to ensure that no evidence was lost in the removal of Wendy's body. Owing to the shortage of space in the bedroom, they would need to work together until Wendy left the house.

It is not always what you see that is important. Nowhere were there signs of a struggle – not in the hallway, nor the kitchen, nor where Wendy was found. Whoever the killer was, this woman did not believe she would be killed until it was too late to fight.

There were strange features to the crime. New stockings not worn but tied in loops, and the shoes as well, but it was too early to make any definite judgment. It would be easy to assume that she was a willing party to kinky sex games, involving bondage, and then her sexual partner turned on her and killed her, but what was the candlewick rag for?

I walked around the exterior of the house to check out the killer's possible escape routes. I stood on Wendy's front doorstep and gazed to the right, down Balne Lane, with its housing on both sides. To the left was a steep hill sweeping into Wakefield city centre. Opposite was the path that led past the prison to Westgate train station.

I wondered which route I would take if I were the killer. In front of the house was the main road, with moderate traffic in the afternoon, but I noticed that, as 5 pm approached, it was bumper to bumper. There were standing vehicles outside Wendy's house as the road under the railway track allowed only single-line traffic. This could be a good source of witnesses.

By 6 pm, the pathologist and forensics had completed their first task and Wendy had been taken to the mortuary at Clayton Hospital. I followed on with Gerry Dickinson. The hospital is on the outskirts of the city centre, a few minutes from Wendy's home. Its Victorian mortuary was one of the most antiquated and grim looking I had ever been in.

Those experienced in dealing with such places know that there is an aroma in mortuaries which pervades the tightest weave of clothes and lingers for days, so I pulled on my blue paper protective suit as soon as we walked in to cover my wool suit. We then began the essential but undignified procedure of collecting all the available evidence from Wendy's corpse. Professor Green would determine the cause of death and assist us with any other information or evidence that he might happen across.

I often feel a sense of futility about the human race when I stand in a mortuary and look at what was a living, breathing human being – in this case a mother, a sister, a friend – until some animal comes along and robs them of their right to live. How do they feel about that? What did Wendy's killer feel now about what he had done? Would it be genuine remorse or would he just appear quiet for a few days and then everything in his life would spring back to normal? Not if I have anything to do with it, I thought, as I pulled on the blue plastic overshoes and ridiculous blue cap that would stop the smell invading what little hair I had left.

Over two hours later, we left with all the exhibits we needed and a cause of death. Wendy had nine stab wounds in her back and two in the left side of her neck. Professor Green disclosed, 'Death was due to shock and haemorrhage resulting from the stab wounds.' Although there was not too much external bleeding, I saw him take several pints of blood from Wendy's chest cavity. There was evidence of sexual interference, and vaginal and anal swabs would go for forensic analysis to ascertain whether any semen was present.

I had known Professor Green for twenty years, since the first homicide I was involved in. In 1975 Vincent De Paul Vokes died after a punch-up outside a pub. It wasn't the punch which killed him but the skull fracture as he fell and crashed his head on the hard surface of the Cherry Tree pub carpark in Leeds.

I asked Professor Green what type of weapon we were looking for. 'A kitchen knife with a blade four and a half inches long, like one of those Kitchen Devils, Bob.' Hilary Parkinson said the killer had left an outline in blood of the knife blade on the duvet when he had put it down, either during or after the attack. It backed up Professor Green's findings.

Gerry and I proceeded to the incident room on the third floor at Wood Street police station. Detective Inspector Steve Palmer was made office manager, and he began pulling the staff together. I briefed them as to what we knew. Wendy was killed twelve to twenty-four hours before she was found, some time between leaving work and midnight.

Professor Green said Wendy had died in a cowering position at the side of the bed. I was not happy with this. I had seen the bloodstaining on the duvet consistent with the neck wounds and with Wendy having been knelt over the edge of the bed when these wounds were inflicted. I was of the opinion that, after being stabbed, she slid off the bed and onto the floor, leaving one arm on the bed in death.

Gerry, Steve Palmer and myself prioritised what needed doing first. Next day I would have over twenty-four detectives for enquiries, so I'd expect to get through a fair amount of work. The teams would work twelve-hour days, with one day off in seven.

One priority was to get officers to sit down with Tracey and Leah and learn as much as they could about their mother. Blond-haired Wendy was a slim, attractive woman. Did she know her killer? If so, it would be a matter of methodically working through her associates and carefully checking their alibis to pick up on a suspect.

In bereavement, most people want to grieve in peace. Unfortunately, in a murder investigation, the police need to intrude into that very private situation as we seek to build up a picture of the victim. As Wendy lived alone, Leah and Tracey were invaluable to the investigation, but they needed to be treated with sympathy and tact. They had as many questions as we did, and being rightfully keen to find their mother's killer helped focus their grief.

Wendy's employers and colleagues at Albatross would help fill in the picture of who she knew and what her movements were. House-to-house enquiries would be essential, especially around Wendy's house, to determine whether anyone saw her come home. Was she with anyone or alone? Were any callers seen by passers-by? This would be a job for the task force, who were well organised regarding this aspect of work. We'd begin close to Wendy's home and work outward, looking for witnesses. The information would be fed back to the incident room and followed up by my officers.

We would also look at any red-hot suspects. Ex-husbands are best alibied and out of the frame early, as are boyfriends and ex-boyfriends. They can be a constant source of doubt if they cannot be totally eliminated. We'd need to look at sex offenders and prison releases – with Wakefield jail on our doorstep, who could tell who might be living near by?

Also, we'd need to start enquiries with respect to the items found at the scene, particularly the stockings, whose packet bore a 'Superdrug' store label, and the candlewick rag. We would also need to search for the murder weapon. There was always the hope of fingerprints on it or something that would link it with the killer.

Did the Cliffe Tree play any part in events? Was Wendy a regular there? The pub itself was small and appeared to have a very local clientèle. A visit had already been made and had not established anything of any significance. We would need to trace and interview every customer who'd been in the pub on the night of the sixteenth, and probably in the weeks leading up to that date.

I had two excellent detective inspectors working on the inquiry, Chris Gregg and Paul Johnston. They would run the inquiry teams. Neither suffered fools gladly, so I knew what I wanted doing would get done. I discussed at length with them the examination of the scene, the necessity of getting it right and of things being done in the right order.

There was blood smearing on the wall next to the inside handle of the front door, as well as on the handle itself. I concluded that the killer had entered and left by the same door. He was most probably bloodstained from the attack, and the blood on the wall was more than likely Wendy's. I ordered the whole door to be removed and a replacement fitted so the lab could do a detailed examination of it.

I knew that the killer had at least gone down the hallway, through the kitchen and up the stairs. They were so steep that wooden banister rails were fitted on both sides; it would be very difficult to go up or down the stairs without using a rail to steady oneself. I ordered that they be removed and examined. I would not miss even a partial fingerprint of the killer, should one be there.

Paul Johnston was given the task of being the scene manager. His job would be to liaise with the specialists to ensure that every inch of the place was looked at for traces of the killer. Though the force had a forensic manager, who was a scientist, for me this was a detective's job. We would only have one chance at it. Fortunately for us, the house was now unoccupied, so we could have the scene for as long as we wanted, and that, I envisaged, might be several weeks. We would put right any damage we did and have the place redecorated if necessary.

By 8 am next morning, I was briefing the team. It would be an important day, filling in as much information as possible. I would spend a considerable amount of time doing press interviews. It was essential that I touch the hearts of as many of the Wakefield residents as possible, as well as reaching out to people farther afield who might also have vital information.

By now I knew Wendy's last movements. After finishing work in Ossett as normal on the Tuesday, she caught the bus into Wakefield with colleague James Ackroyd. He lived in Leeds and got off the bus at Westgate station to catch his train. He presumed that Wendy would, as usual, have got off at the next stop at the top of Westgate.

There were no other sightings of Wendy after that. I assumed she would have alighted from the bus and walked the six hundred yards to her home.

I estimated that the bus arrived at her stop at around 5.50 to 6 pm. It was a fifteen- to twenty-minute walk from there, so she would have been home no later than 6.20 pm. Of course, she could have gone into Wakefield, met someone and gone home with him later, but I had to work on what I thought was her normal routine. My first instincts were that she had been followed home, or that the killer saw her arrive back.

There are hundreds of fingerprints in any house. If we could eliminate those that were there legitimately, theoretically we should be left with the killer's. Before we routinely took fingerprints from suspects, I needed to know whether I had any unexplained prints.

I felt that the killer did not have legitimate access to the house. There was no sign of burglary, no forced entry, but that did not in itself indicate it was a person Wendy knew, though I could not discount this.

By day two, the picture was becoming clearer. Paul Downing, who worked at Green Print across from Wendy's, saw a man at her door between 5.30 and 6.45 pm. Paul had been working at a machine by a window that overlooked her house. He saw Wendy wearing her black slippers, standing on the top step with her front door open.

He described the man as white, aged thirty-five to forty-five, of medium to slim build with straight dark brown hair cut above the ears and with a thinning patch at the crown. He wore a light grey ski jacket which had a dark coloured band around the top of the sleeve.

The man walked from the rear of the house to where Wendy was standing. They held a short conversation lasting around thirty seconds. The man then returned round the side of the house to the back. Paul saw Wendy stand at the door with her arms folded. A minute later the man reappeared at the front door and continued talking.

Paul looked away to concentrate on his work, and some time later, when he gazed back across the road, he saw the same man leave the house through the front door. He was on the top step and was closing the door behind him. He walked down the steps to the gate, looked to his right towards the pub, turned left, walked for a couple of yards, then started running. Paul saw him run twenty yards up the hill towards the city centre before disappearing from view.

This was a vitally important sighting. Paul Downing could well have seen the killer within seconds of his taking Wendy's life. He had also provided another little gem in that he had described Wendy standing at the door wearing slippers, the very ones we saw in the bedroom where she had been killed. Yet when she was found, she was wearing cheap-looking powder-blue mules. What did that mean?

A picture was starting to develop of a killer who had gone to Wendy's home with the intention of killing her, taking with him the tools of his murderous trade – a knife, a candlewick rag to gag her, the black stockings and maybe the tacky blue shoes. All these things had significance in her death and the manner in which she died. The pair of black shoes on the dressing table next to Wendy's body also had a meaning.

A major line of enquiry had developed with respect to another incident that occurred at 5 pm, an hour before Wendy arrived home, at a house off Flanshaw Lane, just a mile from Wendy's and with a fairly direct route between them. The woman was in her early twenties and lived with her boyfriend. For legal reasons I cannot identify her, so I will call her Woman 'A'.

Woman 'A' contacted us after seeing media reports on the murder. She told officers about an incident with a man on the day of Wendy's death. She had first seen him at 9.30 am that Tuesday while waiting for a bus.

She had been standing alone at the bus stop for only a matter of seconds when she looked back in the direction from which she had come and saw a man walking towards her. She felt he was acting furtively, and was conscious that he was looking at her as he passed and walked on along Flanshaw Lane.

She looked to see where he had gone, only to find he had turned around and was walking back towards her. His actions so disturbed her that she began to wonder what he was up to. He then walked past her again, heading in the direction of her home.

As the bus approached her stop, she stopped taking notice of him. She travelled into Wakefield, went to work (she worked at a shop in the Ridings shopping centre in the heart of Wakefield) and forgot about him for the rest of the morning.

When she left work at 2 pm, she walked from the Ridings to Superdrug, where she did some shopping. She then walked up Westgate, where Wendy Speakes would later get off the bus, and went to a friend's house on the Darnley estate, halfway between Wendy's house and her own.

She left her friend's at 4.50 pm and caught the bus home. She barely had time to take off her coat, open the back door to let her dog out and put the kettle on before she heard a knock at the front door.

She opened the door and a man was standing there. She did not immediately recognise him as the man she had seen that morning, but knew she had seen him before. As she spoke, she thought it was him but wasn't sure.

He wore the same clothing, a grey cotton bomber jacket with an elasticated waist, zip-up front and a blue collar. It was faded and appeared old. He also had a pair of well-worn blue jeans, faded especially at the creases and noticeably around the groin area.

Woman 'A' related what happened next: 'The man said he'd been looking around for two hours for Flanshaw Drive. I didn't think it was true, if he was the same man I'd seen earlier in the day. "Have you any idea where it is?" he asked. Although I didn't not know where it was, or even if it existed, I decided to try and help him. I directed him to where the Flanshaws were but he said he'd already looked there and couldn't find it.

'As he spoke, I was conscious he was looking up and down my street. He was stood at an angle to me and had his hands in his jacket pockets. I was now sure it was the same man I'd seen earlier and began to feel very nervous. But something was telling me to give him the benefit of the doubt.

'He said, "I'll give that street a try but could you get a pen and a piece of paper and write down the directions?" A terrible feeling came over me as I stood looking at him. I was rooted to the spot, unable to move, with a sense of foreboding he was going to push me back into the house, walk in and shut the door behind him. I daren't move, stupid words were coming from my mouth. I said, "Oh I'm better off just saying it to you."

'Then my dog started to bark at the sitting-room door. "I can't think where you're on about," he said. "Can I have that pen and paper? It's my granddad's house I'm looking for and I haven't been for years, but I've got the phone number. Could I borrow your phone so he can give me directions?"

'The dog's barking brought me back to reality. I made an excuse and said he couldn't come in as my boyfriend was in the house with his friends. My sense of danger had reached the point where I really felt that something was going to happen. I said he could use the phone at the Flanshaw Hotel on the main road. But he said it wasn't open. I knew he was lying as it's open all day. This added to my sense of urgency to get rid of him. Panic rising, I said I could not help him any more and slammed the door.'

She did not realise it then but Woman 'A' had just saved her own life.

She was so disturbed by him that she ran to the back door and locked it. She then went back to the front door and double-checked it was locked. She looked out of the window but could not see him, then rang her sister, who came to the house and took her away. She described the man as white, five foot seven to five foot nine inches tall, of medium build with a lean face. His brown hair was greying at the sides, cut short, and he was balding on top.

I read her statement and spoke to the officers who had seen her. She was described as a very attractive young woman whom they considered truthful and honest. It struck me immediately that the description of the man and his clothing was similar to what Paul Downing had described. If it was the same man, then Wendy Speakes might have been the second-choice victim and Woman 'A' his first.

If that was so, the killer knew there was a witness alive who could identify him, and, as Michael Sams said, you don't get any more for two murders than one. This young woman would need protection until the killer was found. I was hopeful that she would be able to provide a good E-fit. The final twist was that Woman 'A' had been in the Cliffe Tree pub next to Wendy's home on a number of occasions. There had to be a link.

There were still no clear favourites emerging as the murderer, though we were resolving some of the issues. There was no mystery with regard to Wendy leaving her job, as her daughter Tracey told us she was intending to move near her.

We had obtained invaluable information from Tracey and Leah. Both were sensible young women whose grief over the death of their mother in these tragic circumstances was immeasurable. We would have to continue intruding into their shattered lives, as you never know what might be relevant. I appointed Nigel Finan and Karen Hardisty as family liaison officers. They would spend days with the sisters to tease every morsel of information from them.

Wendy's daily routine was as regular as clockwork. As I listened to what her daughters said, it was clear that some of what I had seen at the murder scene fitted in and could assist us greatly to make a best guess as to what time she died.

Their mother was not a great socialite. She spoke with her daughters on a regular basis but spent virtually every evening at home. Their parents had met in the RAF, married and, after their two girls were born, left the service and settled in Wakefield. Wendy had no current close male friends and really had not had a man in her life since her divorce.

Any thoughts of a lover going berserk because she was moving south were not likely to lead anywhere. Neither daughter could suggest anyone, except the occasional customer at the Forrester's pub, who had shown any interest in her at all. One, a taxi-driver, had asked her out, and she had told her daughters about him as she was concerned about the attention he was showing her. She was so careful that when she did agree to him taking her home she got him to drop her a hundred yards from her house and waited for him to drive off before she walked home.

Tracey and Leah told us that when their mother got up of a morning she read her newspaper in bed, marking with a 'V' the programmes she would video and ringing the times of those she would watch. She would go to work, leaving the paper on the bed, where we found that day's marked exactly as they described.

One important point they made us aware of was that Wendy never used the front door. She always left and entered the house through the conservatory at the back. Tracey described her mother's routine: 'On getting home, Mum would hang her bag over the breakfast stool, her coat in the hall, take off her shoes and put her slippers on.

'She'd place her shoes neatly together by the dresser or by the radiator in the kitchen. If it was a night that Mum would shower, usually Tuesday and Thursdays, she would go upstairs and, after showering, put on her nightclothes.

'She'd then go downstairs, unpack her shopping, go into the living room, close the curtains and put on the TV. She'd usually make something light like beans on toast and eat it in the living room while watching TV. At ten pm, she'd go to bed and read for half an hour.' The daughters also added that she would sit watching TV wrapped in a duvet to save on heating. That solved the mystery of the bed made up on the settee.

Clearly Wendy's routine had been interrupted. Her coat was hanging in the hall, her bag was on the kitchen chair and her shoes were by the dresser, as described. The television page of the paper was still on the unmade bed; she had ringed the first programme she would watch at 7 pm. The television was turned off and the lounge curtains were open.

The plates in the sink must have been from the previous night, as the pathologist told us she had fruit for her last meal, which was lunch at work.

I noticed at the post-mortem that she was fully made up. She had not progressed her routine farther than taking her coat off and putting her slippers on. Her unwelcome visitor must have called within minutes of her arriving home.

The other pointer to the visitor being a stranger was that all regular callers would go to the back of the house. This man went to the front. Then there was the issue of the blue mules marked inside with 'R P Ellen of Oxford Street'. They were a backless, open-toed slip-on shoe with two leather strips across the foot. The sides of the stubby heels and the bands were covered in a powder-blue material that was now wrinkled, scratched and bubbled. They now looked shabby but were not a cheap shoe.

Why was Wendy wearing them? Did the killer bring them? Neither of her daughters recognised the mules; they were not the type that their mother would wear, they insisted. Tracey was adamant they did not belong to their mother. Paul Downing was quite sure that the woman he had seen at the door was wearing slippers. There could be no confusing these two completely different types of footwear.

Then there were the stockings. I established that they had been bought either on Monday or Tuesday from Superdrug on Little Westgate, the same store that Woman 'A' had visited. If the visit to Woman 'A's home was connected, the killer may have followed her into Superdrug and bought the stockings while she was in the shop. One of the shop's staff recalled a man buying a pair of black stockings but could not remember the time.

There was no knife missing from Wendy's as far as we knew. It seemed the killer had come prepared or intending to kill his victim and, to satisfy his own fantasies, would bind her with the black stockings and make her wear the mules. I asked myself what the chances were of this person killing again – they had to be high.

I was starting to get an insight into the killer. If Wendy and Woman 'A' were both potential victims of the killer, then he had been in Wakefield from early morning until teatime carrying around a knife and a gag. He had purchased the black stockings presumably to tie up his victim while he raped and killed her. Taking account also of the shoes, it all seemed to be a staged sexual ritual.

All officers working on a murder hunt have a picture of the killer in their minds, though invariably this mental E-fit varies from person to person. We look at what the killer has done, hang his description around it, then imagine who could have done this. The brutality of the crime forces us to the conclusion that the killer is a monster, a fiend, some indescribable demon who will look so evil he will be noticeable. The reality is that this is rarely the case.

That which makes one person different from another can rarely be seen. It lies in the darkness behind the eyes, and their evil is apparent only to those who find it is too late to escape the destiny that this person has decided for them. This was the case for Julie Dart, and probably also for Wendy Speakes. This case was developing in such a way that I decided offender profiling could be useful. If this was a sexual killing with a ritualistic element, it would be useful to speak to someone who had dealt with such people.

If the killer was a stranger to Woman 'A' and Wendy, how did he know their routine? Woman 'A' certainly did not know him, and it appeared that Wendy probably did not either. One thing that bugged me was that while I could accept that the killer saw Wendy come home to an empty house, how could he be sure she lived alone, and that when he got into her home there would be no husband or sixteen-stone Wakefield Trinity prop-forward son about to walk through the door and beat the hell out of him?

Wendy's front door was several steps up from street level, ensuring that passers-by could not see through the lounge window. You could see into the conservatory and kitchen by walking down the side of her house, and also from the pub's lounge-bar window, but strangers were unknown in the pub. He would need to have stalked Wendy for some time to work out her routine, and in so doing surely someone would have noticed him.

Another point that bothered me was the killer's route from the scene. Trudy Milnes was walking down Balne Lane towards Wendy's house on her way home at 6.40 pm when a man jogged towards her as she passed

LEFT Christopher Farrow being led from court. (*Phil Callaghan*)

BELOW Serial rapist Clive Barwell at his wedding to Margaret Teasdale in 1994, while he was still a serving prisoner at Sudbury Prison. (picture research by *Phil Callaghan*)

under the railway bridge. She gave a vague description and said she thought he was wearing sports-type clothing.

Terry Clough, head of security at Wakefield District College, situated at the top of the hill leading down to the murder scene, saw a man running up the hill at 6.30 pm. He described him as stockily built, five foot eight to nine inches tall, in his thirties with short or very thin hair, clean shaven and with staring eyes. He wore a grey bomber jacket with elasticated cuffs and light-coloured trousers.

Both sightings may have been of the killer. I was fairly confident that Terry's was. It left me wondering why he had left the scene by the most difficult route. He had exposed himself to possible identification within seconds of taking Wendy's life by drawing attention to himself running up a steep hill away from her home. I had pondered the escape routes before, and this was the least likely one, I thought.

Was he a stranger to Wakefield and, after following her home, knew only that route? Was his car parked up there? He could have gone through the fields at the back, and caught a bus back into Wakefield. He could have gone down the path at the side of Green Print, past the prison and out onto the bottom of Westgate. I felt he did not know Wakefield well.

But this was slightly at odds with my other theory that he had stalked both Wendy and Woman 'A' for some time. Had he done so, then surely he would have known the lie of the land well. Maybe he knew the area where Woman 'A' lived well and, as his plan to attack her had failed, he had come upon Wendy on her way home from work and taken a risk when he tricked his way into her house. The answer lay somewhere in between, maybe in a combination of different theories. We would not know until we caught him.

One revelation was bound to generate a tremendous amount of work. The man's clothing that witnesses described – the grey ski jacket with tight cuffs and a black band round the top of the sleeves – was identical to a type available to prisoners on their release.

I had some good witnesses who had clearly seen the killer, yet only Woman 'A' could prepare an E-fit which could be relied upon. The information had been pumped out to the press and the response was good, but the problem with an E-fit is that it is rarely a good likeness, so there has to be a process of sorting the wheat from the chaff, as many callers would ring in and give information that it was not really possible to follow up, such as: 'I saw a man who looks like the E-fit on a number seventy-two bus in Bradford and he looked odd.'

The blue mules were interesting. I had doubts that the killer had brought them with him. They did not quite fit with buying black stockings and were not a size that would fit Woman 'A', if she were the first-choice victim. But if he did bring them, where did he get them from – a girlfriend maybe? Would anybody recognise them as being missing and provide the link to the killer we were searching for?

It is unusual, to say the least, to hold a press conference and reveal that we believe the killer brought a pair of shoes to the victim's home and made her wear them while killing her. This was an interesting development for the media, and turned our investigation into something of a unique inquiry. I knew I would be asked the question: 'Are you saying, Mr Taylor, that the killer has a shoe fetish?' My answer was simple. 'Yes.'

The Crime Faculty at Bramshill Police College recommended Dr Richard Badcock to me as an offender profiler. He was local, working as a consultant forensic psychiatrist at Newton Lodge, a secure unit in Wakefield and the regional centre for forensic psychiatry.

It was 5 pm and a little over a week into the inquiry when, with Gerry Dickinson, I met Richard Badcock. A quietly spoken man, he immediately put us at ease. Had we not known he was a psychiatrist, I might have thought him slightly eccentric in his bow tie. I guessed this familiar psychiatrists' attire had less to do with looking smart and more with denying patients an easy method of strangling them. He exuded enthusiasm for the task as Gerry and I briefed him on the case.

We went through every detail, however mundane, as we did not know what he might or might not consider significant. I was hopeful that he could enlighten me on some aspects of this inquiry, in particular the foot fetish. I gave him witness statements and photographs to study. We sat and watched the murder scene video and explained the events leading up to Wendy's death.

He was immediately drawn to the man's visit to Woman 'A'. His first instincts were that the two events might well be connected. He said that stalkers often stalk more than one person; he might have had a first- and second-choice victim. Such people have been known to stalk for months prior to an attack and, for many of them, this was part of the thrill. He could have been watching both women for some time.

He would need time to study the statements and visit the scene of the killing to develop his profile, but he said that given what we already knew, the probability of the man reoffending was high. We also talked about whether he might have offended previously and what his history might be. Richard Badcock's assessment at that stage was that he might have committed crimes in the past but that this was probably his first murder.

I would share what he had told me with my team at my briefings. I told Dr Badcock, as I did all experts I consulted during an inquiry, that I did not want to hear anything that could not be supported.

There were a number of questions that my team had asked me to put to him. What would be this man's reaction when confronted by one of the team? How would he react to questioning? This stemmed from a preconception that many officers and the public had that this man would act strangely. Richard's answer was: 'He knows that society thinks what he has done is wrong; though he doesn't, otherwise he would not have done what he did. He will appear normal. He can defend himself in a conversation and will lie to cover up what he has done.'

I felt he was making a bold statement and asked him to justify it. 'Wendy was not frightened of him. She stood on her doorstep while he went down the side of the house. She did not feel threatened otherwise she would have shut the door and locked herself in. He is obviously plausible, as whatever he said to her to keep her there appeared genuine.'

I wondered why I had not worked that out, but this was the advantage of having a person other than a police officer looking at the case. He was considering it from a different perspective to us. This would change our mental pictures of the killer from a troll-like creature to someone vaguely human, whom any person could consider normal.

I also asked Richard about the shoe fetish issue. I had already enlightened myself with the dictionary definition: 'A material or object believed among primitive cultures to have magical powers.' In terms of psychology it states, 'An abnormal sexual attraction to some object or part of the body not normally considered erogenous zones.' Richard explained, 'A person with a fetish would achieve sexual arousal only with the aid of this additional stimulus.'

In other words, I said, 'The sights and smells that would arouse the average person would not sexually arouse him.'

Richard agreed and went on, 'A shoe or foot fetish is the second-most common fetish. Women's underwear is the most common – bras, knickers, stockings.' I was intrigued and asked why this was so. 'It's because they are worn normally on parts of the body associated with sexual pleasure. Fetishes are classless and predominantly occur in males. Many fetishists live a normal life and their partners will often be aware of it and have no problem, so long as it is under control. The most common shoe fetish picture is the one of a woman's legs in a standing position, wearing red high-heel shoes showing the legs from the knee down.'

'So what will my officers find in this guy's locker at work? What would give them a clue he has a fetish?'

'They might find women's shoes, but generally pornography,' he said.

I knew from the way the conversation was going that this would not be what I thought of as pornography. 'What do you mean by that?' I felt obliged to ask.

'Pictures of women's legs, feet and shoes,' he said.

'That, in my view, is not pornographic,' I remarked.

'Oh, it is to him,' he responded immediately. 'Often if you go in their prison cells they'll have posters on the wall. One might be an innocuous picture of Princess Diana in a coat, but the only part of it they will focus on is the legs or the shoes.'

I was being taken into a world I had rarely even considered. I felt more confident now about briefing my team. I would need to explain it carefully, as I did not want every poor sod with a picture of Princess Diana on their locker getting thrown into a cell.

I knew this would take the inquiry into a world none of us had ever stepped into, so to speak, so I asked Richard to explain the use of the shoes in the crime. He told me that the selection of the shoes would be significant, as were the black stockings and the black shoes on the dresser. They would be placed where he could see them as he raped and killed her. Richard found it strange that he had left the shoes behind. He would have expected him to take them with him for use later as an aid to masturbation to take him back to that night.

I wondered whether he might have taken some of Wendy's shoes for this purpose, or some of her underwear. We would need to check that with Wendy's daughters. I surmised that any item he took away would for him be charged in some way with power that would sexually arouse him at a later date. I needed to know whether this killing would satisfy him, or whether he would commit another similar crime; if so, when that was likely to be, and why Richard thought this was his first murder.

'He will no doubt have watched you doing the TV appeals. He'll be kicking himself for leaving so many clues at the scene – the stockings, shoes and rag. All could conceivably lead you to him. That's why I think it is his first. He will have learned from this for the next time. If he does strike again, do not expect to see the clues you have this time. He may not kill again if he did not enjoy the experience or if it did not meet his expectations, but more than likely he will in time.'

'When will that be?' I asked.

'Difficult to say. When the urge takes him, when the power of the memory of what he did has faded and no longer excites him.'

Richard and I discussed the slippery slope that people can slide down, and how our killer could well be careering down it. I needed to know more about the nature of the beast. How did the killer arrive at a point where he needed to take this innocent woman's life just to satisfy his own sexual needs? Where did he come from and where was he going? He told me that academic research suggested the potential for progressive behaviour. It started with voyeurism, watching couples through car windows or women in their homes, then progressed to theft of women's underwear or shoes. There is then a phase that is regarded as optional – sexual cruelty to animals. The next stage is indecent exposure, 'flashing'.

Things are getting serious when he progresses to control, bondage and domination, which may take the form of a sexual attack or piquerism, where the knife is symbolic of the penis and its penetration of the body has a sexual connotation; then cannibalism, where the killer eats parts of the victim's body; finally, even more grotesque, necrophilia, a sexual fascination with corpses.

In the latter stages, there are those who would say the slipperiness and angle of the slope prevent a person's rehabilitation, or, as one academic psychologist put it to me, there comes a point on the slope where treatment can do nothing and the best solution is execution.

Richard talked about the possibility of the wounds to Wendy being piquerism. He detailed instances where women out shopping arrived home to find a stab wound in their buttocks. Someone had unbeknown to them got a sexual kick from brushing against them in the street or a shop and stabbing them in the behind.

I would have to wait for Dr Badcock's report, but he had excited my imagination with regard to the killer. I had been impressed with our meeting, gaining an incredible insight into another world. He also told me of a magazine called *Footsie* and an association called FLASC, the Foot Lovers

Appreciation Society. I decided we had to look at both to see whether they could advance the inquiry in any way.

It is important to know what makes a killer tick – why did he kill in the manner he did, why did he choose a victim in her own home rather that pick an easier target such as a street prostitute and take her to a secluded location to carry out his bestial deeds? What was this man's motive?

I now felt I was getting inside the killer's mind. Everything about this crime told me something about him. I was confident now that he had bought the stockings for Woman 'A' to wear while he raped and killed her. In Wendy's attack he had used them to tie her wrists. The mules Wendy had been wearing had been pulled out of the cupboard downstairs, and the black shoes on the dresser next to where he killed her were part of the sexual stimulus he needed to carry out the attack. I had been reading about Andrei Chikatilo, one of the world's worst serial killers, who murdered and mutilated up to fifty-three young girls and boys in Russia between 1982 and 1990. The motivation for Chikatilo's crimes was sexual gratification, as was the case with Wendy's killer, who I knew was a walking time bomb who could kill again at any moment. Like Chikatilo, he would be accepted as a normal member of the community until he was caught and his true character revealed.

I was pursuing a number of different lines of enquiry, one of which was the prison. Our in-force intelligence system had identified 140 prison releases to West Yorkshire from jails elsewhere in the two weeks before Wendy's death. If that was an average figure, and was projected over six months, it meant that nearly 2,000 prisoners had been released into the community in my county. I would look at white males, aged between thirty and fifty, with convictions for indecency or theft of shoes.

Birmingham clothing manufacturers Rose & Co. supplied ski jackets to forty prisons. We would research prisoners who had been issued a jacket in the previous six months, check them against the suspect criteria and look at their convictions. We would also check them against the thirty-nine fingerprints and fragments of prints that were unaccounted for at Wendy's house.

The fingerprint inquiry was a huge task, and we had no chance of checking all the outstanding marks nationally until we had eliminated all innocent marks left by legitimate visitors to the scene. We had two fingerprints in places where we knew the killer had been – one on the edge of the front inside door handle, and one on the stocking packet the killer had left

on the bed. We traced double glazers and window cleaners, and even eliminated one fingerprint as belonging to the man who had fitted Wendy's
bedroom wardrobes ten years earlier.

There were problems with AFR (Automatic Fingerprint Retrieval).
Not all forces nationally were on the system, so even if we launched a
search it would only be with those that had put their prints on the system.
The others would have to be done manually – if their force fingerprint
departments were prepared do it – or I would have to send staff to the
Police National Computer Bureau in London and do them there.

We were following up enquiries at places that sold rags, of which there
were a few in Wakefield. They would buy old bedding, in particular candlewick, as when torn into handy-sized rags these are useful to the likes of
engineers and mechanics for cleaning their hands. The rag left at the scene
was definitely one of these, as one of the short sides showed a dog-leg tear
commonly seen when they are ripped into hand-size rags on the spikes at
such places.

Hilary Parkinson from forensics told me that the rag had saliva on it.
The distribution was in a haphazard fashion, indicative of it having been
screwed up. I presumed it had been used as a gag on Wendy. I knew there
was no semen on it but it was bloodstained, and I reckoned the killer had
used it to wipe blood off his hands.

Two weeks into the inquiry, I was delighted to get a DNA profile of
the killer from semen found on the anal swab. The lab had also been testing all the different areas of bloodstaining, and their analysis showed an
area of blood on the duvet that was not the same type as Wendy's. The
killer had cut himself.

The combination of the DNA and blood grouping was my Cinderella's
slipper (an unfortunate term given the killer's predilection for shoes). We
had a piece of evidence that would be a major factor in catching the killer,
as well as in eliminating the innocent. The problem we had was to find
someone to fit the slipper.

Our ability to eliminate through DNA was a great relief to our only
real suspect at that time, the taxi-driver who had taken a fancy to Wendy.
A search of his bachelor flat revealed a pair of women's tights which had a
more than liberal distribution of semen on them. DNA categorically eliminated him; nor did he fit the blood group.

Descriptions are always a problem, apart from clothing, which people
can be reasonably consistent about. Sometimes short people see anyone

taller as much taller and vice versa. Stocky people see themselves as of average build, while thin people think everyone else is fat. Age is often pure guesswork, as it comes down to how old the witness thinks people look, not how old they actually are. They can quite easily be ten years out on suspects aged between thirty and fifty. For this reason, although our witnesses might think the man they saw was aged forty, I would not eliminate anyone on account of age unless they were younger than thirty or over fifty.

The mules provided another avenue of enquiry. After a television appeal, Edna Dodd, the deputy manageress at a charity shop in Wakefield, came forward. She had seen the shoes on the appeal and thought she had sold them to a man around the time of the murder, probably the Saturday before.

He had come into the shop and selected the shoes from the display, even asking Edna to try them on for him. The description she gave was of a man slightly taller and older than the one seen at Wendy's door, but she described his jacket as grey with a zip-up front. When shown the blue shoes, she was pretty sure they were the same ones.

This seemed a positive step, yet I had problems with it. If he bought the shoes for Wendy to wear, how did he know they would fit? Also, if they were so important to the ritual of killing Wendy, why didn't he take them away with him? Wendy's daughters were adamant that they were not hers, but there was the matter of the shoes at the bottom of the stairs having been pulled out of the cupboard. This tended to suggest that the killer had chosen the shoes at the house and they were Wendy's.

The stockings were not proving to be a rewarding line of enquiry. The price label led us to Superdrug on Little Westgate – they had come from a display in the shop that had been restacked on the Monday and Tuesday by an employee who did not normally work at that branch but whose fingerprints were on the packet.

Our research extended to similar offences locally, nationally and internationally, to establish whether our suspect had approached any other women in their homes. It revealed a number of murders in which women had been killed at home, but insufficient information to link them with our crime. One that might be relevant involved a thirty-nine-year-old married woman whom I will refer to for legal reasons as Woman 'B'. She lived in Meltham, south-west of Huddersfield, and worked in a women's clothes shop in the town.

She told us what happened on 10 January 1994, three months before

Wendy's death. Her movements were similar to those of Woman 'A'. She worked in the shop until 2.55 pm and walked to the bus station to get a bus home. As she waited in the queue, she noticed a man standing behind her. She got on the bus and sat downstairs, unaware that the man was near her.

Arriving at Meltham, she got off and walked the forty yards to her home. As she opened her gate, she noticed the same man walking along the lane in her direction, ten yards away.

Once in the house, she had just put the kettle on when there was a knock at the door. It was the man who had been in the bus-station queue, but she did not appreciate this until later. He appeared agitated, said he was concerned about his father, and asked whether he could use her phone.

He was shaking his hands in front of him, as if he were talking with them. He said he had been to his father's house but could get no answer; the television was on and he was frightened that something might have happened to him. He again asked to use the phone.

Although hesitant, as she was alone in the house, the woman reluctantly agreed. She did not feel threatened by the man, just concerned that she was alone. She stayed in the kitchen and watched him go into the lounge. After a while he put the phone down and said he couldn't get an answer. 'I'll go and try again. I'll come back and let you know.'

She reckoned he must have got only as far as the gate before he was back. 'I'm still not able to get an answer. I'm really worried, perhaps something might have happened to him. Do you think I could use your phone again?'

She let him in again and stood three yards from him while he made the call. She could hear BT's recorded message for an unobtainable number. He turned to her and asked, 'How do I get out on the phone?' She told him just to dial the number. He redialled and got the same unobtainable message.

He turned to face her and said, 'I still can't get through. I'm frightened something might have happened to my father.' He then asked her what time her husband would get home. As they were now face to face, she realised it was the man from the bus station and that he must have been the man walking behind her after she got off the bus.

She told him her husband would be home soon. She now felt uneasy, alone in the house with a stranger whose behaviour was odd. She was frightened. He asked for a ladder. 'There is a window open but I'm not very good with heights. I thought your husband could help if you knew what time he would be back.'

Thinking quickly, she offered to get a ladder from a neighbour. She'd spotted his van outside his house when she came in. He was not interested. 'I don't want to bother anyone else.' This made her feel even more uncomfortable, and she decided she should keep him talking. She asked whether anyone else had a key and he said he would try again. If he did not get an answer, he would ring his mother. As they were talking, she sidled into the kitchen and grabbed an umbrella for protection.

She picked up on his comment about his mother and asked him why he did not ring her house. At this, he said he would come back and let her know how he got on, and walked out of the house again.

As soon as he was out of her garden, she ran to the neighbour's. She told him what had happened and he came back to her house with her. As they got to her door, the man was already there, and when he saw them he said, 'It's all right now. I've got an answer,' claiming his father had said to him, 'Why are you knocking at my door, you silly bugger?' He then walked off.

She described him as aged thirty-five, five foot ten to six feet tall, of very thin build, with short dark brown hair receding at the front. He wore light blue jeans, a blue/grey bomber-style jacket with a narrow band around the upper arm of the sleeve, and white trainers. His accent was Northern rather than local, meaning it was not a Huddersfield accent and he could be from anywhere in the north.

The description was not dissimilar to the ones we had of the man at Wendy's door. This man was perhaps taller and slimmer, but his approach to Woman 'B' was an important similarity with Wendy's murder and the incident with Woman 'A'.

Although this had happened months before, we examined the house for fingerprints and obtained an E-fit from her which turned out to be similar to Woman 'A's.

Dr Badcock's offender profile was sent to me. It made interesting reading. He believed Wendy's killer was single and probably in his forties. The age was largely based, he said, on older men's interest in stockings. The psychopathology, referring to the level of violence and the manner in which he carried out the attack, would take time to evolve. He thought he would be of normal physical appearance and voice, with a polite but firm social manner, and unlikely to appear aggressive. This was based on his ability to engage Wendy in conversation as he did without alarming or frightening her.

I could go along with that. It seemed logical enough to me. I read on. He also considered that our man might be socially inadequate, based upon the nature of the attack, and be unable to sustain normal relations. He might also have an obsessional character, based on his sadomasochistic pathology. His intelligence level would be normal, and he would be from a working-class background, based on the social group of his victim, which would reflect his own. The assumption that he would choose his victim from the same social class was something I questioned, as I knew of murder cases which did not follow that principle.

Richard took the view that our man lived in a broadly local area on his own, or in organised accommodation, which was likely to be tidy but bare. If he was in work, he would be regarded as capable but not sociable.

I had mixed feelings about where he lived. A compelling argument could be made out that he was local, but his departure from the scene taking the worst route, causing him to be seen, suggested a stranger retracing his steps, maybe along the route on which he had followed Wendy home.

The sexual fantasy side of his nature was such that Richard thought he could have a collection of sadomasochistic pornography, and a collection of women's shoes or pictures of shoes. He would likely have written records of the targeted victims, their routines, and a trophy from the killing, such as clothing.

The possibility that he might revisit the crime scene to relive his fantasies could not be dismissed, nor that he would have learned from the killing. There was also a likelihood he might change his behaviour to enhance fantasy fulfilment, though not necessarily his modus operandi.

Hilary Parkinson and Mike Barber, the DNA specialist at the Forensic Science Laboratory, were testing the blood on clothing and swabs, trying to separate Wendy's from the killer's. They found that blood on the inside front door handle, the wall next to the door, Wendy's clothing and the duvet was from the same person. And it was not Wendy's.

There was blood on the waistband of Wendy's underwear and on her blouse. Neither stains were hers. At some stage during the attack, the killer had, I thought, cut his left hand, judging by the position of the blood on her underwear. Although the blood on her clothing was likely to be the killer's, the smear on the handle and the wall could have been that of an everyday visitor.

I had the killer's DNA, his blood group, a description of him and his clothing, but I did not have him. I just needed a name.

Because the killer had a shoe fetish, I decided to look at massage parlours. Where had he gone to satisfy his fantasies before he killed Wendy? Perhaps he went to a parlour and took the mules with him. We had calls from prostitutes with some weird tales of punters wanting to buy their shoes from them after sex.

The services these girls offered were varied and went beyond a quick rub-down with baby oil. One told us about a man who brought a pair of women's shoes for her to wear. She had to stand on paper cuttings of an unknown woman while he poured fake blood on the shoes, masturbated, ejaculated and then licked the shoes.

Another punter (a professional man) would bring a pair of his mother-in-law's shoes. He made the prostitute wear the shoes and assume the mother-in-law's name while they had sex. None of my team was surprised to hear that the man's wife was divorcing him.

We traced the 'left shoe man', a young local man who stole women's left shoes from shop displays, these being the only one of the pair displayed. He was well known to shoe-shop staff, who would regularly chase him off. His mother, with whom he lived, was aware of his problem. She did not mind as long as he did not use her shoes for his sexual gratification.

I was considering an appeal on *Crimewatch* within weeks of the murder, but felt it was too early. We could be deluged by national calls, taking my officers all over the country before we had done the basics in Wakefield. As time went on I became more convinced that the killer did not live in Wakefield and that a wider viewing audience might be helpful, so I met with a director and arranged to go on the next programme, on Thursday, 12 July.

Four of us travelled down for the programme – myself and DCs Jan Whincup, Nev Hanley and Mick Crossland. We took the mules, but I doubted we would be allowed to show the stockings as they were a bit risqué, and I suspected the programme-makers did not want hundreds of phone calls from people whose only interest was talking about being tied up with stockings.

The programme went smoothly, and although we had a good response there were no calls that set me alight, though we did have numerous serving and ex-prison officers ringing in with names of possible suspects.

I could present convincing arguments that the killer was local, had identified his victim and had gathered information on her lifestyle from walking past the house. Yet at the same time I could pull other facts from the case and convince someone that he caught a bus, a train or even drove into Wakefield from another city.

I could not hope to DNA-profile all males in the surrounding towns and cities, but I could concentrate on those who lived close enough to the scene to have targeted Wendy or Woman 'A'. I decided to look at all males in my suspect age group who lived within a half-mile of Wendy's home.

This was no easy task, but I believed that as we had DNA I had a responsibility to go out and look for the killer, in contrast to some, more senior to me, who could not wait to shut down the inquiry, stick the DNA profile on the national database, and wait for a hit at minimal cost. I had to fight at meetings to keep my staff and be allowed to look for the killer, arguing that the next enquiry we undertook might lead us to his door and save another woman's life and the cost of a second murder hunt.

I never felt I had the support that I got from Tom Cook on the Julie Dart murder, where I was told if I needed more money then as police officers retired they would hold the vacancies and divert the savings to me. At a meeting to review the Wendy Speakes murder there was a proposal that the inquiry be shut down. We had lines of enquiry that previous meetings had agreed should be completed but now I felt the draught on my neck as the axe was falling.

As the weeks and months passed, five thousand men were blooded for DNA without us identifying the killer. I considered the possibility that he might have committed suicide and asked to be notified of such cases where there was no apparent reason.

I researched all murders of women nationally, with one at Salcombe catching my attention. Sandra Parkinson was found near a cliff path above the Devon town. The young woman had been sexually assaulted and asphyxiated. Her killer, Alan Connors, hanged himself from a tree miles away in Cambridgeshire. The Salcombe inquiry team did not know him, and had he not left a suicide note declaring his guilt the inquiry would still be open to this day. They took a sample of DNA from his body which matched the DNA from semen left at the scene, but he was not Wendy's killer.

I was looking at suicides in surrounding force areas but could not cope with it as a national task. If my killer died in circumstances other than suicide or in force areas I was not looking at, I knew I would miss him.

I now believe that when a person dies, from whatever cause, a DNA sample should be taken so that it can be checked against outstanding DNA profiles for unsolved crimes. It seems sensible. DNA is a positive tool, but without everyone in the country being on a national register it is like looking for a needle in a haystack. What has an innocent person to hide?

Another option I had was fingerprints. We had two good prints in the sense that they were in places which made them more likely to be the killer's. They were sent to all member countries of Interpol to check on their fingerprint systems, but we had no success there either.

There was only one other crime at that time which caught my eye, and that was the murder of Julie Pacey, who was murdered at her Grantham home on 26 September 1994, six months after Wendy.

Found on the bathroom floor, the married thirty-nine-year-old had bruises on her head and had been strangled with a ligature. Her tights and underwear had been pulled down and she had been sexually assaulted, but otherwise her clothing was undisturbed. She was found by her fourteen-year-old daughter at 4.15 pm.

It appeared to me that she was probably attacked shortly after arriving home. Mrs Pacey probably went upstairs to the toilet. Her killer entered the house through the unlocked door and was able to walk up the wooden stairs without detection, as the flushing toilet would have drowned out any noise.

The Pacey house was completely different to Wendy's and Woman 'A's. It was a decent-sized detached; anyone approaching it could be clearly seen. Lincolnshire Police used Richard Badcock to profile the killer. His view was that the killing was a sexual homicide, and he could not exclude the killer being the same man as ours. Had he refined his techniques? There was no DNA, no matching fingerprints and no description of a suspect, so a definite link couldn't be made.

Hundreds of murders and sex attacks nationally going back twenty years were researched, but I was no nearer to catching our killer or connecting him to any other crimes.

Meanwhile, Michael Sams was never far from my professional life. There was always something happening with him. I read about an author who had written a book suggesting that Sams was also responsible for the abduction and murder of London estate agent Suzie Lamplugh. I knew I would have to see him to clear this up.

There had never been any evidence that Sams was Suzie's killer, except that he had kidnapped an estate agent. Conveniently for me, Sams was in Wakefield prison – just four hundred yards from the Wendy Speakes incident room. His constant battling with the prison authorities ensured he was regularly moved. Tim Grogan and I met Sams's solicitor, David Payne, at the prison on 21 April 1995.

Mr Payne spoke to the prison authorities, who had been withholding a copy of Stephanie Slater's book *Beyond Fear*, from Sams, and they reluctantly agreed to give him a copy. We were shown into the interview room, set between two corridors, with one entrance for us and one for him. As we went in, Sams stood up and nodded. 'Hello, Mr Payne. Hello, Mr Taylor,' he said politely. I was shocked by the extent to which his appearance had changed in the last two years. He looked like Cat Weasel – his hair was long and unkempt and he had a wispy beard and moustache. David Payne sat next to him, Tim and I opposite them. He was agitated and launched into a vitriolic diatribe against a prisoner he suspected of grassing him up to the screws.

'I wired up my radio to the mains electric in my cell to save on batteries but the screws turned my cell over and found the radio.' 'So what are you going to do?' I said. 'I will blind the person who grassed me up 'cos being blind is worse than being dead,' he explained. It was nice to see while his looks had changed, his true nature hadn't.

His only expense in prison, as he did not smoke or do drugs, was his radio batteries. In an attempt to save money he had somehow wired his radio through a transformer to the prison mains. He had his radio confiscated.

As I was about to broach the Lamplugh issue, he bristled: 'Anyway, Mr Taylor, you called me a fiend. I'm not a fiend.' I knew he did not like to be called a fiend but looked amazed: 'When? Where?' 'In the newspaper,' he said. 'Oh, they will have added it to a quote. Journalistic licence, Michael.' 'Anyway', he said, 'I rung you up.' 'From where?' 'From here, prison, rang that Wendy Speakes Incident Room.' I knew I had not had a call from him so I asked, 'Who did you speak to?' 'Detective Chief Inspector Gerry Dickinson', he said accentuating each individual word. I knew he must have rung. Sams has an excellent memory and he would know exactly who he spoke to.

I wondered why Gerry had not mentioned it. 'What did he say?' I asked. 'I said, "It's Michael Sams here. Can I speak to Detective Superintendent Taylor?" He just said. "Fuck off," and slammed the phone down.' I looked at Tim, we were both fighting back the tears of laughter. 'I'll speak with Mr Dickinson, Michael,' I said earnestly. It was typical of his arrogance to try to ring me, but Gerry had put him in his place.

As I looked away trying to suppress a smile, I saw a face I knew in the corridor behind Sams. It was John Cannan, named as a strong suspect for Suzie's death. Cannan was convicted of murdering Shirley Banks, a Bristol newlywed, who disappeared while shopping in October 1987. Her body was found a year later in Somerset.

I was amazed. Here I was to speak to Sams about Suzie Lamplugh and there, feet away, was Cannan. It might have been a coincidence that he was in the same prison as Sams but beyond that, I knew Sams had some-how orchestrated Cannan's presence there. As we began to talk about the Lamplugh case, Sams motioned with his head over his right shoulder and said, 'Do you know who that is?' This was his test. I suppose I would have lost face had I not known. 'John Cannan,' I said, looking at him. I spoke to Sams at length and was satisfied there was nothing new to connect him with Suzie Lamplugh. We then left.

However, Gerry Dickinson could not be allowed to get away with his faux pas. He was there when I got back to the incident room, 'Did Michael Sams ring up for me one day?' 'Told you,' he said. 'No, you didn't.' 'Er, I thought it was a wind up.' 'That would be why you told him to fuck off was it?' I said, 'Er, yes.'

We did not speak of this again, but strangely over the next few days Gerry began receiving phone calls asking for me from Lord Lucan and the missing racehorse Shergar, to name but a few.

Wendy Speakes's case was my only unsolved murder when, in September 1996, I was seconded to the Regional Crime Squad, later to become the National Crime Squad. But Wendy's was always my job. Although I had physically left the case, it was never far from my thoughts, and I kept in touch with Steve Palmer, the office manager. Over the years, if I came across anyone who looked a good candidate for the Speakes murder, I would ring it through to Steve to be checked out.

While the years rolled on, I never forgot the murder inquiries I was involved in, or the people I worked with, though some affect you more than others. Wendy Speakes was one such investigation. I had many discussions over the years on the shoe fetish angle as many people who did not have the in-depth knowledge of the inquiry would air their doubts, usually behind my back.

One Friday afternoon, 10 March 2000, nearly six years after the murder of Wendy, I was sitting in my office in Wakefield as Head of Operations for the Northern Area of the National Crime Squad when I received a call. 'Mr Taylor, it's Rod Holdsworth, Fingerprints.'

'Yes, Rod, what can I do for you?'

What he said left me stunned.

The words I had waited six years for finally came. 'We have a match with the fingerprint on the door handle on Speakes. I've rung you because we have you down as the Senior Investigating Officer.'

Rod then gave me what I had waited a long time for – a name. Christopher John Farrow, thirty-nine, born 5 September 1961. He told me Farrow had been fingerprinted in 1996 but they had only just got a match.

'Is it good enough for court?'

'Yes,' he said.

This was pretty good evidence against a man whose name meant nothing to me. I knew he was not likely to be in the Holmes computer system, otherwise we would have blooded him.

Urgent research was needed. Did the family know him? Could he have had legitimate access to Wendy's and left his print on the door handle that way? Where was he living? The address we had for him was four years out of date. Over the weekend, enquiries revealed that he had been living in Bradford in 1994 but had moved on, and no one knew either where he worked or where he lived. By Monday morning we were no farther forward, though we had contacts who might be able to assist us.

Farrow had never reapplied for his licence after his disqualification from a drink-driving conviction in June 1996 ended. It was not normal practice to take the fingerprints of people arrested for drink-driving, but his had been – a stroke of luck for us. When he was arrested, he elected unusually to be kept in custody over the weekend and dealt with on the Monday morning. Normally, people are bailed to appear at a later date. He had obviously done this to get to court, get convicted and hopefully disappear into oblivion before his prints were checked and maybe matched with any he had left at the murder scene.

He allowed his passport to expire and had not applied for a new one.

The picture was developing of a man who might be a ghost to the systems that play a large part in daily life. As the Monday progressed, we came up with an address in Cookridge, north-west Leeds. He worked as a printer for a company in Holbeck, south Leeds, just eight miles from Wendy's home.

We had a briefing in the afternoon. I knew Wendy's family did not know Farrow, and I was trying to suppress my elation at the thought that this was the man I had been looking for. We established that he lived with a woman and her young children, but we did not know whether he was working away or not. A number of the original team were called back in – DCs Mick Kelly and Mick Tedder were but two. They would interview Farrow when he was arrested.

The local night CID in Leeds was drafted in to keep an eye on his home, and a briefing was arranged for the following morning. A DNA sample was needed from Farrow, as this would prove or disprove his involvement in the murder. His sample would be fast-tracked at the only lab that could give a result in twenty-four hours, the London forensic lab. However, we could get an early indication if we also took another blood sample and sent it to Wetherby, where forensics could get us a result in four hours.

After a 6.30 am briefing the following morning, arrest, interview and search teams were dispatched to do their duties. I watched from the incident room as their cars left. I felt it was going to be a good day. Just after 7 am, officers arrived at the unassuming semi-detached house in Kirkwood Close, Cookridge. The lives of the people inside would never be the same from the second the knock on the door sounded.

A man came to the upstairs window. Officers were stunned at the remarkable likeness he had to Woman 'A's E-fit. He was arrested and brought to Wood Street police station.

The first interview would not be demanding, as a number of issues had to be resolved. We would have to show he had had the opportunity to commit the murder. If he had a cast-iron alibi, the fingerprint and DNA evidence would be open to challenge. There was always a chance that when interviewed he would offer a perfectly reasonable explanation for being at Wendy's house.

The print might be his, but how did it get on the door handle? I knew he had never worked for the firm that had fitted the door eighteen months prior to Wendy's death. But of course if the print was his, which we were certain it was, but the blood group was not, we would have to wait for the DNA result. Developments in DNA technology since 1994 had permitted the blood on the door handle, previously too small to test, to be profiled. It showed that the blood had the same DNA profile as the semen.

Everyone who saw Christopher John Farrow was stunned by his sheer ordinariness. A clean-shaven man, balding with short hair at the sides and back, he was casually dressed and walked with a pronounced limp, an injury from a motorcycle accident when he was seventeen resulting in surgery and a metal pin being inserted in his leg, but no one had mentioned a man with a limp.

While we prepared to interview him his background was being feverishly researched.

His history was traced back to his first wife, Michele Heyslip, whom he married in 1985. They lived in Horsforth, north Leeds. They had a son, Mathew, but split up shortly after his birth. They got back together just over a year later, and in 1989 they had a daughter, Danielle. The marriage once again hit the rocks in 1992, and he moved in with his parents until he went to live in a caravan on a site at Baildon, near Keighley.

While living there he met Lesley Hill. Their relationship was stormy but they moved into a flat together on the Thorpe Edge estate, Bradford, in January 1994, a few months before Wendy's murder. Just weeks after the killing, Lesley gave birth to their daughter. Their relationship ended in 1996.

Farrow then lived in various bed-and-breakfast accommodations in Leeds until he found a flat in Horsforth and met his current partner, Jane Messenger, in a local pub in early 1999. He moved in with her and her children and was living there until we came calling.

His work record was good. He had served an apprenticeship in the printing industry and worked in that trade all his adult life. The records at his present firm were abysmal, to say the least. There was no way of knowing whether or not he had been in work at the time of the murder.

Farrow's previous criminal history gave no insight into his character. As a juvenile he was fined for bizarrely trying to steal a steak from a diner's plate in a restaurant in Skipton, North Yorkshire. His only other serious brush with the law was his 1996 drink-driving offence.

The first interview was merely for the purpose of taking blood samples, so they could be dispatched to the forensics laboratory. The following interviews would be about the specific details of the crime. The first milestone was to establish whether or not the print was his. When it was put to him that his fingerprint was found at the scene of the murder, he offered no explanation. He said he had only once been to Wakefield, shopping with his partner. He had not gone out of the city centre and certainly did not know Wendy Speakes, Balne Lane or the Cliffe Tree pub.

This was a good start. His fingerprint had not got there from a legitimate visit, though proving the print did not prove the killer.

It was put to Farrow that he had been to Wakefield and was lying, as his boss had told us that the two of them had visited when they did some printing work for a club in the city.

He stuck to his guns. By the end of the first day, I was certain we had our murderer. He gave no explanation for his fingerprint being at the murder scene. I guessed he was banking on it being some object that was movable, an envelope or the stockings packet, so he could try to explain it without admitting going into Wendy's home.

The enormity of what he had actually done might be too much for him to come to terms with, even without having to speak about it.

There was plenty to do as more information came in. The search teams at his home had not found any startling evidence, but they did make one interesting discovery. Concealed between the mattress and the base of the bed he shared with Jane Messenger lay a poster-sized picture of a naked woman in high-heeled shoes, a classic shoe fetish picture.

I hoped to get the DNA result by 4.30 pm on Wednesday, ironically the sixth anniversary of Wendy's murder.

The interviews started again on the Wednesday with DCs Mick Kelly and Mick Tedder. This time he was told the fingerprint was on a non-movable object in a place we knew the killer had been. He was still unmoved. 'I did not have a car at that time and had no reason to come to Wakefield,' he said.

The turning point was the telephone call from the forensic science laboratory at Wetherby. They had been doing the blood tests – Farrow's blood was the same as the killer's. If it had been different we would have been sunk. The DNA profile would surely now prove to be the same. I was delighted.

I doubted that his being the same blood group would break him down. I thought he might be waiting for the DNA result. I had been observing the interviews on a TV monitor from an adjacent room. I watched as he was told that the blood at the scene was the same type as his and belonged to only 6.4

per cent of the population. It was then that he totally crumbled.

His head dropped and he muttered, 'She was in the wrong place at the wrong time.' I felt a surge of triumph mixed with sadness for Wendy. I knew this would herald his confession.

'Tell us what happened.'

Farrow began: 'I had a bad day, I had an argument with Lesley. She was pregnant, it was only a few weeks before the baby was born. I wasn't getting any sex either. I went to work but finished early in the morning and took the rest of the day off. I got a bus to Wakefield and up to Ossett and back into Wakefield.

'Someone was going to get it.

'I wandered around Wakefield and ended up at Wendy Speakes's house.

'I saw her arrive home, went over and knocked at the front door. When she opened it, I pushed her inside the house, shut the door, took her upstairs and raped her. I walked out of the bedroom and realised she could recognise me, so I went back and killed her.'

And there you have a murderer explaining why he took a life. He had had six years to repeatedly turn over in his mind what he had done. Some parts he could not deny, such as the fact that he raped and killed Wendy Speakes. But why he did it would have changed slightly every time he thought about it, until he reached a point where what he did was as acceptable to him as he could make it. His confession was subtle. Without saying it directly, he blamed his partner Lesley – it was her fault that he was bad that day. He said he murdered Wendy as an afterthought because she could recognise him rather than admitting the truth that he set out to kill that day.

He was asked what he meant by 'get it'. 'I intended to rape a woman, not to kill someone,' he explained. When asked why he had a knife and the rag he used to gag Wendy if it was not premeditated, he said, 'They were in my pockets. I used them at work. The rag was normally used at work to clean my hands but I put it in Wendy's mouth to stop her crying out. I put the knife and my clothes in a skip outside my work premises.'

He said he arrived in Wakefield at 10 am but could not account for his movements between then and 6 pm, when he must have been at Wendy's home. He admitted buying the stockings as he wandered around, but couldn't or wouldn't give an explanation as to what they were for.

I had always wondered how he knew Wendy lived alone. 'I didn't. She told me her husband would be home soon.' Then he said: 'I read what was said about the killer having a shoe fetish. You're wrong there, I haven't got one.' The remark cut no ice with me. I knew he had. Later in the interview, he returned to the point and confessed: 'I suppose I do have a shoe fetish,' before explaining how he chose the shoes from the cupboard for Wendy to wear while he raped her. So the powder-blue shoes were hers.

The evidence of his shoe fetish was unmistakable. In choosing the blue shoes for Wendy to wear and putting the black shoes on the dresser next to where he raped her, he could not hope to hide it. His first wife told us how he would choose her shoes for her and even made her dig the garden in high-heeled shoes. When I did my TV appeal, his first wife saw it and the E-fit and heard me state that the killer had a shoe fetish. She actually said to a friend, 'That could be Chris.' Unfortunately she dismissed the idea from her mind, just as Susan Oake did with Sams until she saw the *Crimewatch* appeal.

When and why Farrow decided to kill Wendy were critical issues. He undoubtedly arrived at her door with his killer's kit. Significantly, he had made no effort to cover his face, and because of the motorcycle injury to his hip he could not perform sexual intercourse in the traditional missionary position, so he forced Wendy to kneel over the side of the bed. If Wendy realised there was something wrong with his leg and provided a half-decent E-fit, his arrest would be inevitable. Wendy Speakes's murder was no afterthought.

The pattern and amount of blood on the duvet suggested the neck wounds were the last to be inflicted, as they had not bled as profusely as they would have had they been inflicted first, suggesting she had already lost a lot of blood through the other stab wounds. The rest of the wounds were in Wendy's back, indicative of her being stabbed while Farrow had raped her. She was dying before he left the room. Had he, as he said, left her uninjured, then returned to the room knife in hand, Wendy would surely have realised what was going to happen and fought. Yet there was no sign of a struggle and no defence wounds. I believe he stabbed Wendy while he raped her, and this was put to him, but he dismissed it as untrue. When asked how he cut himself, he said, 'No idea, didn't even know I had.'

His vagueness on how he spent eight hours that day in Wakefield was in my view because he could not tell the truth, which was that he was stalking Woman 'A'. Farrow said, 'I wandered around the Wakefield centre and eventually ended up outside Wendy Speakes's house, when I saw her arrive home.' The truth more likely was that he spent the day stalking Woman 'A' and, after his failed attempt to get into her house, reverted to Wendy as someone he had seen when stalking Woman 'A', which was possible as there was a connection between the two in terms of the pub next door to Wendy's. If so, he knew she lived alone. Or was Wendy really in the wrong place at the wrong time? Did he choose her by chance, having seen her for the first time getting off the bus in Wakefield and following her home?

I had no doubt that Woman 'A' was his first-choice victim. Nor was it a coincidence that Farrow purchased the black stockings from Superdrug, a shop Woman 'A' had been in. He probably followed her in there. Why did he tie loops in the stockings? Simply to restrain her, or were the stockings really for his first-choice victim to wear in the attack he planned on her? Did he always intend to kill his victim? Or did his failure with his first-choice victim anger him to the point where he decided to kill Wendy?

The difficulty in unlocking Farrow's secret was that he vehemently denied calling at Woman 'A's home or at any other. Was he the same man that she had seen early that morning? If he did go into work first, could he have got to her home at the time he said? I somehow felt that this was not something that happened because he was having a bad day. I believe he probably made several visits to Wakefield that we did not know about and stalked both Woman 'A' and Wendy.

On whether the killing was premeditated he said finally, 'Look, I accept I am a rapist who killed but I am not a killer who raped.' I believed that this was also a product of the six years' wait for the knock on his door and was the least repulsive form of words he could think of to explain the brutal act he had performed.

On the evening of 15 March 2000, DI Steve Palmer charged Farrow with the murder, rape and buggery of Wendy Speakes. The neighbour of Woman 'B' later identified him on an identification parade, but neither Woman 'A' nor Woman 'B' did. He was also charged with the offences of burglary with intent to rape in respect of both Woman 'A' and Woman 'B'.

The question left unanswered was why it had taken four years to get the 'fingerprint hit' from the time Farrow's prints were taken and put on the Automatic Fingerprint Recognition (AFR) computer to his arrest. The answer must lie in the vagaries of the computer and the manner in which prints are assessed. The AFR computer is in Tacoma in Washington State,

USA. Thirty-three of the forty-three forces in England and Wales use the system and it contains the fingerprints of 3.5 million convicted people.

The partial print from the door handle was regularly run through the system as new prints were entered every day. The partial print had been checked against the database of prints several hundred times, but it was not until the day Rod Holdsworth from the fingerprint department rang me that a match was made. They would usually ask for the hundred nearest prints to our mark and then they would manually check the results they got. Farrow had never been among the hundred until that day, and then he came out for the first time ever – at number one.

## chapter nine

# A Day Out from Jail

It had been worthwhile coming back to the university, reflected the twenty-two-year-old student as she made her way back to her car. She'd spent the afternoon in the library putting the finishing touches to her dissertation – and now she could enjoy the rest of summer. But as she started up her mother's car, her carefree life came to a grinding halt.

The young woman was about to leave Woodhouse Lane multistorey carpark in Leeds when she heard someone running towards her. Before she sensed the danger, a man leaned in the car, put a knife to her neck and growled: 'The police are after me. Don't do anything stupid.'

'Don't hurt me,' she pleaded. He pushed her over to the passenger side and made her kneel in the footwell, saying, 'I'm not going to. I just want your car. Keep your head down and eyes shut.'

It was 4.20 pm on Wednesday, 26 July 1995.

She noticed he had problems selecting reverse gear as he manoeuvred from the parking space. Then he drove to the top floor, parked, and told her to put her hands behind her back and keep her eyes closed. He bound her wrists together with sticky tape and pushed her back in the seat.

Though her eyes were already shut, he ordered: 'Keep them closed or it'll burn.' Using his finger, he brushed glue across her eyelids, causing them immediately to seal together. Then he put her in a normal sitting position and drove into Leeds.

237

He pulled her purse from her shorts pocket and asked how much he could get on her Midland Bank Switch card. 'Fifty pounds,' she said.

'Just want to go for a mile, let you out and go to the A1,' he muttered.

She twice complained that the wrist bindings were painfully tight before he stopped the car and cut them. 'Do you mind if I cut your arm?' he said, almost politely.

'I'd prefer it if you didn't,' she replied.

He rebound her wrists less tightly with Sellotape. 'What's the PIN number for your bank card?' he said. Fearing for her safety, she told him.

In her handbag was a letter addressed to a man in Germany. Her abductor asked who he was and she said it was her boyfriend. At that moment he pulled her towards him and tried to kiss her. She did not react. He tried again, with the same result.

On his third attempt, she tried to avoid his kisses by moving her head. Annoyed, he slapped her hard on her left cheek. 'You do what I want you to do, do you hear me?' She asked him not to hurt her. 'If I wanted to, I'd use this.' He pressed the cold tip of a knife blade into her waist and then against her right nipple, threatening to cut it off.

Suddenly he ripped open her shirt to reveal her bra. Then he slid his hand under her bra and felt her breasts. She became angry. She knew where this was leading and spat at him: 'Come on, if we're going to have sex, let's do it.'

He was irked: 'Shut up. You're getting on my nerves.' Apparently rattled, he drove off, stopping at a grassy embankment.

She dropped back with a jolt as he reclined her seat, pulled up her bra and again fondled her breasts. She heard the clunk as he let his seat down, then a shuffling sound which she knew was him removing his clothes. She sensed he was moving over to rape her. With all her strength, she wrenched her wrists apart, breaking the Sellotape, at the same time as she brought her knees up to her chest and pushed out, forcing him away from her.

Fighting blind, she struggled as he twice hit her on her face. He must have been holding the knife as she cut two fingers in the struggle. He forced her onto her stomach and held her down, pulling the old tape from her hands and retying them behind her back with a piece of her torn shirt.

She was relieved when he got out of the car. For the moment the attack had ended, and from the sounds and the rocking of the car she assumed he was trying to wipe away his fingerprints. He got back in and drove off with her now kneeling on the passenger-side floor, facing the seat and with her hands tied behind her. During the journey he stopped three times.

The last time he stopped, he got out of the car and said, 'I'm going to dust it. Tell them I'm English.' She waited until she thought he had gone, then started frantically to rub her eyes against the car seat in an attempt to get them open, but still she could not see. She stretched across the seats and thumped the car horn with her foot to frighten him off and attract attention. She then climbed out of the car, distressed, crying and shouting for help.

Just after 6 pm, a number of people saw the young woman staggering dishevelled and distraught in Globe Road, Leeds. Her eyelids remained glued together, her hands bound behind her back, and she was shouting: 'Help me. I've been kidnapped.' Her face was red from where he'd slapped her; she was practically topless with her shirt in tatters where it had been ripped. Her nightmare had lasted nearly two hours before he dumped her at the busy roadside.

My week had not got off to a good start. Monday morning blues set in at 2 am when I was called out to a murder at Bramley in Leeds. Malcolm Dunkerley, forty-three, had died after being stabbed twice in the chest and once in the stomach. We were closing in on the killer, whose identity I now knew, and it was only a matter of time before he'd be locked up.

By 8 am on Thursday, 27 July, I was in the incident room at Pudsey police station in west Leeds, from where I was conducting the inquiry. I started on my routine morning calls to the managers of the CID officers on my patch. 'Got anything overnight?' I said to DS Paul Langan, at Millgarth. 'Just one funny job.' I knew what he meant by funny. After that phone call, I was to launch what was to become the biggest manhunt since the Sams inquiry, which at one point was to involve every force in the country.

Paul told me of the student's horrendous ordeal. 'Any suspects?'

'No,' Paul replied.

'Got a statement yet?'

'Yes,' said Paul.

'I'll pop down later in the day to read it.'

Crimes involving women being abducted in their cars and sexually assaulted are rare. Sexual attacks usually form part of a series, so put the two together and we had an unusual beast on our hands. Only I didn't know what a truly appalling creature he would turn out to be.

I landed at Millgarth later that afternoon. After looking at a supergrass case I was running, and with the Wendy Speakes murder now in its second year, I sat in my office to read the victim's statement.

I felt for this woman. Her eyes were left tender and sore. They had to be bathed to remove the glue and allow her to see again. She was unable to describe in any detail her attacker's face. But from the fleeting glance she had managed, she said he was white with a tanned complexion, aged twenty-eight, five foot ten inches tall, of average build with gingery-brown hair, green eyes and an Irish accent. The weapon was a kitchen knife with an eight-and-a-half-inch blade.

Although she could not see what he was doing, he'd taken her bank card and £30 cash. Her bank later told us the card was used to withdraw £50 at 8.10 pm, two hours after her release, at a cashpoint thirteen miles away in Dewsbury.

When the student's car was examined there were four cuts in the front seats where the abductor had stabbed them with his knife. A forensic examination revealed bloodstaining in several places, including both the driver's and passenger doors. The student was adamant she had never touched the driver's door. Swabs of all stains were taken for DNA analysis.

Paul arranged for the victim to hear tapes compiled by the Linguistics Department at York's University of Ripon and St John, to try to identify the accent. She was fairly certain it was similar to a Belfast one.

Two years later, ironically while watching an episode of *The Bill*, she heard an actor speak with the same accent as her attacker. He was contacted and told us he came from Dundee and that he had used his own accent in the police series.

On 8 November, a phone call from the forensic lab confirmed that DNA had been obtained from a smear of blood. There was also a fingerprint on her love letter which the abductor had handled. The print could not be eliminated but was too small a fragment to test on the computer using the Automatic Fingerprint Retrieval system.

It was a nasty attack which would have ended in rape had it not been for the young woman's brave fight. It was also unusual. I could not recall another where the victim's eyes were glued together. And neither were kidnapping a victim in her own car and stealing money regular features of such attacks.

But I knew of two incidents in Leeds and Bradford in the early 1980s where two women were abducted in their cars, raped and had property stolen. One aspect bore heavily on my mind – one of the women was thrown into the canal yards from Globe Road, where the student had escaped from her attacker. The earlier cases were investigated at Holbeck police station, where hopefully the papers would be still filed.

Although it was a busy time when the student was abducted and abandoned, no one had seen her or the attacker. We had no E-fit and his description was so vague it was of little help. Because of the unusual nature of the attack, I decided to do a national search for similar offences, and came across an incident in Nottingham two years earlier which shared some key elements with my case. Could it be the same man? If so, the attacks were seventy miles apart. I got a copy of the report. It did not make pleasant reading.

At 2.25 pm on Friday, 14 May 1993, a young air hostess was driving her Volvo into the multistorey carpark at Broadmarsh shopping centre on the edge of the city centre. The twenty-three-year-old manoeuvred her car into a ground-floor parking space and was rummaging in her handbag when suddenly the driver's door opened and there, leaning into the car, was a man she thought she had seen moments earlier walking up the ramp that she had just driven down.

In an instant, his arm was around her head and a knife thrust at her throat. 'The police are after me. I need the car,' he barked, as he forced her into the passenger-side footwell. As he drove off, he told her not look at his face and threatened her if she gave him any trouble. Finally, he told her to take off her leather jacket and waistcoat, which he then put over her head.

His driving was erratic and he seemed to have difficulty finding reverse gear. 'How do I get to London from here?' he said.

After driving for some time, he parked up. She knew he was searching her handbag by the conversation. 'I need enough money to get back down South,' he said. He asked whether she was religious and she told him she was a Catholic. 'So am I, would you believe. You'd better start fucking praying, then,' he said, before adding that he did not trust women.

She was still crouched down in the footwell as he warned: 'Don't fucking move or I'll slit your throat.' He also asked whether she had any alcohol or cigarettes in the car, and why she was shaking. 'Because I'm terrified,' she said. He just laughed.

He found her bank card in her bag and quizzed her on the PIN number. Hoping to pacify him, she said, 'You can get money from my

Halifax building society account.' Immediately and aggressively he spat back: 'What, and get my face on fucking camera?'

Next time he stopped, she sensed they were at a secluded location. From the tyre noise, she knew he had turned off the main road and onto a gravel surface. Despite being trained to deal with hijack situations and difficult passengers, the hostess knew she was powerless as he forced her to strip and then raped and buggered her. As he did so, he pinched her breasts and stomach, slapped and kneaded her buttocks, and ran a knife blade over her body. 'Have you got a boyfriend?' he asked.

'Yes,' she answered.

'You'd better start fucking praying hard, then,' he retorted. He called her a whore and a blonde bitch, and likened her to his wife in that respect. He also blamed his wife for the 'mess he was in' and made derogatory comments about women generally.

But her ordeal was not over. He threatened to kill her before dragging her from the car and shoving her into the boot. He tied her hands together, forced a glove into her mouth and covered her with a coat. He then laid her, like a parcel, under the shelf.

They were on the move again. He asked her where the nearest city was, but as she hadn't a clue where she was she could not tell him. Later he announced they were in Derby town centre. When he stopped the car, he prodded her with his knife as he warned: 'You'd better not be lying about the PIN number. You'd better hope the cashpoint pays out.'

Five minutes later he returned, his mood aggressive as he put his knife to her eye. 'You lied about the number.' She repeated it and assured him it was right. He left again, returning a short while later with the money, and drove off.

Fifteen minutes later he stopped again and asked her whether she had a match. 'No, but there's a cigarette lighter on the dashboard,' she said, in an effort to placate him.

'That's no fucking good,' he said. About forty-five minutes later he pulled up again. She heard him unscrew the petrol cap, but no fuel being poured in over a two- to three-minute period. He drove off, stopping a short time later. 'You move within fifteen minutes and I'll murder the next woman I see. And the next one will suffer at the hands of you,' he warned, before cutting her bonds and fleeing.

A woman walking with her child spotted the car at 5.10 pm on Peverill Drive, Nottingham, only half a mile from where the stewardess was abducted. Her ordeal had lasted over three and a half hours. She was hysterical and in deep shock as she got out the car, crying: 'Phone the police. I've been raped.'

She described the rapist as white, six foot two, aged thirty-five to thirty-nine, with a thin gangly build, and speaking with a Glaswegian accent. He had collar-length, dirty blond hair, and she likened him to TV actor Dennis Waterman. A fingerprint on the seat belt was believed to be the man's. His DNA was obtained from semen after intimate swabs were taken from the victim.

Nottinghamshire Police were unaware of the attacks in Leeds and Bradford in the early 1980s. In fact, I felt they seemed to have done very little considering the seriousness of the crime. I knew they had doubts that the man the victim had passed on the ramp was the man who had attacked her. If not, then the description was of the wrong person. She had assumed this was her attacker as she had seen no one else near her.

I assumed it was for this reason that they had not done what I would have expected when investigating such a brutal attack. Even though they had the rapist's DNA, they appeared to have attempted little in the way of taking samples from suspects for comparison. In fact, to be blunt, they had not taken a single sample. I was disgusted. We had taken five thousand samples on the Speakes case and I was constantly looking for the killer. But here, it appeared, they were content to sit it out and hope that at some time the guy would be arrested for something else and they would get a DNA match.

The wait-and-see option is a cheap one, with no particular expense needing devoting to the hunt for the attacker. The problem was the eventual match might not be with that of a man arrested but might relate to an undetected crime, such as a murder. I was concerned when I read about the petrol cap being removed in the report, and her abductor asking for a light, which she assumed was for a cigarette. I had no doubt, after a petrol-sodden rag was found in the car, that he intended to torch it – with her still inside.

There were no fingerprints or forensic links between the Nottingham attack and ours. But when forensics in Wetherby tested a sample of semen from the Nottingham attack, it matched the DNA profile from the blood on the driver's door handle of our crime.

So we knew it was the same man who had attacked two women two years apart. We just didn't know who he was or where he was.

I was also looking at the attacks from the early 1980s, but trying to make sense of it all was not easy.

I got together the paperwork from those cases and sat in the quiet of my office to study them. My first surprise was that Detective Superintendent John Stainthorpe, who then headed the investigations, had linked a rape in Leicester to his two in Bradford and Leeds. I ordered that the paperwork be sent to me.

As I read the files on the Yorkshire attacks I thought only a fool would not have seen the stunning similarities. The events leading up to the first attack began at 9.40 pm on 3 December 1982, when a mother-of-two drove to Bradford for her regular Friday night out with her girlfriends.

It was foggy as the thirty-year-old housewife drove into the carpark at the rear of St George's Hall near the city centre, but she turned the wrong way and ended up in a secluded area. Unconcerned by the fog and isolation, she opened the door to get out, but as she did so a man pushed her back into the car, putting a gloved hand over her eyes so she could not see him.

He spoke in a staccato manner. 'Right, lassie, move over. Don't look at me. I don't want to hurt you, lass. I need to use your car, that's all I want. I want to get to the other side of Bradford.' His accent was gruff and Scottish.

He pushed her into the passenger seat so she was facing away from him. The speed of the attack stunned her. 'Direct me to the Mecca Dance Hall on Manningham Lane, avoiding the city centre,' he ordered. She noticed he had difficulty changing gear. He followed her directions until they could go no farther without driving through the centre, and she told him so. 'Right, we'll go to the airport and you can direct me there,' he replied.

The fog was thick by now, but he was driving at dangerously high speeds, constantly cursing. When they arrived at the airport, he drove down a back lane to a dirt track. He said he had to catch a plane to Edinburgh at five minutes to midnight. She was terrified as she realised he was not looking for the main entrance. 'Well, this is it, he's going to kill me,' she told herself.

Making small talk, he asked her whether she was married. Hoping to appeal to any compassion in his nature, she said she was divorced with two little daughters who'd be waiting at home for her, but it was to no avail.

'I want to be near the airport lights. I'll tie you up so I can get away before you contact the cops,' he said as he pulled her jumper up around her neck and tied the sleeves in a knot on top of her head.

He bound her hands behind her back with material he had brought with him and then he tore a strip from an old seat cover to blindfold her.

As she lay trussed up, she felt her bra being pulled over her breasts. He was talking of his dislike of prostitutes, then asked whether she had a boyfriend and bit her breasts painfully hard. 'You'd better not be a prostitute,' he growled.

Suddenly he was out of the car and opening the passenger door. He leaned in and pulled off her clothes and boots, throwing them outside. He tried but failed to recline the seat, and told her to move over into the already laid-back driver's seat.

He then violently grabbed her, ripped off her underwear and attempted sex, but failed to get an erection. He pulled the jumper off her head and started kissing her. Then he raped her over a ten-minute period, throughout which he asked her about boyfriends.

She told him she was convinced he was going to kill her. 'I can't, I only have my bare hands. I've enough problems with the police without a murder charge,' he said. He got out of the car, threw her clothes in it and bade her farewell, saying, 'I'm going to get my plane.'

There was barely time for it to dawn on her that she had survived the ordeal when to her unimaginable horror he was back. 'Have you ever been to York?' he asked casually, announcing that they would go there as he had a friend in the city.

He asked her why a red light was flashing on the dashboard. 'Petrol warning light,' she said.

'Will it make Edinburgh on a full tank?'

'No, there's a problem with the cylinder head and it will only go twenty miles at any one time.'

As suddenly as it began, this poor woman's nightmare ended. 'Count to a hundred,' he ordered. She was counting as he left, but a minute later he returned. 'Start counting again,' he said, and left again. When she reached a hundred, she pulled off the blindfold and looked around. She was on a petrol station forecourt.

Her instincts were to get away. Her panic and fear were almost out of control when her car wouldn't start. After five or six attempts, it fired into action and she drove off. In the distance, she spotted blue flashing lights and frantically drove towards them. Traumatised by her ordeal, and dressed only in a jumper and socks with a wool car seat cover wrapped around her, she saw police officers dealing with a road accident. She leapt from her car and ran to them.

Tears streaming down her face, she managed to blurt out what had happened. She had been driven from Bradford, around the outskirts of Leeds and was now on York Road in east Leeds. Her ordeal lasted two hours.

She described her attacker as white, thirty-five or younger and speaking with a strong Scottish accent. There were definite links between the Leeds student attack, the Bradford one and the Nottingham offence. The styles of the attacks, his conversation and the accent were enough similarities for me to be convinced it was the same man. But there was an eleven-year gap between the Bradford and Nottingham offences. Where had he been – prison?

My day drew to a close, but I would not leave work until I'd studied the report on the Leeds assault from the 1980s. I knew that, although the two were years apart, it had a closer link with my crime as both women were left within yards of each other. I did not think it could be as bad as the previous woman's ordeal. I was very wrong.

This attack occurred exactly a month after the Bradford case. At 10 pm on 3 January 1983, a twenty-six-year-old mother-of-two drove to her part-time job at Leeds General Infirmary. Parking her car, she became aware of a man wearing a sheepskin coat near by. He opened the car door and asked whether it belonged to her. Before she could answer, he thrust his hand across her mouth and pushed her over to the passenger seat.

Pinning her down, he shouted: 'Don't scream and you won't get hurt. I'm borrowing your car for ten minutes to go to Pudsey.' He covered her head, told her to face the passenger window, climbed into the car, and set off out of the city.

He stopped in a secluded wooded area. The woman had no idea where she was as he tied her hands behind her back with rope. She was frightened but calm and confident in the belief that if she did what he said he would not hurt her.

He rummaged through her bags before putting her empty shopping bag over her head. 'I don't want you to see my face,' he explained, and she hadn't.

She was lying quietly in the reclined seat, tied up, blindfolded, awaiting her fate, when she felt him touching her. He pulled up her jumper and bra, exposing her breasts, and said he was going to rape her. When she began weeping, he became aggressive.

He pulled off her clothes and threw them outside the car, climbed into the passenger side next to her and removed his trousers. He bit her nipples so hard she complained, and surprisingly he became gentler. She still had the shopping bag over her face. He pushed it up and kissed her on the lips. She smelled his Brut aftershave, along with his sweaty body odour.

He tried to rape her but could not achieve an erection. His second attempt, unfortunately for her, was successful. He sadistically laughed at her fear and distress. 'I'll shoot you in the back of your head,' he threatened.

He let her put some clothes back on before tying her hands behind her back with her bra and gagging her with an old maternity dress from her car.

After searching the boot, he came back with an extension lead, which he used to bind her hands and feet. He replaced the bag on her head and drove back to Leeds city centre.

After a short drive, he stopped the car. It was dark and she was still bound hand and foot, gagged and with the bag over her head. Suddenly he opened the door and part carried, part dragged her from the car. She stumbled and fell over a fence, catching herself on sharp wire. She got back up only to be led a little farther, before he deliberately pushed her backward.

As she fell into the darkness, she fleetingly expected to land on grass. But that was not the case. Our man had much more sinister plans. She plunged into an ice-cold blackness. He pushed her, bound and gagged, into the freezing murky waters of the Leeds and Liverpool Canal.

It was six feet deep and the bag over her head quickly filled with water. She was minutes from drowning, but this courageous woman was not giving up without a fight. Desperately struggling to free herself from her shackles, and with restricted leg movement, she somehow managed to find her saviour – a stone on the canal bottom. Teetering on her tiptoes on the stone for several minutes, she kept her head above water and saved her own life.

Frantic and terrified, she pulled the cable off her hands and feet and the bag from her head and threw them onto the bank. She glanced up to see her abductor standing watching her nearly drown and shouting he was going to get her. Although petrified with cold and fear, she managed to swim to the opposite bank and pull herself out of the water in time to see her would-be killer casually drive off in her car.

He had taken her to a remote carpark by the canal near the Doncaster Monkbridge Engineering Company on Globe Road. Dripping wet and partially clothed, she climbed over a wall to get onto the roadside. At 11.35 pm and in a hysterical state, she flagged down a passing taxi-driver. Her ordeal had lasted just over one and a half hours. She had been raped, thrown in a canal and left for dead.

She said her abductor was aged twenty-five to thirty-five, clean shaven with thick, dark collar-length hair. He had a distinct Scottish accent and looked scruffy, smelling of body odour and Brut aftershave.

As I studied the reports on the attacks, I knew the two in the 1990s were connected, and without doubt the two from the 1980s were also linked. The question was, were all four? If so, it would mean one man had for thirteen years roamed free, attacking women in a cruel manner at will.

I compared all the attacks, and saw that they all displayed five phases. First, he snatched women from carparks. Second, he told them he just wanted their car and then drove out of the city. Third, in most cases, he bit their breasts. Fourth, he raped his victims. Finally, after a further drive, he stole money and other items from them.

An incident room was set up to investigate the 1980s attacks, commanded by Detective Superintendent John Stainthorpe, who linked the two crimes through their similarities and a connection through stolen vehicles. The attack on the hospital worker was treated as abduction, rape and attempted murder.

Bizarrely, it seemed our man was a petty thief first, a rapist second. The sheepskin coat that he wore in the hospital worker attack was stolen from a car in Leeds on 10 December, and was linked to him through the use of a stolen credit card. The places at which he used the cards indicated he lived in the Leeds area.

I then received the report and papers on an attack on a twenty-year-old single office receptionist in Leicester. On 10 May 1984, she was driving her employer's white van into the city centre, intending to visit a nightclub. At 10.15 pm, as the woman parked in Every Street, a stranger opened the car door.

He grabbed her hair and put a knife to her neck. 'Don't make a noise. Move over to the passenger seat.' He got into the driving seat and said, 'I'll drop you off at the other side of town.'

He drove for twenty minutes, repeatedly saying, 'I only want the van to go to London,' before pulling up at a gateway near an access road to the M1.

Knife still in hand, he said, 'No fast moves, lassie.' He asked for her money and she gave him a few pounds from her purse. 'Take your clothes off,' he muttered. When she was naked, he tied her hands behind her back, kissed her, and asked whether she was married.

He fondled and bit her breasts, kissed her between her legs and pushed his fingers in her vagina and anus, causing so much pain she screamed out.

Blindfolding her with her own blouse, he forcibly and violently raped her, causing her to scream again. After the attack he took off her blindfold and she saw that he had scored her breasts and stomach with the knife. She was forced into the passenger footwell with her hands tied behind her back and her blouse covering her head.

After a short drive he stopped again, saying he was filling up with petrol and would knife her if she moved. Terrified after her ordeal, she remained crouching for ten minutes before bursting out of the van to discover she was back in Leicester city centre, only fifty yards from where she had been abducted.

She was taken to the police station by a passer-by. She described her attacker as aged twenty-eight to thirty, with a Geordie accent, mousey unkempt hair and wearing a donkey jacket and denim jeans. The description was similar to that in the two attacks in Bradford and Leeds.

Similarities between the three offences convinced senior investigating officers at West Yorkshire and Leicestershire that they were the work of the same man, but they were not publicly linked at the time, maybe because they had no evidence or fingerprints to link them.

But I had a problem. I was amazed to learn that Leicester Police could not find any trace of their file on the attack. It involved kidnapping, rape and theft, and the way it was carried out suggested it was linked to other crimes. Yet the original investigation papers were missing. The perpetrator would expect a life sentence but could arguably escape prosecution if vital original statements and documents were missing.

The argument that all five offences were linked was interesting. Without doubt the Leeds student and stewardess attacks were, as were the Bradford and 1983 Leeds attacks. There was insufficient information to link the Leicester one. Somehow, I had to find a link between all the incidents beyond the methodology of his crimes – fingerprints, for example.

Did the rapist's movements and the locations of the offences fall into any pattern? Was he at those places by choice or did his work take him there? A serial rapist, a brutal man on the verge of becoming a killer who struck across a large area of the country, could not be caught by just me and another officer working part time on the case. I would need a dedicated team to catch him, so I applied to force HQ for funding to put the whole inquiry on the Holmes computer. I was disappointed when I was given just a few extra staff and limited funding.

Having such a small staff and budget meant I was unable to actively search for him, as the officers were concentrating on pulling together information on the five attacks. I met with the team to discuss how we would tackle the investigation. I kept returning to the same point. 'Where was he between 1984 and 1993? It is hard to believe that he has not struck in those intervening years, unless he was in prison.'

We researched sex offenders nationally, looking for someone of a similar description who was serving a lengthy sentence between the 1980s and 1990s series. It would not be confined to those with a Scottish or Irish accent, as he could have faked that.

Local sex offenders in Nottingham had never been researched. The police there were taking little cognisance of the suspect's description, which in terms of his hair, height and build greatly differed from ours. Yet the DNA told us they were the same man. And then, after initially publicising the Dennis Waterman lookalike E-fit, they decided to withdraw it. I had no problem with that, but couldn't understand why they had done no work on local sex offenders.

So I sent my own officers to Nottingham to make enquiries. I had an agreement with their SIO that a Nottingham officer would pair up with every one I sent. But Nottingham reneged on it and no officers ever materialised, for reasons known only to them. They did not seem to want to become part of a joint investigation into two very serious crimes with undeniable links. There had to be a will to succeed, but I felt it was missing in Nottingham's attitude. They just didn't seem interested.

Equally, West Yorkshire Police were still not being as supportive with staff or money as I felt they should be. It was not like the Julie Dart inquiry, where the potential threat of the attacker was recognised. Attitudes had changed. Saving cash was the priority, not detection of crime, it seemed.

I was convinced that one man was responsible for all five attacks. The clues to link them all lay in the two Leeds abductions. The last victim was picked up at the Woodhouse carpark, a short walk from where the 1983 victim was abducted, and both ended up by the canal in Globe Road just outside the city centre.

I put in another bid for money to headquarters and was given a further limited amount. On 30 January 1996, I launched Operation Dab from the Millgarth incident room. I felt, despite a lack of money, staff and interest on the part of my force and others, that I was finally getting somewhere.

In mid-June 1996, I visited *Crimewatch* to present the five attacks on the programme. I made a straightforward appeal, especially to wives, girlfriends and prison officers. I publicly warned: 'This man is a danger to women and we must catch him at the earliest opportunity.' I believed that if he had not killed already it was inevitable he would. If he thought a victim had seen his face, he could easily kill them. He was happy to watch the 1983 Leeds victim nearly drown in the canal.

The big question I wanted an answer to was what was this man up to after the 1984 attack and the next one we knew of in 1993 in Nottingham.

I also stressed he could be faking his Scottish accent. Between the incident room in Leeds and the *Crimewatch* studio, I had 205 calls. None looked of any great value, except one from a possible victim.

I used the dates and locations of the crimes to eliminate suspects and DNA as a final discriminator. It would be a long road to catch the rapist, and it was not made any easier being dogged with lack of money and officers.

The inquiry continued with uncertainty over funding and no commitment by my bosses to upgrade the investigation to full-blown incident status. But after two years of having the case in my portfolio, I was on the move to the Regional Crime Squad, where I was appointed Regional Co-ordinator. I was sorry to leave the inquiry in its apparent state of limbo and with the rapist still at large.

But I continued to watch its progress from a distance, and in March 1997, six months after I left, the three forces involved – West Yorkshire, Nottingham and Leicester – finally accepted the links between the attacks and added a further three offences to the list. That gave me some satisfaction.

The first of these new incidents came from my *Crimewatch* appeal, when a twenty-year-old shop manager rang in. Her attack had occurred on 15 November 1985, when, at 6 pm, she walked to her car, parked on waste ground adjacent to St George's Church in Doncaster town centre.

Our rapist stuck to his usual routine. As the woman got into her car, he confronted her with a knife. 'Move over. Look away, look that way,' he shouted. He climbed in and instructed her to undo her clothing. He fondled her breasts, put his hand between her legs and rubbed her between her thighs.

When he climbed over to the passenger side, she realised he was going to rape her and shouted at him mockingly, 'If you're going to do it, do it.' Just as when the Leeds student stood up to him, this unsettled him. He immediately stopped, got out of the car and ran off. She straightened her clothing and climbed into the driver's seat, only to see him back at her door. She quickly locked it and he ran off. She reported the incident to the police, but yet again the paperwork relating to the original investigation could not be found.

Another crime that was now being considered part of the series was the death of Shani Warren. She was twenty-six and secretary to the divisional manager of a company, Microscope, which specialised in intelligent electronic systems. The millionaire's daughter left her £70,000 home in Stoke Poges on 17 April 1987 to drive to her parents' house at Gerrards Cross. She was taking a bin-liner full of grass cuttings to dump on their compost heap. Shani never arrived.

The next evening, Easter Sunday, Shani's body was discovered fully dressed in eighteen inches of water in Taplow Lake, Maidenhead. Her hands and feet had been tied behind her with a towrope; she had been gagged with a blue scarf and had a noose round her neck. She had been strangled to death.

The post-mortem revealed that her body had been put in the lake while she was unconscious or dead. There was no sign of sexual assault. Her car was found near by, unlocked, in a lay-by. Her purse and car keys were missing.

Amazingly, the pathologist concluded that she had committed suicide. To do this, she would have had to gag herself and bind her feet and hands behind her back before hopping into the water in her stiletto heels, to die of strangulation. An escapologist later proved she could not have done so.

There was no reason anyone could give as to why she would want to take her own life, and a psychologist who examined her diaries at the time said suicide was 'completely out of tune' with the evidence. And even if she did commit suicide, given Shani's fear of water this would have been the last method she would have chosen.

Thames Valley Police investigated her death. They were unconvinced by the pathologist's findings and considered that she had been murdered, as did her family. If this incident was connected to our series, she was definitely murdered. It is feasible that, like the others, she stopped off somewhere and was kidnapped. Our man tried to kill the Leeds hospital worker by throwing her in the canal and, apart from the noose around the neck, he had tied her up in a similar fashion to Shani. Of course, if it was him, he might have learned from his earlier failure.

The third new offence added to the rapist's catalogue took place on 8 January 1993. A warehouse worker was on a night out. She drove into Leeds city centre, arriving in Belgrave Street at 10 pm, and parked her car. As the mother-of-three locked the door, she noticed a man walking towards her. When level with her, he grabbed her around the neck and put a knife to her side. 'Shut up screaming, you bitch. I want the car,' was his greeting, before he punched her in the back and pressed the knife into her neck.

The woman, aged thirty-nine, offered her car keys and begged: 'Take the car, but don't hurt me.'

He responded: 'Right, you bitch, open the door and get in.'

Then she realised his intentions. 'It's not just the car he wants. It's me as well,' she told herself, terrified.

'I'm not getting in,' she shouted. She struggled free from his grip, buttons ripping from her blouse and coat in the process. His hold broke so suddenly she fell into the bushes behind her and he against the car. He clambered to his feet, grabbed her handbag and ran off.

She suffered cuts, bruising and a severe pain in her kidneys where he had pressed a knife into her side. Her description of the attacker being over six foot with blond hair and having a skin complaint was not in keeping with the others, apart from the stewardess's, and that was considered inaccurate. It was the abduction of a woman in her car in a city centre that was the consistent theme.

The linked inquiry now involved five forces and was renamed Operation Lynx. It was headed by Assistant Chief Constable Lloyd Clarke of West Yorkshire Police, and centred on Detective Superintendent John Stainthorpe's 1983 theory that the man was local to Leeds and involved in other petty crime.

DNA would provide good evidence when the rapist was found, but we had not hit on a match when we checked the database after the 1995 attack in Leeds. We had three poor-quality partial fingerprints, two on the envelope addressed to the student's boyfriend in Germany and one on the seat-belt catch of the air hostess's car. But they lacked enough detail to be run through the Automatic Fingerprint Retrieval (AFR) system.

In May 1997, a decision was taken to manually compare what might be fragments of the offender's fingerprints against prints of known sex offenders from records at Leeds and Leicester, but again it yielded no matches.

The profile of the attacker from the 1982 and 1983 inquiries showed he was actively engaged in petty crime, taking cars and stealing goods and credit cards from his victims, then using the cards to buy petrol, mainly in the Leeds area, indicating that this might be where he lived.

A list was drawn up of men arrested for petty crime between 1982 and 1983, and the laborious process of manually checking each individual's fingerprints against the three partial prints began.

Ten months later, after 7,000 sets of prints were compared over 940 hours, a match was finally made. A fingerprint expert doing routine checks not only matched the mark against the first partial print but when he checked the other two found that they matched as well.

The prints belonged to Clive Barwell, who had been arrested in 1982 for shoplifting. While the quality of the identified prints was not sufficient for them to be used as evidence under court rules at that time, they were good enough to justify the arrest of the forty-year-old.

The icing on the cake tasted all the sweeter when Barwell fitted my theory of being a petty thief first and a rapist second. Born in March 1957 in Leeds, Barwell was the second eldest of five children. His parents had a stormy relationship and he was frequently in trouble, appearing six times before juvenile courts between the ages of eleven and fifteen for burglary, theft, receiving stolen property and stealing cars. His offending continued, and he was sent to borstal for further petty crimes.

His criminal career flourished, and he appeared at Leeds Crown Court in 1975 for stealing vehicles and theft. Regular court appearances followed until 1989, when he was convicted of eight robberies, possessing firearms, eighteen burglaries, conversion of a weapon, taking cars and deception.

The robberies were mainly on post offices and businesses in and around Leeds, where security guards making cash deliveries were attacked and threatened with a sawn-off shotgun. Live shotgun cartridges were found at several of the scenes.

Barwell was jailed for sixteen years. But he had no previous convictions for offences of indecency with women, though he had admitted an offence of taking a car from Water Lane in Leeds, a street next to Globe Road, where the 1983 victim was pushed in the canal and the 1995 one was abandoned.

But when his release dates from prison were checked, there was a problem. His files showed that he was serving his sentence at Sudbury open prison at the time of the 1993 Nottingham rape. How could that be? Sudbury is in Ashbourne, Derbyshire, thirty-three miles from Nottingham.

I was disgusted to find that, just three years into his sentence, Barwell was downgraded from a Category B prisoner to a Category D and transferred to Sudbury in 1992. Open prisons operate a rather relaxed regime, with extensive freedom for home leave, social visits and work placements in the community, known as outwork.

And so it came to be that on Friday, 14 May 1993, a man rightly jailed for a considerable time for a string of serious crimes, but who had served only a quarter of his sentence, freely roamed Nottingham's streets until abducting the stewardess.

He left prison at 7.45 am that day for his outwork. But he never turned up. Instead, he caught a train to Burton upon Trent and collected a car from his then girlfriend, Margaret Teasdale. Barwell was recorded as being booked back in jail at 6.20 pm – seventy minutes after the hostess was found in a Nottingham street.

The prison authorities operated a system of trust, otherwise they would have had checks and balances and known that Barwell had failed to attend his work placement. Sadly the prison service saw fit to trust a man serving sixteen years for serious violent crime.

But it gets worse. In early 1994, Barwell began work in a hotel kitchen in Ashbourne, Derbyshire, visiting it on a daily basis. Prison bosses even allowed him to live at the hotel, were he was promoted to the job of manager! Someone must have realised how this looked, and so the job was given on paper to his now wife, Margaret, whom he had married while serving his sentence.

Barwell made only occasional visits back to prison until, in May 1995, the regime changed and new rules required prisoners to be back by 9 pm on weekday evenings, and so his wife would finish his shift for him. Finally, in June 1995, Barwell left jail, after serving six and a half years of a sixteen-year sentence.

Just thirty-six days later, he abducted the student.

Now working for a haulage firm near Leeds city centre as a long-distance lorry driver, he had assumed his wife's surname and was known as Clive Teasdale.

Finally, in March 1998, sixteen years after his first attack and three years since I got that early-morning call from Paul Langan, a trio of detectives approached Barwell as he parked his lorry at the works premises. He was arrested and taken to the Leeds Central Bridewell, where he was confronted with his suspected crimes, including the murder of Shani Warren. Barwell, never short of words in the confines of his victims' cars, declined to comment.

But he did agree to a further set of fingerprints being taken. The finer detail obtained from the new prints meant the matches from the Leeds student attack and the Nottingham case were now good enough to be used as evidence against him in court.

Detective Sergeants Paul Langan and Rod Bennett interviewed Barwell. He was asked if he understood which offences he was to be questioned about. 'Yes,' he replied. Did he wish to comment on them? 'No.'

He happily discussed his background in the second interview. In the next, he was asked about the 1995 attack in Leeds. 'Yes, it was me,' he declared, and then recalled how he had been in the Merrion Centre when he saw the student. 'I was about twenty yards behind her. She just walked straight past me, didn't look back at all as she went to her car. I went to go behind the car and as she opened it, I moved forward and pushed her in.'

'Why did you decide to attack a woman?' the officers asked him.

'I don't really know at what point I decided. I think it must have been when I parked the car behind the Merrion Centre.'

'Did you intend to rape the woman?' Paul asked him.

'Possibly, yes.'

'Why didn't you?'

'I think it was a combination of how she was acting and how hysterical she was and that sort of got to me more than 'owt. I told her I'd tie her back up and take her back.'

The next interview focused on the air hostess. He knew we had his fingerprints and DNA on this and admitted it as soon as he was asked. 'I drove into Nottingham and parked near the Broadmarsh Centre. I walked into the centre and went to the carpark. A car went past me and parked on my right and, as I walked behind it, I noticed a young girl getting out. I pushed her back in and drove out of the city.

'I parked up on a side road and raped the girl there. I then drove to Long Eaton, took two hundred pounds out of a machine, took her back towards town and left her in the car.'

So far, he had admitted only the offences that could be proved with his fingerprints and DNA. Then he drew the shutters down and would not comment on any other crimes he was quizzed about. However, he was happy to speak of his past and his exploits as a car thief.

Barwell was a master of disguises in an attempt to deceive victims and avoid detection. As well as changing his appearance, he'd put on Scottish or Geordie accents, asked for cigarettes when he was a non-smoker, hinted he'd been drinking although his friends described him as teetotal, lied about being Catholic, and pretended to be a bad driver.

More proof was needed, and so on 8 April 1998 Barwell appeared in an identification parade in Leeds. In a specially designed suite, the victims view the line-up through one-way glass from a separate room. Though sixteen years had passed, and despite his disguises, the victims from the first two attacks in Bradford and Leeds immediately and positively identified him.

If proof were needed of how traumatised the women were by their ordeal, it was visible to those present at the ID parade. When the hospital worker entered the room, she froze and could not continue. After a few minutes, she went back in, but on seeing Barwell standing at position number one in the parade, lost her nerve and fled again. On her third effort, she walked up and down the parade and then became upset and agitated. 'He's here. Oh my God, it's him. It's number one,' she wept.

A short while later, she made her statement: 'The man I immediately recognised was at number one. I felt as though he was staring at me. He had the same smirk on his face as he had in 1983 when he was stood at the canalside, looking down at me struggling to keep my head above water, thinking I was going to die.'

Barwell was charged with sixteen offences in the series, not including the murder of Shani Warren. They ranged from attempted murder, rape, assault and indecent assault to robbery and kidnapping.

Seventeen years after he attacked the Bradford housewife, Barwell entered the dock at Teesside Crown Court on Tuesday, 5 October 1999. At a previous hearing he had entered guilty pleas to the Leeds and Nottingham offences, but we thought he'd deny the other charges.

Unexpectedly, as the trial was about to start, he admitted eleven of the charges, including the hospital worker's attempted murder, rape and kidnapping. Three of his victims watched as Mr Justice Penry-Davey branded Barwell 'dangerous, cunning and chilling'. He was given eight life sentences and is not expected to be considered for parole until 2011 at the earliest.

The 1984 Leicester attack and the 1993 Leeds attack were not proceeded with, as there were no forensic or fingerprint links. The judge asked the jury to return a not guilty verdict for the 1985 Doncaster attack, which was an administrative process requested by the defence to prevent Barwell being tried again at a later date. The prosecution accepted that the charges relating to these three incidents should not go to trial as they could not materially affect the expected life sentence he faced.

Today, in the UK, hundreds of murders of women remain unsolved. Did any of them fall victim to the man who had murder on his mind when he threw a young mother into the ice-cold, black January waters of the Leeds–Liverpool canal and waited to savour the moment of her death, only to be cheated by her luck in finding the stone and her will to live?

As a young teenager, Barwell witnessed his father's violence towards his mother. Both parents indulged in affairs, and in one of the many stormy moments of the marriage his mother left his father, taking his two brothers and leaving him with his father with his sisters.

It appears from this, and the fact that he was given his elder brother Karl's hand-me-down clothes, that his mother did not have much time for him. He stole money from her, and his father's watch, which resulted in him being sent to a detention centre for three months. He was a constant truant from school with his younger brother.

From his early teenage years, he enjoyed active sexual relationships with women, progressing from relationship to relationship, the finding of a new woman ending his current involvement. Many of his past partners described him as a womaniser. He was a double divorcee before marrying his current wife, Margaret, in 1994 at Leeds Registry Office while on home leave from his armed robbery sentence. Barwell clearly held a high opinion of himself as a ladies' man, yet his troubled childhood, the comments he made to his victims and how he treated them suggests he hated women, and this may have been as a result of his poor relationship with his mother.

\*

On 26 May 1996, Operation Enigma was launched to look at the ever-growing number of murders of women. The operation is run from the Crime Faculty at Bramshill Police College in Hampshire. Its aims are to identify good investigative practice and new ideas in crime investigation, particularly in serial crime, and disseminate them to the police service. It provides serious crime analysis, especially in areas of rape, sexually motivated homicide and abduction, by comparing cases and looking at linking factors between crimes.

But the Crime Faculty has no operational capacity and does not investigate cases. Clive Barwell could easily have slipped through the net because of complacency, a lack of interest on the part of various forces, and an inability to recognise a criminal who is offending across regional boundaries.

I had to fight hard on the Barwell case, not just with my own force for money and staff, but also with other forces to make them handle these attacks with the seriousness they warranted. I was disgusted at the leniency Barwell was afforded in prison. After his trial, a Prison Service spokesman said: 'While at Sudbury, Barwell appeared to be a model prisoner and was trying to put his life back in order and stop his reoffending. I don't think we would accept any criticism of any decisions taken back then.'

I hope lessons were learnt, but I am not so sure. Nearly nine hundred offenders carried out serious crimes – including murder – between 1997 and 1999 while on probation or out of jail on licence, according to the Home Office. Barwell was one of these.

But how many other serial rapists are out there? I believe there must be several. There is a pressing need for an FBI-style organisation in the UK to look at serious and serial crimes which cross force boundaries, especially murder and rape. A number of countries have offences designated as federal crimes which are dealt with by the national, not local, law enforcement agency. The rivalry and prejudices of the forty-three forces, along with the bureaucracy they bring to crime investigation on this small island, create problems on a national scale.

I would take the Crime Faculty and integrate it into the National Criminal Intelligence Service, and incorporate them within the National Crime Squad to be Britain's answer to the FBI. Within their scope would be the Drugs Enforcement Branch, and the NCS would also retain its current objectives regarding serious and organised crime.

All Barwell's victims remain psychologically damaged by their ordeals.

The student has built up a successful professional career. However, she never uses multistorey carparks, avoids Leeds, and even the most simple trip out to the postbox terrifies her.

The Bradford housewife was happy, confident and outgoing before that fateful 1982 night. Since then, she has seen a pyschiatrist for acute depression, takes antidepressants and suffers panic attacks. 'There is not a day goes by when I do not think of the attack,' she says.

To this day, the mystery of Shani Warren's death is unresolved. Clive Barwell remains a strong suspect.

# chapter ten

# DRUGS, BOMBS AND MONEY

Many a quiet day has suddenly turned dramatic, as was the case on Wednesday, 17 June 1992, when terrorists struck at the heart of my home city. I still had Michael Sams on my mind, as we had not found the missing ransom money, but was about to have an early finish when at 5.25 pm Inspector Barry Jewitt put a call through to my office.

I had known Barry for years. The consummate police officer, tall, well built, he feared no one. We had been known to take the odd libation together. 'Don't dash off home just yet, we might have something at Marks and Spencer,' he said. I knew it was potentially serious. Two men acting suspiciously had been seen at 5.10 pm by staff in the store in Briggate. One asked an assistant where the tracksuits were and she noted he had an Irish accent.

They were tracked through the store using its newly installed £250,000 security camera system. The duo went down to the basement, where they were observed examining a three-piece suite, lifting the seat cushions and looking around it. At this stage they were viewed as potential shoplifters. The smaller of the two was carrying a blue holdall.

As the staff watched, one of the men slipped something down the side of a settee and the other placed something behind a cushion. They then strode out of the store. Their actions had made staff so suspicious that they immediately went to examine the settee and found an audio cassette case behind the cushion and another down the side of the settee. The store rang the police.

Barry told me he had already started the evacuation procedure, cordoned off the area and contacted the Bomb Disposal Unit from Catterick army camp in North Yorkshire. I knew it was a uniform job at this stage, and until it had been established that a crime had been committed I would not be in play. Bomb disposal would be with us at about 7 pm. I told Barry I would wait and see.

I knew Marks and Spencer staff were well drilled in procedures in the event of bomb hoaxes and evacuation. They held regular practice sessions where a cuddly toy was hidden and staff would have to search for it. These two plastic cassette cases with their contents obscured may have been small and innocuous looking, but the staff rightly were taking no chances.

I went to the CID office to get an officer to link up with the store staff. I did not want to lose any witnesses, and there was also the matter of the pictures of the suspects we'd need so I could dispatch plainclothes officers to covertly locate them. If they had planted bombs, they might hang about to get a thrill from hearing the blast.

By 7.30 pm, bomb disposal officers had disabled the bombs and informed us that they were incendiary devices which had been set to explode between midnight and 2 am. I requested that Special Branch be notified, and then went to meet the captain from Bomb Disposal. I asked him about the devices. He said, 'They have a maximum twelve-hour timer and if exploded would create a pyrotechnic effect – a fire in layman's terms.' I asked him whether the way they were constructed would give us any clues as to who planted them, perhaps animal liberation activists or a political group. He said, 'Their construction is crude, the same as those used by the Provisional IRA in the seventies.'

So we had two suspects – one we knew was Irish, though his accent could have been put on – and an incendiary device that, given the right circumstances, could easily start a fire that would gut a building. The store could be a target for animal rights activists, but a company like this was not on the list of current IRA targets and, in any event, the IRA's devices were far more sophisticated. But were there any more? The holdall had been big enough to hold dozens.

A short time later the divisional commander, the larger-than-life figure of Chief Superintendent David Harry Clarkson, arrived. Dave was never one to shy away from a major production, and he certainly would not on this occasion. He quickly formulated a plan. This was his city centre, and if there were dozens of these things, and they had been planted in the afternoon, they could go off during the night. Most shops close between five and six, but the last ones had just shut at eight. Working on the basis of a twelve-hour timer, and if devices had been planted in the shops last to close, we could still have devices going off up to eight in the morning.

Dave decided he would get shop key-holders to return to their premises and search them with police teams to try to find any other devices that had been planted. I would not like to estimate how many shops were involved, but a radio appeal was made and officers were brought in from all over the force to help with the search.

My task was to find the fire-bombers. I dispatched my teams to search the pubs for them. We had excellent-quality pictures of them from the security cameras. It had not escaped my notice that they could still be out there, pushing their bombs down the backs of pub seats.

The heart of Leeds city centre is bounded by Briggate, the Headrow, Park Row and Boar Lane, and is like many others in that it would not be difficult for fire to spread and set the whole area ablaze. The fire brigade and ambulance services were standing by near Millgarth, as was the bomb disposal unit, ready to go if needed.

Special Branch was checking to see whether there was any intelligence to assist us. The town centre was cordoned off. There are over 150 pubs, clubs and restaurants in the centre, but as the evening wore on the numbers of people in town reduced to a trickle.

At 12.41 am, smoke was seen seeping from the frontage of a shop not two hundred yards from Millgarth. It was cordoned off just as an explosion went off. I was in the incident room at Millgarth, but heard it. The message soon came through as to where it was, and I walked over. The metal shutters of Stop and Shop on New York Street had blown out like crumpled tinfoil and revealed the whole of the inside to be ablaze. This shop sold household goods, many of which were combustible plastic and aerosols, and the whole lot had gone up.

Canisters exploded in the flames and in a short time the shop was gutted. The explosion was caused by the flash-over when the smouldering mass inside caused a build-up of combustible gases and ignited, blowing out the windows and shutters like corks popping out of champagne bottles.

By the time the fire brigade had damped it down it was a mess, with damage running into hundreds of thousands of pounds. This was a main road, and it was sheer luck that a passing pedestrian or car had not been caught in the blast, as without a doubt there would have been serious injuries.

I walked back to the incident room, where I had set up my operation. By this stage it had become a fire watch, with task force officers looking for smoke coming from any building. Stop and Shop and Marks and Spencer were only 250 yards apart, and they were completely different types of businesses. There was no pattern that could be predicted from these two. Stop and Shop was a discount shop, and the row it occupied was not at the heart of the shopping centre.

The next alert came at 1.47 am from one of the task force sergeants. He was in Albion Street, and had spotted smoke coming from Waterstone's bookshop. The fire brigade and bomb disposal team quickly extinguished the fire, which was caused by a similar cassette-type device. As the shelves were searched for further devices, another was found lodged between books. This too was made safe by bomb disposal officers. The second device was set to go off between 3 and 5 am.

I did not know how many devices had been planted at Stop and Shop, but we had now accounted for at least five. Waterstone's would have been gutted had the patrolling officers not been so vigilant. The recovered device was exactly the same as those from Marks and Spencer. The first devices were set to ignite between midnight and 2 am, these for later. Still no pattern, as they were planted indiscriminately, it seemed. The next few hours were tense as the possibility of more bombs was contemplated, but the night passed without further incident.

I stayed on duty until 8.45 am, when DCI Gordon Garfit took over while I grabbed some sleep. I made sure that we had the pictures of our suspects circulated before I left. I had been on duty twenty-four hours. Though this was not commonplace, it was not unusual when an incident broke, especially if it was at the end of the working day.

I returned to work at 2 pm to be updated. At 9 am, the Irish National Liberation Army (INLA) had claimed responsibility for placing twelve devices in the city centre in a call to the BBC in Belfast, using a known code word to authenticate it.

The INLA is a terrorist organisation committed to the end of British rule in Northern Ireland and the incorporation of Ulster into the Irish Republic. It is an offshoot of the Irish Republican Army. Among its activities was the killing of the British MP Airey Neave in 1979.

Another device was found at Rawcliffe's clothes shop on Duncan Street, which was on a direct route from Marks and Spencer to Stop and Shop. At 11.59 am, a member of staff had discovered that a tracksuit top hanging on a display rack had fire damage to it. A closer examination revealed a device in the pocket identical to the others. It had ignited, but after smouldering in the pocket had died out through oxygen starvation.

We had been in touch with the Anti-Terrorist Branch at New Scotland Yard, and when the attacks were confirmed as being INLA initiated they decided to send an inspector and a detective constable up to us to act as liaison officers. I now had my incident room fully functional, and a sizable contingent from our own Special Branch, or the 'Secret Squirrel' department, as they were known.

At 4.10 pm, a further two devices were discovered at Supersave in Albion Street, near Waterstone's. One had been placed among aerosol deodorant sprays, the other between bath sponges on a display in the centre of the store. Fortunately neither had ignited, otherwise they would have had a devastating effect. They were again of identical construction to the others. Twenty-three hours had passed since the devices were first discovered at Marks and Spencer. We could now account for eight, as the forensic fire experts said that only one had been planted at Stop and Shop. There must still be four as yet unexploded, but if the watches had stopped and restarted they could still do so at any time.

Special Branch had been busy. Unbeknown to me, they had identified one of the men on the photograph but had decided to keep it to themselves, presumably so they could make an arrest. Identified through his coming and goings in and out of Leeds and Bradford Airport was Eamonn Patrick O'Donnell, thirty-seven, from Londonderry.

He was studying sociology and living at Bradford and Ilkley College. Special Branch had spotted him in Ilkley town and arrested him in the street. He was taken to Pudsey police station. O'Donnell had previous convictions, including one in 1975 for causing an explosion when a hand grenade was thrown at an RUC police station, and membership of the IRA. He was jailed for six years. He was not being co-operative and refused to speak when he was booked into the station.

His arrest should lead us to the second man, though we would need a more open approach from Special Branch, otherwise we would end up running two separate inquiries. It was agreed that their detectives would be paired off with mine. A specialist team of fingerprint officers were dispatched north from SO13, the anti-terrorist squad. Flat 11, Woodend, at Bradford and Ilkley College, where O'Donnell lived for two years, was about to be taken apart by the best. The additional benefit to West Yorkshire Police was that it would cost us nothing.

The first problem was to establish whether the second man was still in the country, and if so whether he was at O'Donnell's flat. Given the background, this would have to be a firearms operation, and all the flats in the building would have to be cleared.

As the day went on, we attempted to interview O'Donnell, though the only resemblance this had to an interview was that O'Donnell was in the same room as the interviewers. He refused to speak to or look at my officers or even acknowledge their presence, turning his face away from them. It was merely a matter of us presenting the evidence and giving him an opportunity to comment if he wished, though I knew he would not.

We'd have to interview his college friends in the coming days, not only so we could ascertain his movements but also to establish whether the other man had been there. On the Friday morning I went to the college; the search would take some time, and we needed patience and co-operation from the staff and students. An attitude was developing to the effect that we had targeted Eamonn because he was Irish. They were unaware that we had the video evidence. I saw Assistant Principal Pat Williamson and explained what we would need, and I addressed the students to dispel any fears they had with respect to what we were doing and why we were doing it.

O'Donnell had been detained under the provisions of the Prevention of Terrorism Act, which allowed a longer than usual detention period. On Saturday, 20 June, at 2.15 pm, he was charged with twelve offences of conspiring to commit arson, arson at Stop and Shop, possessing explosives and placing explosives at each shop. Not surprisingly, he had not uttered a single word during any of his three interviews.

He appeared in court the following Monday and spoke for the first time since his arrest when he acknowledged his name to the magistrates. He was then remanded in custody to the high-security Hull prison.

We established from witnesses that the second man in the Marks and Spencer security pictures had been at O'Donnell's flat and had probably stayed with him the night the devices were planted.

Within days we had identified him as a known INLA member. He had recently changed his hairstyle to a close-cropped cut, so this had made identification slightly trickier. Sean Paul Martin Cruickshank, twenty-one and also from Londonderry, was arrested on 25 June at Stranraer, having boarded the Larne–Stranraer ferry the previous night. He drove for his father's firm, Foyle Freight, regularly making deliveries from Northern Ireland to England.

We went through the same interview procedure with Cruickshank, who, like O'Donnell, never said a word from his arrest until he appeared in court. He was charged with the same offences. Although he was a member of the INLA, he did not have the same ideological background as O'Donnell, though this did not stop him completely blanking his interviewers. He appeared in court a few days later and he was remanded to Armley jail, Leeds.

Enquiries revealed that there was another man in O'Donnell's flat on the day of the fire-bombings. He was identified by a fingerprint as Martin Columba McMonagle, a thirty-year-old with strong INLA connections. The Home Secretary had excluded McMonagle, a native of Londonderry, from mainland Britain in 1988 owing to his suspected terrorist activities. Being in O'Donnell's flat was in breach of the exclusion order.

I obtained copies of further security videos from the railway station and Albion Street. The latter showed O'Donnell, Cruickshank and a third man walking down the street shortly before the Marks and Spencer fire-bombs were planted. The station's video footage showed just O'Donnell and Cruickshank passing through the ticket barrier to catch their train to Ilkley shortly after 6 pm.

Cruickshank travelled to England on Tuesday, 16 June, as a passenger in a Foyle Freight lorry, and had caught the 8 pm Larne–Cairnryan ferry, probably with McMonagle hidden in the back of his wagon. I reached this conclusion on the basis that two men were seen being dropped in Bradford from a Foyle Freight wagon, which then continued south to make deliveries. The two men caught a taxi. The cab firm's night controller recalled being approached at 5.10 am on Wednesday, 17 June, by an Irish man in his late twenties, casually dressed, wearing a baseball cap and carrying a holdall. Although he did not see him, he knew he was with a second man.

The cabbie drove the two men to the Bradford and Ilkley College. He described one as having a large bag and the other a smaller one. They had shown him a piece of paper with the address on it, and he had been paid with an Irish banknote. O'Donnell was at this time in the halls of residence, so he could not be one of the two men.

Around 8 am that Wednesday, the assistant principal saw a man at the college wearing a grey blouson jacket, shell-suit bottoms and a baseball cap. He had a ginger moustache and spoke with an Irish accent. She identified him as Cruickshank. A number of students and cleaning staff also saw a second person on the campus and in the communal kitchen on O'Donnell's floor.

Throughout the morning, O'Donnell was seen by several student friends with a man who introduced himself as Sean. O'Donnell was well known among students and staff, and there appeared to be two conflicting descriptions of the man seen in company with him. The reason for this was that they were different people – one described as short haired, virtually a skinhead, the other with curly hair.

Enquiries made of British Rail revealed that the conductor on the 2.43 pm to Leeds remembered three men together on the train. He described two who fitted the description of O'Donnell and Cruickshank and a mousey-haired man in his late twenties who paid for the tickets with an Irish £20 note.

When they got off the train, O'Donnell and Cruickshank, who was carrying a dark-coloured sports bag, were walking together and the third man was walking in front when they were caught on the Albion Street camera. It was my belief that the third man returned to the station and left on the train before O'Donnell and Cruickshank planted any devices.

Fingerprint examinations had proved positive as Cruickshank and McMonagle's prints were found in a number of places in O'Donnell's flat, such as on newspapers and a door frame. I could now prove that McMonagle had been to the flat and was there within a narrow time limit.

The difficulty was that McMonagle was now likely to be back in Londonderry. It would be no simple task to arrest him. It wasn't as if we could walk up his garden path, knock on his door and say, 'You're nicked, mate.' It would be a major police and army operation. In any event, when they did attempt it a few days later, he had fled to Limerick and so was out of our reach, unless he came back to the North.

Our British Rail enquiries revealed that two computerised Leeds–Belfast tickets had been bought on Wednesday. The first, a return, was bought at a time when I knew all three men were in Ilkley. The second, a single, was bought between 3. 21 and 3.36 pm, minutes after the trio arrived at Leeds at 3.13 pm. If McMonagle had bought that ticket he could not have been with them at 5.02 pm when they went to Marks and Spencer, as his train left Leeds at 4.48 pm.

I did not know whether the Marks and Spencer fire-bombs were the first or last planted, and as McMonagle was with the others in the town centre for over an hour before he caught his train, he too could have planted some. The third person with Cruickshank and O'Donnell on the Albion Street video could not be clearly seen owing to his peaked cap shadowing his face. What could be seen was the shape of a tattoo on his left forearm, identical to McMonagle's. When O'Donnell and Cruickshank returned to Ilkley on the 6.15 pm train, the third man was not with them.

The force's underwater team was searching the River Aire, which runs along the bottom of Briggate, after reports that a man had been seen throwing a gun into the river. The divers didn't find it, but did discover three more devices that must have been cast into the water.

All the eight unexploded devices, and I expect the three that had activated, were cassette cases containing a combustible mixture, a timer and detonator. The fire-bomb mixture was wrapped in pieces of the *Belfast Telegraph* from editions dated between 9 and 13 June, a few days before they were planted.

Although the video of O'Donnell and Cruickshank was good enough for a juror to positively identify them, witnesses who saw them in the store could reinforce the case. To obtain their evidence, Cruickshank and O'Donnell would have to stand on an identification parade, but their co-operation could not be guaranteed, and there was also the question of the security problems. The only practical course was a video identification. This could be done with or without their co-operation.

The prison authorities didn't make it any easier for us, as they decided for security reasons to move the two to Durham prison. This meant they had to be brought to Leeds by armed escort each time they were due to appear in court. They did not have to appear every week but had exercised their right to do so to create maximum disruption and inconvenience.

O'Donnell went on a dirty campaign; he refused to wash or wear prison clothes, claiming he was a political prisoner. He preferred to smear his excreta around his cell walls rather than pull the chain. Consequently, he was unshaven, stunk to high heaven and appeared in court with long hair, bearded and naked but for a grey blanket draped around his shoulders. On at least one occasion, Cruickshank, having insisted on exercising his right to attend court, refused to come up the steps to the dock and was remanded in his absence.

Durham was far enough from Leeds for their activities to pass me by to a great extent. I was not too concerned that O'Donnell was increasingly becoming a health hazard to himself, prison officers and fellow inmates; nor that he was occasionally hosed down in an attempt to avert an outbreak of cholera. Well, not until I had to do the video identification. As neither had spoken in interview, I needed Cruickshank identified as one of the two men at O'Donnell's flat, as his fingerprints could have been left on a previous visit.

Barry Jewitt was appointed to deal with all aspects of the identification. This would involve an element of co-operation from O'Donnell, such as filling in the necessary consent forms in his solicitor's presence. A video identification would require a shot of O'Donnell and eight other people who resembled him in age, height and general appearance. The other eight would not be a problem. If O'Donnell refused to co-operate we could covertly video him. When the video was complete, Barry would show copies to witnesses.

When Barry arrived at Durham prison to see O'Donnell, speaking only through his solicitor O'Donnell indicated that he could not read the video consent forms as we still had his glasses. They had not been returned and he had not asked for them until now. I had to dispatch a motorcyclist to Durham with his glasses before the whole process could start.

With his long beard and straggly hair, O'Donnell now looked nothing like he did on Wednesday, 17 June. There was no way we could proceed until something was done about smartening him up.

Barry was not famous for his diplomatic skills, but somehow he talked O'Donnell into having a shave and cleaning himself up for the video shot. When the tape was completed, Barry supervised over thirty identification procedures. On each occasion a tape was chosen at random and the seals were broken in the presence of the solicitor.

It is amazing how quickly amnesia sets in when witnesses are required to finger a terrorist. Most members of the public and staff who saw O'Donnell and Cruickshank in Marks and Spencer appeared afraid to identify them. But I did get enough identifications of both of them for a strong case, considering that neither had spoken in interview. We also recovered the jacket Cruickshank wore on his fire-bombing campaign.

McMonagle was arrested in February 1993 in the Avon and Somerset Police area while taking part in an attempted burglary on a Semtex store near Bristol. He was charged with conspiracy to cause explosions in the UK and firearms offences.

On 5 October 1993, O'Donnell and Cruickshank appeared at Newcastle Crown Court. The trial was intended to be at Durham Crown Court, as a secure tunnel joins it to the prison. Unfortunately Durham Constabulary scuttled the plan when their ACC declared that court security was inadequate. The trial was transferred to Newcastle, so instead of walking them through a tunnel an armed escort had to take them to and from the prison each day.

I believed O'Donnell and Cruickshank, like all the other Irish terrorists, would refuse to recognise the court or enter a plea and answer questions. The court would treat their silence as a not guilty plea. Instead, in a moment of pure drama, they unexpectedly pleaded guilty to conspiring to commit arson. O'Donnell was sentenced to twenty years in jail and Cruickshank fifteen years. McMonagle was sentenced at crown court in December 1993 to twenty-five years' imprisonment.

O'Donnell and Cruickshank are believed to be the first terrorists to plead guilty to terrorist offences in England. It was a mystery to me then and still is now why they changed their plea, unless the arrest of McMonagle in some way influenced their decision.

McMonagle was interviewed by two of my officers while in custody in Southeast London's Belmarsh prison. He refused to answer any questions. The Crown Prosecution Service made the decision not to proceed with charges against him, no doubt owing to the length of his existing sentence.

As I scanned through the 2001 *Sunday Times* Rich List, many names caught my eye. There was the usual crop of royalty, property millionaires and the odd Formula One racing chief, but there were also a couple of other names that were familiar to me for very different reasons. Side by side with the Queen, ranked at joint 105th with an estimated £300 million fortune, was time-share con man John Palmer. Several years earlier drugs baron Curtis Warren had appeared ranked 461, his wealth estimated at £40 million.

Liverpudlian Warren is an example of a petty criminal who became immensely rich through crime. His entry in the *Sunday Times* Rich List read, 'Warren is a major property player and trader in the North West, particularly the Merseyside area where he is a well-known figure in the local community. He also has extensive interests on the continent.' The implication was that his wealth was from doubtful origins.

The thirty-three-year-old was sentenced to the maximum twelve years' imprisonment in Holland for drug trafficking in June 1997. Warren was one of nine Britons and a Colombian arrested in Holland with a haul of cocaine, heroin, cannabis and Ecstasy with a street value of £125 million. In the UK, this offence carries a maximum of life imprisonment and sentences of over twenty years are not unusual. It is the more lenient sentences handed down in Holland which encourage those who traffic drugs into the UK to operate from there. Attempts to trace Warren's criminal assets continue.

Organised crime and drugs in particular are big business. Annual world turnover in illicit drugs was estimated by the United Nations to be £250 billion in 1996.

Serious and organised crime investigation focuses on professional criminals rather than the crimes they commit. They may alternate between trafficking Class A drugs such as cocaine or heroin one day and importing cigarettes, cannabis or firearms the next.

They are generally organised in a hierarchical structure and will often operate with other criminal groups. Their success is built upon operating criminal ventures behind legitimate businesses, which are used both as a front and as a means of laundering their criminal assets. Violence is often used either as a threat or an example to enforce loyalty to the group and to protect their market, their territory and their criminal business interests. It is not unusual for the premier league of crooks to build and operate multi-million-pound empires.

The profit margin between the raw product and the street price in the UK for drugs such as cocaine can be as much as a thousand per cent. It is these obscene profits which drive the drugs trade. Today, there are dozens of drugs millionaires in every major UK city, with many more springing up every month.

Another criminal who rose from petty crook to millionaire is Kenneth Noye. Born in Bexleyheath, Kent, his criminal career progressed from handling stolen goods as a nineteen-year-old to smuggling gold Krugerrands, with offices and a smelter in Eindhoven, the Netherlands. In 1982, his activities made an annual profit of £1.3 million. Noye joined the Freemasons around this time to widen his business contacts, being proposed and seconded by police officers, which enraged masons in other lodges. He enjoyed the fruits from his rotten criminal tree, driving a Rolls-Royce, buying a squash club in Dartford for his wife, and residing in a mock Tudor mansion with twenty acres of land and a heated swimming pool.

In 1983 four masked men robbed Brink's-Mat of £26,369,778 in gold bullion. Tragically, DC John Fordham died at Noye's hands while carrying out covert observations on his home during the investigation. During a search of Noye's cottage after his arrest, eleven gold bars and traces of a gold smelting process were found, linking him with the Brink's-Mat robbery.

Noye went on trial for John Fordham's murder at the Old Bailey in 1985. The jury accepted his claim of self-defence and found him not guilty. He was, however, later sentenced to fourteen years' imprisonment for offences relating to handling the gold bullion and VAT irregularities.

While on a hostel release scheme he became involved in a £50,000 cocaine deal, but ditched the plan when he found the American Drug Enforcement Administration (DEA) hard on his heels. He then moved into Ecstasy, which by the mid-1990s had become a £500 million drugs trade nationally.

Noye, although a multimillionaire, was still a violent criminal at heart, and in 1996 a road rage incident turned into murder when he stabbed to death Stephen Cameron, twenty-one, near the M25/M20 intersection, in front of Stephen's fiancée, Danielle Cable, nineteen.

Callous Noye walked away after the stabbing and, using his criminal contacts, fled to Spain. He was on the run for two years before he was arrested at a restaurant in Barbette, Spain, in 1998.

Extradited, he appeared at the Old Bailey in March 2000, where he pleaded self-defence, as he had done fifteen years earlier. The jury rejected his defence and he was jailed for life. Noye was supported by legal aid as his wealth was now hidden. His house in Spain was reportedly sold for £500,000, his vehicle for another £15,000.

Wealthy businessman John Palmer, fifty-one, was found not guilty of handling stolen bullion from the Brink's-Mat robbery. He built up a time-share empire, which accounted for his joint 105th position in the *Sunday Times* Rich List. However, he was jailed for eight years at the Old Bailey in May 2001 after he was found responsible for swindling up to 17,000 people out of an estimated £30 million.

The time-share tycoon, nicknamed Goldfinger through his Brink's-Mat involvement, kept a smelter in the grounds of his home in Battlefield, Bath. He had melted down gold, but the jury accepted he had not known it was stolen in the robbery. Palmer's wealth gave him a jet-set lifestyle, with a string of expensive sports cars, a £6 million private yacht, a jet and a helicopter.

Unfortunately, court appearances on the part of those involved in top-level organised crime are rare. Most of the top-flight criminals are known to law enforcement agencies, which are constantly collecting intelligence on them. MI5 believe there are four hundred Mr Bigs operating in Britain, earning more than £440 million a year, with just forty of them accounting for half of that. That is an average £5.5 million a year each. Some live lavish lifestyles, the trappings of their sudden wealth drawing attention to them. But other millionaire criminals live in council houses, opting for a low-profile life.

The major stumbling-blocks in tackling these sophisticated criminal syndicates are a lack of resources and funding, restrictive legislation and, in my view, a dysfunctional relationship between the proliferation of organisations trying to catch them. The newly formed National Crime Squad (NCS), England's answer to the FBI, set up to tackle the higher echelon of crime bosses, is too inadequately staffed and funded to seriously tackle the problem.

If the battle against organised crime and in particular drugs is to succeed, then I believe extraordinary measures must be taken. The Prevention of Terrorism Act was passed to deal with terrorists, so while drugs continue to be an ever-spreading cancer throughout society, special anti-racketeering legislation should be considered. Offences such as being a member of an organised crime group and living off criminal proceeds should be created, together with restrictions imposed on those in jail who try to continue to run their organisations from behind bars. The Italians introduced anti-Mafia legislation along these lines by limiting the visits and phone calls of the gang bosses in prison.

One drug trafficker currently on the run used a specialist tax QC to put his money in offshore trust accounts, a quite legitimate process – the same QC had performed this service for a serving high-profile MP. In this case, unbeknown to the lawyer, his work facilitated the movement of drugs money. The top-level criminals have the cash to buy the best advice and legal representation in pursuit of their illegal activities.

The dysfunctional nature of our law enforcement agencies stems from the fact that too many organisations are looking at the same groups of people. At ground level in England and Wales, there are forty-three police forces. Then there are the Scottish forces, whose officers have no jurisdiction in England and Wales, and vice versa, except for some limited cross-border powers under the Crime and Disorder Act. At this level, drugs squads and major crime units tackle the criminals on their own patches.

At the top level, there are four intelligence agencies. The National Criminal Intelligence Service (NCIS) draws its staff from many police forces and other intelligence agencies. It has a responsibility to provide intelligence services to UK police forces, the NCS and many other agencies. The other intelligence organisations are the Security Service (MI5), the Secret Intelligence Service (SIS) and GCHQ. All these devote part of their time to supporting law enforcement agencies.

The proactive organisations at the top level are the National Crime Squad, whose area of operation includes England and Wales, as well as an international remit; the National Investigation Service (NIS) of HM Customs and Excise (HMCE) also operates at home and abroad; the Scottish Drugs Enforcement Agency and the Crime Squad of the Police Service of Northern Ireland, formerly the Royal Ulster Constabulary, have responsibility for their respective areas.

The result is that each agency's crime operations overlap those of several other law enforcement agencies, leading to arguments over who has primacy and who leads the multi-organisational operation. There can only be one lead agency, one person in charge making decisions that all then abide by. The absence of an efficient and effective working relationship only benefits the criminal.

Drugs in the UK have now become a more serious problem than the Black Death. The thrust of the government's response was the ten-year drugs plan and the appointment of the drugs czar, a former Chief Constable of mine, Keith Hellawell. Well meaning, it has focused on education to achieve a reduction in use, treatment programmes to rehabilitate drug users from their habit, and increasing public awareness. But it has all been rather cosmetic.

Why are we trying to stop drugs coming into this country instead of stopping them leave where they are produced, or trying to intercept them in the transit countries *en route* to the UK?

Too little is being done. If I am being stung by a swarm of wasps, what is better? Treating the wasp stings or looking for the nest and destroying it? There have been many occasions in history when sanctions have been imposed on other countries whose antisocial activities have been regarded as unacceptable to our government. So why not impose sanctions on Colombia and take action against Afghanistan, the major sources of our cocaine and heroin, as well as the governments who support their regimes by doing little to prevent the drugs being transported across their countries.

Only after the terrorist attacks on New York's World Trade Center on 11 September 2001 did the government publicly acknowledge and determine to stop what we in law enforcement and they themselves have known for years: that 95 per cent of the UK heroin supply comes from Afghanistan. It is estimated that the country has sufficient opium stockpiled to produce 300 tonnes of pure heroin with a street value in the UK of £20 billion. Neither do I doubt that the Afghan Taliban rulers' purpose in permitting the export of the drug was to destabilise the West as well as to fund their military activities. They would raise £6 million by collecting a 10 per cent tax on the £20-a-kilo stockpiled crop the local farmers produce.

There needs to be one national UK agency dealing with drugs trafficking, whether it be the National Crime Squad merged with the Scottish DEA and the Northern Ireland Crime Squad or the NIS of HM Customs and Excise, supported by dedicated intelligence support from the NCIS. My preferred option would be to create a super-agency by merging the National Crime Squad and the other police agencies with the NIS. Terrorism is also organised crime, and force Special Branches should also be part of the new agency as well.

Why *can't* these agencies jointly work together? Surely they all have the same objective? Sadly, no. The police agencies mainly target crime's Mr Bigs, but Customs target the goods and seize them before they reach the Mr Bigs.

Both objectives have their merits, but disruption of the criminal enterprise by seizing the goods (drugs, firearms) is easier to achieve. Dismantling a well-organised criminal group can rarely be achieved, and would generally require everyone in the organisation to be arrested and held incommunicado throughout their sentence so they could not continue to operate or rebuild their criminal enterprises.

Will the government's proposed Proceeds of Crime Bill go far enough in dealing with these crime barons, stripping them and anyone who lives off their criminal proceeds of their ill-gotten gains? Or will it be challenged and diluted by the host of lawyers the Mr Bigs employ, exploiting loopholes to the point where the act becomes a toothless tiger?

At present, a conviction is necessary to pursue the benefits of crime. The government has grasped the nettle by introducing in the bill radical legislation whereby assets considered as the proceeds of crime can be calculated and seized without a conviction.

The bill also introduces other long-awaited measures to take the criminal benefit, the amount the court calculates is their financial gain from crime, from professional crooks. But it could go farther in dealing with others who might also benefit. The bill creates a Criminal Assets Recovery Agency, to track the assets of criminals. But will it be as efficient as police and Customs are now, or will it become a white elephant like the Serious Fraud Office and fail to achieve its objective?

The agency will have powers to tax suspected criminal assets where no source of income has been identified. My view is that if the source cannot be identified we should presume such assets are the proceeds of crime and seize them until proof of legitimate origins can be shown.

Wives, husbands, partners, parents and children of criminals now live in properties financed by crime. They can and should be stripped of them under the act. Their Ferraris, cruise boats and aeroplanes can also be seized. The bill does not but should create an offence of living off the proceeds of crime, in the same way that pimps can be prosecuted for living off the immoral earnings of prostitution. There is no difference in principle, only in the amount and manner in which such earnings are obtained.

Over £2.6 billion of dirty money from the drugs trade and international terrorism is laundered through bureaux de change every year. As much as 65 per cent of the money they deal with is estimated to be illegal, acting as a front for drugs and terrorist money laundering and as the soft underbelly of organised crime financing. The system operates by legitimising dirty sterling, exchanging it for clean foreign notes.

Is there really enough money in criminal hands to justify these reforms? A Home Office report of November 2000 painted a depressing picture drawn from a study of two inner-city drugs markets. It revealed a network based around four main suppliers, seventeen sellers and twenty runners, who brought the drugs from safe houses and conducted the deals. The low-level runners reported earning £800 a day, potentially £200,000 a year, tax free.

Higher up the supply chain, other dealers allege that they can earn over £50,000 a week, a staggering £2.6 million pounds annually. The traffickers above them will make even more, so it is not ridiculous to suggest that every major city will have numerous drugs millionaires. These figures come as no surprise to me at all.

The other side of the coin is the drug users who commit crime to finance their habit. A pair of drug addicts convicted at Leeds Crown Court in February 2001 admitted that to feed their heroin habit they had stolen cars and goods from cars to the value of £1 million in an eight-month spree.

These two men, aged twenty-seven and twenty-eight, admitted over 650 criminal offences between them. Their sentences, after such an orgy of theft, were an insult to their victims. One was jailed for two years, the other for twenty-eight months. When a drug addict who has no cash and maybe no home, everything having been spent on drugs, is convicted, there is no way that a court can make an order to compensate victims for their losses. The court should be able to impose extended sentences on those who cannot pay compensation. Thus a sentence for crimes totalling £1 million pounds might be ten years without compensation, reducing to two years if all the compensation is paid.

Is the jury system the best means of determining a person's innocence or guilt? Would there be fewer miscarriages of justice if a professional panel of judges heard all or some cases? Is public participation in the criminal justice system now outdated?

People's involvement as jurors in the administration of justice has, in my view, no validity today. Juries are no longer drawn from the communities in which criminals live and commit their crimes, justifying their sitting in judgment on their behaviour. In fact, if they did, the conviction rate would be lower through intimidation and fear of reprisals on jurors.

Magistrates do not use juries when they hear cases; nor does the Court of Appeal or the House of Lords. So how do we justify the system in the crown courts? Apart from the principle of being tried by your peers, the advantages seem few and the disadvantages many.

Most barristers I speak to do not want to lose the jury system. I suspect their reasons are not based on fear of giving the judiciary too much power. The simple fact of life is that barristers can pursue outrageous and outlandish defences in the certain knowledge that the judge will not interfere for fear of creating a ground for appeal. The judge is there to guide the jury on matters of law, but not on matters of fact. The interpretation of the evidence is down to the jury. So the judge's influence does not come into play unless that fateful word 'guilty' is uttered by the jury foreperson.

Would there be fewer miscarriages of justice if the evidence were heard and interpreted by a panel of judges? A panel could also sit with an expert adviser such as an accountant in complex fraud cases. If the system can deliver a better standard of justice, can it do so more cost effectively? I have sat for hours listening to barrister's speeches throwing sand into jurors' eyes, seeking to confuse them to the point where they don't know what day it is, never mind being equipped to decide the issue of a person's innocence or guilt. Under the alternative system the final and, at times, endless speeches to the jury would be unnecessary. Trials would have far fewer theatricals than they now do, so would be shorter, saving time and money.

The major problem I experienced in the trial of the Woodhouse rapist, David Jackson, was the challenge over the DNA evidence. With a panel of judges the case could have been stood down to await the result of a further DNA test. Instead, we had to forge ahead, not knowing whether the jury would believe Jackson's preposterous allegation regarding his blood sample being swapped. It would have been a miscarriage of justice to his victims if he had been declared innocent.

My final point is even more compelling. Juries are seen as fickle, and any prejudicial media publicity can bring a trial grinding to a halt if there is a possibility they may have been tainted by it. Judges are regarded as being above such contamination of opinion, so there would be fewer retrials.

Before DNA revolutionised criminal investigation, the fingerprint was the ultimate discriminator, and it still has great value today. Both DNA and fingerprints can lead to an individual's door. Identical twins will have the same DNA, but oddly their fingerprints will be different. The amount required for a DNA profile was originally a blood spot the size of 5p coin; now a single blood cell can be enough.

Fingerprints are comparable worldwide as all countries use the same classification system. But countries are at different stages in using DNA analysis, if they use it at all, and those who do DNA profiling use different systems. So a sample taken from a suspect in America cannot be accurately compared with a DNA profile obtained in France from a semen sample at a crime scene. This was the case with Francisco Montez, fifty-one, arrested in Miami and accused of raping and strangling thirteen-year-old Caroline

Dickinson in a French hostel in 1996. Montez will be extradited to France and he will be DNA-tested there.

I had DNA on the Wendy Speakes murder which I knew was the killer's. At that time there was no DNA database and so no samples to compare it with. Four months after Wendy's murder, the body of Sandra Parkinson was found on the cliffs at Salcombe, Devon. She had been raped and strangled. Her killer left his DNA. Alan Connors hung himself from a tree in Huntingdon, Cambridgeshire, and left a suicide note in his pocket claiming he was Sandra's killer. A check revealed that his DNA matched. Connors had a history of rape and burglary, but these had occurred before DNA sampling started.

A DNA database for convicted sex attackers would not have saved Wendy Speakes's life as her killer had no previous sex convictions. Nor would a national database have saved her life, as there are no prior crimes with samples that matched his. But what did Farrow do in the intervening six years between his crime and arrest? If a database existed in 1994 with everyone in the country on it, Farrow would have been arrested within days.

If there had been a national DNA database in 1992 Sandra Parkinson would be alive today, as the DNA taken from Connors after his death matched that from a rape he committed that year at Ludlow, Shropshire. Had Connors not left a suicide note, the murder squad at Salcombe would to this day still be looking for Sandra's killer, costing time and money. There is no requirement or legal basis for which to take DNA when we die. Though that would be unnecessary if it was taken at birth from every British subject, and all those entering the country provided a sample as an entry condition.

The UK national DNA database we currently have went live in April 1995 at the Birmingham Forensic Science Laboratory. It holds over one million profiles, but represents only 1.6 per cent of the population and the profiles are of criminals only. A truly national DNA database could be linked with a national identity card system. It would also help root out those who make fraudulent benefit claims and to identify illegal immigrants. But from a criminal detection viewpoint it would be a marvellous tool.

The current state of the homicide laws is a mess, to be frank. The sentencing gap between murder and manslaughter is unsatisfactory and juries often struggle to understand the distinction between the two.

Murder is the unlawful killing of a human being by another human with malice aforethought expressed or implied. Murder requires an intention to actually kill a person or to cause grievous bodily harm, or transferred malice, which is as an intention to kill one person but mistakenly killing a third party instead. This is still murder, as the law transfers the malice from the intended victim to the one killed.

Provocation and diminished responsibility can reduce murder to voluntary manslaughter, although the killer may have malicious intent in both. Provocation is self-explanatory; diminished responsibility applies when the killer is not insane, but suffering a temporary imbalance of the mind at the time of the killing.

Manslaughter is unlawful killing without intention, either by acting recklessly or by an unlawful act. Reckless manslaughter may occur in the course of a legal act but in circumstances where the consequences of the actions should have been foreseen, such as knocking down a ten-foot wall without looking round the other side first, thereby killing a sunbather. Unlawful-act manslaughter is where death results through illegal conduct, such as supplying heroin to someone who overdoses and dies as a result.

Murder carries a fixed life sentence, whereas manslaughter carries a maximum sentence of life, which is rarely if ever imposed. I have seen probation supervision orders given for manslaughter convictions, but rarely anything over ten years' imprisonment. The average sentence is around four years. The majority of those sentenced to life for murder will serve less than ten years' imprisonment.

Murder and manslaughter are two very different crimes and should be kept completely separate. But I believe the murder laws should be changed. I would like to see two degrees of murder rather than the reduction of murder to manslaughter, as often happens now. First-degree murder should attract life imprisonment without parole; second-degree murder should carry a minimum sentence of ten years; manslaughter would remain unchanged at a maximum of life imprisonment with no minimum limit.

First-degree murder would be defined as premeditated murder or killing in pursuance of a serious crime such as rape or kidnapping, as it is in many US states. Peter Sutcliffe would come under the first definition, as his crimes were premeditated. Michael Sams and Christopher Farrow would also be guilty of first-degree murder, but by virtue of their killing in pursuance of some other criminal offence, such as kidnapping or rape, in their case there would be no need to prove premeditation. The sentence would be mandatory life without parole.

On proof of provocation or diminished responsibility, first-degree murder could be reduced to second-degree murder, not manslaughter. The essential difference between first- and second-degree murder is planned premeditation rather than spur-of-the-moment action. A man killing his wife's lover as an immediate reaction would be second-degree murder whether argued on the grounds of provocation or lack of premeditation. But if the husband catches his wife and lover in bed and two days later buys a gun and waits outside the lover's house to shoot him dead, that would be first-degree murder. The definition of manslaughter would be unchanged.

These changes would give more clarity to a jury when they attempt to relate actions to the crime. At the moment juries must feel intimidated by the stark choices available to them, regardless of the facts – murder carrying life imprisonment or manslaughter with the prospect of release in a couple of years.

# chapter eleven

# ONE HUNDRED PER CENT

And so, on 14 November 2000, I pondered what sentence Christopher Farrow would receive. His case was set to be heard at Leeds Crown Court, ironically the very place I had left at the end of the Woodhouse rapist trial only an hour before Wendy was murdered. Robert Smith, QC, was the defence barrister in that case. Now he was prosecuting Wendy's killer.

At 10.29 am, Christopher John Farrow stood in the dock feet away from Tracey and Leah, Wendy's daughters. The charges were read to him. To the murder, rape and buggery of Wendy Speakes, he pleaded guilty. To charges of burglary with intent to rape Women 'A' and 'B' he pleaded not guilty.

The case would be stood down for a jury to be sworn in at 12.30 pm. As I returned to the court, there was a flurry of activity. Farrow had said he would plead guilty to visiting the home of Woman 'A' but not that of Woman 'B'. This was acceptable to the prosecution, as it would show he had spent the day looking for a victim and Wendy had indeed not been his first choice.

At 2 pm, in front of a packed court, Farrow pleaded guilty to burglary with intent to rape Woman 'A' at her home an hour before he went to Wendy's.

Mr Justice Morland jailed him for life for the murder, plus fourteen years each for rape and buggery and finally four years for the offence against Woman 'A'. He told Farrow: 'You decided to rape a woman to take out on her the frustration and anger you felt towards your then partner, and when you failed to gain entry into the house of the first woman you targeted, you selected another victim, a complete stranger, Mrs Speakes.

'You forced your way into her house, tied her hands behind her back, gagged her and brutally and savagely raped and buggered her, then you murdered her, stabbing her many times. Your motive was self-preservation. Your terrible crimes remained undetected for six years; my recommendation will be that you remain in custody for very, very many years.'

Farrow's counsel, Douglas Hogg, QC, the ex-Tory minister, suggested in mitigation that the crime was committed as an afterthought when Farrow realised that Wendy could identify him. The judge gave Mr Hogg a terse rebuttal: 'Killing because the victim can identify you is no mitigation at all.'

The last-minute capitulation to Woman 'A's charge left me with no doubt that she was Farrow's intended victim. I cast my mind back to his inadequate explanation as to what he had been doing during the hours he was in Wakefield. He had without doubt stalked Woman 'A' all day while Wendy was at work. So was he lucky to find another victim an hour later, following Wendy, a stranger, from the bus stop to her home? Or was he reverting to her, knowing her routine from previous visits to the city? Also, Woman 'A' had visited the Cliffe Tree pub next door to Wendy's home a number of times. Without doubt Farrow had stalked Woman 'A' and Wendy separately for some time. Whether he saw Woman 'A' first then Wendy, or vice versa, is a secret Farrow has taken with him to his prison cell.

My theory is that Farrow used Wendy Speakes to vent his anger and frustration over the problems he was having with his partner Lesley. Was it a planned act of degradation, sexual gratification and death? I believe so. Would his preferred victim have been Lesley, if she had not been pregnant with his child? Did he instead slip into a fantasy world as he hunted down and stalked a victim, ending up at Wendy's door? When he confronted and pushed her into the hallway, what were Wendy's options – fight or flight? She had nowhere to escape to, so she had to confront the situation. I now know that her nature was not to fight but to be subservient to her attacker, if the worst that was going to happen was rape. Had she expected her encounter with Farrow to end in her death, she would surely have fought, as she had nothing to lose.

The wounds in her back were the first to be inflicted. She may only have felt a thump as he stabbed and punctured her right lung. Her life was already draining away when he inflicted the final two neck wounds.

Farrow no doubt hopes that some day he will be released on parole, but he will always be a danger to women if an argument with his partner can trigger such brutality in him. Julie Pacey's murder is still unsolved, and Farrow cannot be eliminated as a suspect.

I watched as prison security officers took Farrow from the dock to begin his sentence. It was a sight I had seen many times in my service, but this ranked among the most gratifying. It was the last time I would see it. I had the feeling of having travelled a very long road, but now I had come to the end. I had headed many murder inquiries since the start of the hunt for Wendy's killer, but this had been the only instance where the killer had not been caught.

I am proud of my hundred per cent detection and conviction record. I had luck on my side on occasions, but I also worked hard and with many good officers, and my wealth of experience saw me through many a tough time. I worked my last shift of operational duty eighteen days before Farrow was jailed. My business was finished. My casebook closed. It was like retiring after scoring the winning goal at a World Cup final.

*If you have enjoyed reading this book, you may be interested in other titles published by Piatkus. These include:*

**BENT COPS**
**The inside story of Scotland Yard's battle against police corruption**
Graeme McLagan

In the early 1990s, shocked by the extent of corruption within the Metropolitan Police, Scotland Yard set up an Anti-Corruption Unit.

This is the amazing, untold story of how the Anti-Corruption Unit tried to combat the problem – the resistance it encountered, the subterfuges to which it has resorted, and the effect its campaign has had on criminals and coppers alike. Graeme McLagan, the BBC's resident expert on police corruption, has followed the work of the Unit from its inception. He has interviewed policemen on both sides of the divide – those who have thieved, fitted up people, sold information to cripple court cases, and even been suspected of murder; and those who have been pursuing them, bugging their homes, tapping their phones and posing as criminals wanting to do business.

**£15.99**     0 7499 2287 7     Hardback
*to be published in June 2002*

**TOTAL SURVEILLANCE**
John Parker
**Investigating the Big Brother World of E-Spies,
Eavesdroppers and CCTV**

Big Brother is no longer fiction. CCTVs, electronic databases, even e-mail interceptors are being used to monitor virtually every aspect of our daily lives. We are being watched, filmed, listened to, recorded, tracked, entered on databases and put on lists. If you thought that because you are a law-abiding citizen you are safe from surveillance, you are sadly mistaken. We have become targets for government and private agents, eavesdroppers, big business, computer hackers, fraudsters and organised crime equipped with a daunting array of electronic gear. This brilliantly researched book reveals:

- The alarming effect computer technology has had on our privacy
- The secret worldwide listening operation run by the UK and US involving MI5, GCHQ and the Secret Intelligence Service (MI6)
- What today's spies do – and who they investigate
- Details of the world's largest spy station – Menwith Hill in North Yorkshire – and the extraordinary capabilities of the Echelon system
- Why the Data Protection Act is too little, too late

**£10.99**      0 7499 2226 5      Paperback